WHAT T[...]
THE JO[...]

MW00764075

"... A superior series of job hunt directories."

-Cornell University
Career Center
WHERE TO START

"A timely book for Chicago job hunters follows books from the same publisher that were well received in New York and Boston...A fine tool for job hunters..."

-Clarence Petersen
THE CHICAGO TRIBUNE

"Job hunting is never fun, but this book can ease the ordeal...The Southern California Job Bank will help allay fears, build confidence and avoid wheel-spinning."

-Robert W. Ross
THE LOS ANGELES TIMES

"This well-researched, well-edited job hunter's aid includes most major businesses and institutional entities in the New York metropolitan area...Highly recommended."

-Cheryl Gregory-Pindell
LIBRARY JOURNAL

"Here's the book for your job hunt...Trying to get a job in New York? I would recommend a good look through the Metropolitan New York Job Bank..."

-Maxwell Norton
NEW YORK POST

"Help on the job hunt...Anyone who is job-hunting in the New York area can find a lot of useful ideas in a new paperback called The Metropolitan New York Job Bank..."

-Angela Taylor
THE NEW YORK TIMES

"If you are looking for a job...before you go to the newspapers and the help-wanted ads, listen to Bob Adams, editor of The Metropolitan New York Job Bank."

-Tom Brokaw
NBC TELEVISION

"No longer can job seekers feel secure about finding employment just through want ads. With the tough competition in the job market, particularly in the Boston area, they need much more help. For this reason, The Boston Job Bank will have a wide and appreciative audience of new graduates, job changers, and people relocating to Boston. It provides a good place to start a search for entry-level professional positions."

-from a review in
THE JOURNAL OF
COLLEGE PLACEMENT

What makes the JOB BANK SERIES the nation's premier line of employment guides:

With vital employment information on thousands of the nation's largest companies, the **JOB BANK SERIES** is the most comprehensive and authoritative set of career directories available today.

Each of the entries provides contact information, telephone numbers, addresses and a thumbnail sketch of the firm's business. Many entries also include a listing of the firm's typical professional job categories, the principal educational backgrounds sought, and the fringe benefits offered.

All of the reference information in the **JOB BANK SERIES** is as up-to-date and accurate as possible. Every year, the entire database is thoroughly researched and verified, first by mail and then by telephone. More local **JOB BANK** books come out more often than any other comparable publications.

In addition, the **JOB BANK SERIES** features important information about the local job scene--forecasts on which industries are the hottest, overviews of local economic trends, and even lists of regional professional associations, so you can get your job hunt started off right!

 Looking for a particular kind of employer? Each **JOB BANK** Book features a comprehensive cross-index, which lists entries both by industry and, in multi-state job markets, by state. This means a person seeking a job in, say, finance, can identify major employers quickly and accurately.

 Hundreds of discussions with job-hunters show they prefer information organized geographically, because most people look for jobs in specific areas. The **JOB BANK SERIES** offers sixteen regional titles, from Minneapolis to Houston, and from Washington, D.C., to San Francisco. The future employee moving to a particular area can review the local employment data and get a feel not only for the type of industry most common to that region, but also for major employers.

 A condensed, but thorough, review of the entire job search process is presented in the chapter, 'The Basics of Job Winning', a feature that has received many compliments from career counselors. In addition, each **JOB BANK** directory is completed by a section on resumes and cover letters **The New York Times** has acclaimed as "excellent".

 The **JOB BANK SERIES** gives job-hunters the most comprehensive, most timely, and most accurate career information, organized and indexed to facilitate the job search. An entire career reference library, **JOB BANK** books are the consummate employment guides.

The Metropolitan
Washington
Job Bank

Top career publications from Bob Adams, Inc.:

THE JOB BANK SERIES:

The Atlanta Job Bank ($10.95)
The Boston Job Bank ($12.95)
The Chicago Job Bank ($12.95)
The Dallas Job Bank ($12.95)
The Denver Job Bank ($12.95)
The Detroit Job Bank ($12.95)
The Florida Job Bank ($12.95)
The Houston Job Bank ($12.95)
The Los Angeles Job Bank
  ($12.95)
The Minneapolis Job Bank
  ($12.95)
The New York Job Bank ($12.95)
The Ohio Job Bank ($12.95)
The Philadelphia Job Bank
  ($12.95)
The San Francisco Job Bank
  ($12.95)
The Seattle Job Bank ($12.95)
The St. Louis Job Bank ($12.95)
The Washington D.C. Job Bank
  ($12.95)

The Job Bank Guide to
Employment Services (covers 50
  states: $129.95)
The National Job Bank ($189.95)

CAREERS/BUSINESS:

Careers and the College Grad
  1990 ($12.95)
Careers and the Engineer
  ($12.95)
Careers and the MBA ($14.95)

Cold Calling Techniques That
  Really Work ($6.95)
The Consultant's Handbook
  ($12.95)
Harvard Guide to Careers in
  Mass Media ($7.95)
Hiring the Best ($9.95)
How to Get a Job in Education
  ($6.95)
Job Search Handbook ($6.95)
Knock 'Em Dead, with Great
Answers to Tough Interview
  Questions ($6.95)
Marketing Without a Marketing
  Budget ($9.95)
Power Sales Presentations
  ($10.95)
Resume Handbook ($5.95)
Resumes that Knock 'Em Dead
  ($7.95)
Ten Second Business Forms
  ($12.95)
Which Niche? (Answers to the
Most Common Questions About
  Careers and Job Hunting) ($4.95)

To order these books or
additional copies of this book,
send check or money order
(including $2.75 for postage) to:

Bob Adams, Inc.
260 Center Street
Holbrook MA 02343

Ordering by credit card?
Just call 1-800-USA-JOBS toll
free. (In Massachusetts call 617-
767-8100)

The Metropolitan
Washington
Job Bank

Managing Editor: Carter Smith

Associate Editors: Casey Sims, Peter Weiss

HOW TO USE THIS BOOK

A copy of *The Metropolitan Washington DC Job Bank* is one of the most effective tools you can find for your professional job hunt. Use this guide for the most up-to-date information on most major businesses in the Greater Washington DC area. It will supply you with specific addresses, phone numbers, and personnel contact information.

Separate yourself from the flock of candidates who answer the help-wanted advertisements "looking for a job." The method this book offers, direct employer contact, boasts twice the success rate of any other. Exploit it.

Read and use *The Metropolitan Washington DC Job Bank* to uncover new opportunities. Here's how:

Read the introductory economic overview section in order to gain insight on what the overall trends are for the city's economy.

Map out your job-seeking strategy by reading the "Basics of Job Winning" section. It's a condensed review of the most effective job search methods.

Write a winning resume and learn how to sell yourself most effectively on paper, by using the "Resumes and Cover Letters" section.

Focus your career goals by reading the "Jobs in Each Industry" section. This chapter lists salary ranges, educational background requirements, and forecasts for future growth of many of today's most common professional positions.

Formulate a target list of potential employers in your field. Consult the company listings in the "Primary Washington Employers" section. Use that information to supplement your own research, so that you'll be knowledgeable about the firm - before the interview.

Increase your knowledge of your field, as well as your connections within it, by using our listings of some of the area's major professional and trade associations.

Whether you are just out of college starting your first job search, looking for a new position in your current field, or entering an entirely new sector of the job market, *The Metropolitan Washington DC Job Bank* will give you an idea of the incredible diversity of employment possibilities in the country's capital. Your ultimate success will largely depend upon how rigorously you use the information provided herein. This one-of-a-kind employment guide can lead you to a company, and a job, that would otherwise have remained undiscovered. With a willingness to apply yourself, a winning attitude, and the research within these covers, you can attain your career objective.

TABLE OF CONTENTS

INTRODUCTION/13

A complete and informative economic overview designed to help you understand all of the forces shaping Washington DC's job market.

THE BASICS OF JOB WINNING/19

A condensed review of the basic elements of a successful job search campaign. Includes advice on developing an effective strategy, time planning, preparing for interviews, interview techniques, etc.

RESUMES AND COVER LETTERS/35

Advice on creating a strong resume. Includes sample resumes and cover letters.

JOBS IN EACH INDUSTRY/59

Descriptions of many of the most common professional positions, with forecasts of their growth potential for the 1990's. Also includes current salary ranges for each position.

PRIMARY WASHINGTON EMPLOYERS/115

Metropolitan Washington's employers organized according to industry. Includes the address, phone number, description of the company's basic product lines and services, and for most firms, the name of the contact person for professional hiring.

GOVERNMENT JOBS/211

An overview of employment opportunities within the federal government.

EMPLOYMENT SERVICES/241

Includes the address, phone number, description of the company's services, contact name, and a list of positions commonly filled.

PROFESSIONAL AND TRADE ASSOCIATIONS/265

Includes the address and phone number of professional and trade associations in each field.

ALPHABETICAL INDEX OF EMPLOYERS/291

INTRODUCTION

Looking to change jobs? Perhaps you're looking for your first job or for an opportunity to re-enter the workforce after years of full-time childrearing or retirement? Whatever your career status, age or experience level, all indications suggest your timing couldn't be better. One of the country's enviable job markets where job creation has exceeded population growth so substantially in recent years as to have created a labor shortage, metro Washington today holds abundant opportunities for experienced professionals and new entry level workers alike.

The area's continuing attraction to retailers, for instance, will be bringing new department and specialty stores and thousands of new jobs to the region this year. Early this summer, hiring at Tysons II and the Fashion Centre at Pentagon City will account for an estimated 3,000 new jobs. Hecht's also has five new stores planned for opening by the mid-1990s... and the list goes on. For those interested in sales positions, depending on the products sold, earnings can reach into the $50,000 bracket.

Although retail has traditionally been an industry that welcomed entry-level employees of all ages, with the national and regional decline of teenagers entering the job market, employers are even more aggressively pursuing alternate population groups for entry-level positions. Retirees, re-entering homemakers and military spouses are among those in demand by area retailers.

Also seeking the talents of non-traditional employee groups are banks and savings and loans, who say they're having difficulty finding sufficient numbers of quality candidates for entry-level teller, customer service, and clerical positions.

Those who hire and place accounting professionals report similar shortages at the entry level, as well as a willingness by somewhat desperate employers, to provide the on-the-job training to those with a good math aptitude and keyboard skills; most accounting today is computerized and so even entry-level work requires basic computer keyboard expertise.

On-the-job training is also provided by retail and financial institutions to enhance the communication, supervisory and customer service skills of new staff. Like many other fields, these service sector employers believe in "promotion from within" whenever possible, so, landing one of the many entry-level roles available today can be the launch of a challenging and lucrative long-term career.

Another career track where positions are numerous and offer excellent advancement potential is the secretarial and office support area.

Far from being the dead-end career many feminists purported it to be in the last decade, being a secretary today and in Washington, can launch you in any number of professional, managerial or executive positions.

Success stories are common of these local residents who began their careers as secretaries, and today have careers as public relations directors, human resources managers and recruiters, sales and marketing executives, lawyers, and entrepreneurs.

And with BLS (Bureau of Labor Statistics) projections indicating continuing shortages of secretaries for the oncoming decade, this appears to be an extremely available and desirable entry-level avenue. In metro Washington, earnings for secretaries can reach into the $30,000-$40,000 plus bracket.

Of course, the nursing shortage in the area has been well-publicized. What may not be as well known is how attractive the shortage is making the nursing field for new graduates and nurses who have taken a number of years off from their careers. The shortages have resulted in improved wages, enhanced scheduling flexibility, more rapid access to specialization, more on-the-job training and tuition reimbursement from area hospitals, as well as hospital-supported day care programs.

Shortages in the allied health or professional services arena, although not as well publicized, are also creating numerous attractive options for local residents seeking an alternate path into the health care industry. Radiology technicians and technologists, physical therapists, and pharmacists are just a few of the many health care specialists in demand by area hospitals and clinics. Here again, shortages of qualified professionals are prompting improvements in earning power, more opportunities for cross training and employer sponsored on-the-job training as well as tuition reimbursement for relevant courses taken.

Not to be overlooked, either, are the many jobs being created in local city and county government agencies to accommodate the area's growing population and increasing demand for services. From law enforcement to child care and social services, from entry-level clerical roles to very senior one-of-a-kind slots, local government are creating new positions and filling existing openings made vacant by those who have retired, been promoted, or decided to change careers.

Finally, for those who prefer the flexibility and variety of temporary work, the temporary industry in metro Washington proclaims more numerous and lucrative opportunities than ever. In addition to the industry's continuing popularity and growth of revenues due to private sector usage, the Washington area temporary industry anticipates significant growth in temporary assignments as a result of recent legislation enabling the Federal government to hire temporary employees from private temporary services firms.

Here, too, with demand in some areas exceeding the number of available candidates, temporary service firms are more aggressively seeking out retirees, military spouses, and homemakers to fill available assignments. To help attract and retain a skilled pool of temporaries, more and more agencies are also offering health benefits, vacation days and performance bonuses to those who work with them a designated number of hours.

What about the future? How secure are those thousands of new jobs? How resilient is the Washington area economy?

Although few are bold or arrogant enough to use the term "recession-proof" to describe the metro Washington job market, many employers certainly admit to a feeling of confidence about the continuing strength and growth of the area's economy. Many acknowledge that the rate of growth may be slowing somewhat, and in fact, some believe efforts to attract new businesses to the area should be curtailed temporarily to ensure adequate staffing, affordable housing and public services for existing businesses in the region.

What few deny, however, is that they're happy they're here, and certainly are not interested in exchanging the difficulty and even the cost of recruiting and retention efforts in the metro area with the alternative--a less healthy economy with high unemployment, less affluent consumers, and ultimately, less business potential.

As a jobseeker--whether you're looking for a first job or simply a different job--consider yourself lucky as well. You couldn't be looking in a better place. The metro area is rich with opportunities for newcomers and experienced professionals alike.

Reprinted with permission of The Washington Post

THE BASICS OF JOB WINNING

THE BASICS OF JOB WINNING: A CONDENSED REVIEW

The best way to obtain a better professional job is to contact the employer directly. Broad-based statistical studies by the Department of Labor show that job seekers have found employment more successfully by contacting employers directly, than by using any other method.

However, given the current diversity, and increased specialization of both industry and job tasks it is possible that in some situations other job seeking methods may prove at least equally successful. Three of the other most commonly used methods are: relying on personal contacts, using employment services, and following up help wanted advertisements. Many professionals have been successful in finding better jobs using one of these methods. However, the Direct Contact method has an overall success rate twice that of any other method and it has been successfully used by many more professionals. So unless you have specific reasons to believe that another method would work best for you, the Direct Contact method should form the foundation of your job search effort.

The Objective

With any business task, you must develop a strategy for meeting a goal. This is especially true when it comes to obtaining a better job. First you need to clearly define your objectives.

Setting your job objectives is better known as career planning (or life planning for those who wish to emphasize the importance of combining the two). Career planning has become a field of study in and of itself. Since most of our readers are probably well-entrenched in their career path, we will touch on career planning just briefly.

If you are thinking of choosing or switching careers, we particularly emphasize two things. First choose a career where you will enjoy most of the day-to-day tasks. Sure, this sounds obvious, but most of us have at one point or another been attracted by a glamour industry or a prestigious sounding job without thinking of the most important consideration: Would we enjoy performing the everyday tasks the position entailed?

The second key consideration is that you are not merely choosing a career, but also a lifestyle. Career counselors indicate that one of the most common problems people encounter in job seeking is a lack of consideration for how well-suited they are for a particular position or career. For example, some people, attracted to management consulting by good salaries, early responsibility and high level corporate exposure, do not adapt well to the long hours, heavy travel demands, and the constant pressure to produce. So be sure to determine both for your career as a whole and for each position that you apply for, if you will easily adapt to both the day-to-day duties that the position entails and the working environment.

The Strategy

Assuming that you have now established your career objectives, the next step of the job search is to develop a strategy. If you don't take the time to develop a strategy and lay out a plan you will probably find yourself going in circles after several weeks making a random search for opportunities that always seem just beyond your reach.

Your strategy can be thought as having three simple elements:

1.   Choose a method of contacting employers.

2.   Allocating your scarce resources (in most job searches the key scarce resource will be time, but financial considerations will become important in some searches too).

3.   Evaluating how the selected contact method is working and then considering adopting other methods.

We suggest you give serious consideration to using the Direct Contact method exclusively. However, we realize it is human nature to avoid putting all your eggs in one basket. So, if you prefer to use other methods as well, try to expend at least half your effort on the Direct Contact method, spending the rest on all of the other methods combined. Millions of other job seekers have already proven that Direct Contact has been twice as effective in obtaining employment, so why not benefit from their effort?

With your strategy in mind, the next step is to develop the details of the plan, or scheduling. Of course, job searches are not something that most people do regularly so it is difficult to estimate how long each step will take. Nonetheless, it is important to have a plan so that your effort can be allocated the way you have chosen, so that you can see yourself progressing, and to facilitate reconsideration of your chosen strategy.

It is important to have a realistic time frame in mind. If you will be job searching full-time, your search will probably take at least two months and very likely, substantially longer. If you can only devote part-time effort, it will probably take four months.

You probably know a few people who seem to spend their whole lives searching for a better job in their part time. Don't be one of them. Once you begin your job search, on a part-time basis, give it your whole-hearted effort. If you don't really feel like devoting a lot of energy to job seeking right now, then wait. Focus on enjoying your present position, performing your best on the job, and storing up energy for when you are really ready to begin your job search.

Those of you currently unemployed, should remember that job hunting is tough work physically and emotionally. It is also intellectually demanding - requiring your best. So don't tire yourself out by working on your job campaign around the clock. It would be counter-productive. At the same time be sure to discipline yourself. The most logical approach to time management is to keep your regular working hours.

For those of you who are still employed, job searching will be particularly tiring because it must be done in addition to your regular duties. So don't work yourself to the point where you show up to interviews appearing exhausted and slip behind at your current job. But don't be tempted to quit!

The long hours are worth it - it is much easier to sell your skills from a position of strength (as someone currently employed).

If you are searching full-time and have decided to choose a mixture of contact methods, we recommend that you divide up each week allowing some time for each method. For instance, you might devote Mondays to following-up newspaper ads because most of them appear in Sunday papers. Then you might devote Tuesdays, and Wednesday mornings to working and developing the personal contacts you have, in addition to trying a few employment services. Then you could devote the rest of the week to the Direct Contact method. This is just one plan that may succeed for you.

By trying several methods at once, job-searching will be more interesting for you, and you will be able to evaluate how promising each of the methods seems, altering your time allocation accordingly. Be very careful in your evaluation, however, and don't judge the success of a particular method just by the sheer number of interviews you obtain. Positions advertised in the newspaper, for instance, are likely to generate many more interviews per opening than positions that are filled without being advertised.

If you are searching part-time and decide to try several different contact methods, we recommend that you try them sequentially. You simply won't have enough time to put a meaningful amount of effort into more than one method at once. So decide how long your job search might take. (Only a guess, of course.) And then allocate so many weeks or months for each contact method you choose to use. (We suggest that you try Direct Contact first).

If you are expected to be in your office during the business day then you have an additional time problem to deal with. How can you work interviews into the business day? And if you work in an open office, how can you even call to set up interviews? As much as possible you should keep up the effort and the appearances on your present job. So maximize your use of the lunch hour, early in the morning and late in the afternoon for calling. If you really keep trying you will be surprised how often you will be able to reach the executive you are trying to contact during your out-of-office hours. The lunch hour for different executives will vary between 12 and 3. Also you can catch people as early as 8 AM and as late as 6 PM on frequent occasions. Jot out a plan each night on how you will be using each minute of your precious lunch break.

Your inability to interview at any time other than lunch just might work to your advantage. If you can, try to set up as many interviews as possible for your lunch hour. This will go a long way to creating a relaxed rapport. (Who isn't happy when eating?) But be sure the interviews don't stray too far from the agenda on hand.

Lunchtime inteviews will be much easier for the person with substantial career experience to obtain. People with less experience will often find that they have no alternative other than taking time off for interviewing. If you have to take time off, you have to take time off. But try to do this as little as possible. Usually you should take the whole day off so that it is not blatantly obvious that you are job searching. Try to schedule in at least two, or at the most three, interviews for the same day. (It is very difficult to maintain an optimum level of energy at more than three interviews in one day.) Explain to the interviewer why you might have to juggle your interview schedule - he/she should honor the respect you are showing your current employer by minimizing your days off and will probably appreciate the fact that another prospective employer is showing an interest in you.

Once again we need to emphasize if you are searching for a job, especially part-time, get out there and do the necessary tasks to the best of your ability and get it over with. Don't let your job search drag on endlessly.

Remember that all schedules are meant to be broken. The purpose of a schedule in your job search is not to rush you to your goal, its purpose is to map out the road ahead of you and to evaluate the progress of your chosen strategy to date.

The Direct Contact Method

Once you have scheduled a time you are ready to begin using the job search method that you have chosen. In the text we will restrict discussion to use of the Direct Contact method. Sideboards will comment briefly on developing your personal contacts and using newspaper advertisements.

The first step in preparing for Direct Contact is to develop a check list for categorizing the types of firms for which you would prefer working. You might categorize firms by their product line, their size, their customer-type (such as industrial or consumer), their growth prospects, or, of course, by their geographical locations. Your list of important considerations might be very short. If if is, good! The shorter it is, the easier it will be to find appropriate firms.

Then try to decide at which firms you are most likely to be able to obtain employment. You might wish to consider to what degree your particular skills might be in demand, the degree of competition for employment, and the employment outlook at the firm.

Now you are ready to assemble your list of prospective employers. Build up your list to at least 100 prospects. Then separate your prospect list into three groups. The first tier of maybe 25 firms will be your primary target market, the second group of another 25 firms will be your secondary market, and the remaining names you will keep in reserve.

This book will help you greatly in developing your prospect list. Turn to the industry cross index to get started. Then refer back to the alphabetically ordered employer listings to obtain more information about each firm.

At this stage, once you have gotten your prospect list together and have an idea of the firms for which you might wish to work, it is best to get to work on your resume. Refer to formats of the sample resumes included in this section of the book.

Once your resume is at the printer, begin research for the first batch of 25 prospective employers. You will want to determine whether you would be happy working at the firmsyou are researching and also get a better idea of what their employment needs might be. You also need to obtain enough information to sound highly informed about the company during phone conversations and in mail correspondence. But don't go all out on your research yet! At some of these firms you probably will not be able to arrange interviews, so save your big research effort until you start to arrange interviews. Nevertheless, you should plan to spend about 3 or 4 hours, on average, researching each firm. Do your research in batches to save time and energy. Go into one resource at a time and find out what you can about each of the 25 firms in the batch. Start with the easiest resources to use (such as this book). Keep organized. Maintain a folder on each firm.

If you discover something that really disturbs you about the firm (i.e. perhaps they are about to close their only local office) or if you discover that

Developing Your Contacts (Networking)

Some career counselors feel that the best route to a better job is through somebody you already know or through somebody to whom you can be introduced. The counselors recommend you build your contact base beyond your current acquaintances by asking them to each introduce you, or refer you, to additional people in your field of interest.

The theory goes like this: You might start with 15 personal contacts, each of whom introduces you to 3 additional people, for a total of 45 additional contacts. Then each of these people introduces you to 3 additional people which adds 135 additional contacts. Who in turn introduce you to 405 additional contacts. Theoretically you will soon know every person in the entire industry.

Of course, developing your personal contacts does not usually work quite as smoothly as the theory suggests because some people will not be able to introduce you to several relevant additional contacts. The further you stray from your initial contact base, the weaker your references will be. So, if you do try developing your own contacts, try to begin with as large an initial group of people you personally know as possible. Dig into your personal phone book and your holiday greeting card list and locate old classmates from school. Be particularly sure to approach people who perform your personal business such as your lawyer, accountant, banker, doctor, stockbroker and insurance agent. These people develop a very broad contact base due to the nature of their professions.

your chances of getting a job there are practically nil (i.e. perhaps they just instituted a hiring freeze) then cross them off your prospect list.

If possible, supplement your research efforts with contacts to individuals who know the firm well. Ideally you should make an informal contact with someone at the particular firm, but often a contact at a direct competitor, or a major supplier or customer will be able to supply you with just as much information. At the very least try to obtain whatever printed information that the company has available, not just annual reports, but product brochures and anything else. The company might very well have printed information about career opportunities.

Getting The Interview

Now it is time to arrange an interview, time to make the Direct Contact. If you have read many books on job searching you have probably noticed that virtually all tell you to avoid the personnel office like the plague. It is said that the personnel office never hires people, they just screen out candidates. In some cases you may be able to identify and contact the appropriate manager with the authority to hire you. However, this will take a lot of time and effort in each case. Often you'll be bounced back to personnel. So we suggest that you begin your Direct Contact campaign through personnel offices. If it seems that in the firms on your prospect list that little hiring is done through personnel, you might consider an alternative course of action.

The three obvious means of initiating Direct Contact are:

-Showing up unannounced
-Phone calls
-Mail

Cross out the first one right away. You should never show up to seek a professional position without an appointment. Even if you are somehow lucky enough to obtain an interview, you will appear so unprofessional that you will not even be seriously considered.

Mail contact seems to be a good choice if you have not been in the job market for a while. You can take your time to prepare a careful letter, say exactly what you want, tuck your resume in, and then the addressee can read the material at leisure. But employers receive many resumes every day. Don't be surprised if you do not get a response to your inquiry. So don't spend weeks waiting for responses that never come. If you do send a cover letter, follow-up (or precede it) with a phone call. This will increase your impact, and underscore both your interest in the firm and the fact that you are familiar with it (because of the initial research you did).

Another alternative is to make a "Cover Call." Your Cover Call should be just like your cover letter: concise. Your first sentence should interest the employer in you. Then try to subtly mention your familiarity with the firm. Don't be overbearing; keep your introduction to three sentences or less. Be pleasant, self confident and relaxed. This will greatly increase the chances of the person at the other end of the line developing the conversation. But don't press. When you are asked to follow up "with something in the mail" don't try to prolong the conversation once it has ended. Don't ask what they want to receive in the mail. Always send your resume and a highly personalized follow-up letter, reminding the addressee

Don't Bother To Try
Mass Mail or Phone Call Barrages

Direct Contact does not mean burying every firm within a one-hundred mile radius with mail and phone calls. Mass-mail techniques very very seldom work. This applies equally to those letters that are personalized (but dehumanized) on an automatic typewriter. Don't waste your time or money on such a project; you will fool no one but yourself. The same applies for making a barrage of phone calls.

The worst part of sending out a mass mailing or making unplanned phone calls is that you are likely to be remembered only as someone with little genuine interest in the firm, as someone who lacks sincerity, and as someone that nobody wants to hire.

Help-Wanted Advertisements

Only a small fraction of professional job openings are advertised. Yet a majority of job seekers (and a lot of people not in the job market) spend much time studying the help-wanted ads. As a result the competition for advertised openings is often severe.

A moderate-sized Manhattan employer told us this about an experience advertising in the help-wanted section of a major Sunday newspaper:

> It was a disaster. We had over 500 responses from this relatively small ad in just one week. We have only two phone lines in this office and one was totally knocked out. We will never do it (advertise for professional help) again.

If you still insist on following-up the help-wanted ads, then research a firm before you reply to the ad so that you can ascertain the fact that you would really be a suitable candidate and that you would enjoy working at a particular firm. Also such preliminary research might help to separate you from all of the other professionals responding to the ad, many of whom will only have a passing interest in the opportunity. However, as your odds of obtaining a better job through the want ads are still small, do not invest a lot of effort in this job-seeking method.

of the phone conversation. Always include a cover letter even if you are requested to send a resume. (It is assumed that you will send a cover letter too).

Unless you are in telephone sales, making smooth and relaxed Cover Calls will probably not come easily. Practice them on your own and then with your friends or relatives (friends are likely to be more objective and hence, better participants).

If you obtain an interview over the telephone, be sure to send a thank you note reiterating the points you made during the conversation. You will appear more professional and increase your impact. However, don't mail your resume once an interview has been arranged unless it is specifically requested. Take it with you to the interview instead.

Preparing For The Interview

Once the interview has been arranged, begin your in-depth research. You have got to arrive at the interview knowing the company upside down and inside out. You need to know their products, their types of customers, their subsidiaries, their parent, their principle locations, their rank in the industry, their sales and profit trends, their type of ownership, their size, their current plans and much more. By this time you have probably narrowed your job search to one industry, but if you haven't then you need to be familiar with the trends in this firm's industry, the firm's principle competitors and their relative performance, and the direction that the industry leaders are headed. Dig into every resource you can! All the company literature, the trade press, the business press, and if they are public call your stockbroker and ask for still additional information. If possible, speak to someone at the firm before the interview, or if not, speak to someone at a competing firm. Clearly the more time you spend, the better. Even if you feel extremely pressed for time, you should set aside at least 12 hours for pre-interview research.

If you have been out of the job market for some time, don't be surprised if you find yourself tense during your first few interviews. It will probably happen every time you re-enter the market, not just when you seek your first job after getting out of school.

Tension is natural during an interview, but if you can be relaxed you will have an advantage over the competition. Knowing you have done a thorough research job should help you relax for an interview. Also make a list of the questions that you think might be asked in an interview. Think out your answers carefully. Then practice reviewing them with a friend. Tape record your responses to the questions he/she raises in the role as interviewer. If you feel particularly unsure of your interviewing skills, arrange your first interviews at firms in which you are not very interested. (But remember it is common courtesy to seem excited about the possibility of working for any firm at which you interview.) Then practice again on your own after these first few interviews. Go over each of the questions that you were asked.

How important is the proper dress for a job interview? Buying a complete wardrobe of Brooks Brothers pinstripes, donning new wing tip shoes and having your hair trimmed every morning is not enough to guarantee your obtaining a career position as an investment banker. But on the other hand, if you can't find a clean, conservative suit and a narrow tie, or won't take the time to polish your shoes and trim and wash your hair--then you are just wasting your time by interviewing at all.

Very rarely will the final selection of candidates for a job opening be determined by dress. So don't spend a fortune on a new wardrobe. But be sure that your clothes are adequate.   Men applying for any professional position should wear a suit; women should either wear a dress or a suit (not a pant suit). Your clothes should be at least as formal or slightly more formal than those worn by the people on the level of position for which you are applying. When in doubt it is better to be slightly more formal and more conservative than the position would suggest.

Top personal grooming is more important than finding the perfect clothes for a job interview. Careful grooming indicates both a sense of thoroughness and self-confidence.

Be sure that your clothes fit well and that they are immaculately clean. Hair must be neatly trimmed and freshly washed. Shoes should be newly polished. Women need to avoid excessive jewelry and excessive make-up. Men ought to appear freshly shaven, even if the interview is late in the day.

Be complete. Everyone needs a watch and a pen and pad of paper (for taking notes). Finally a briefcase or folder (containing extra copies of your resume) will help complete the look of professionalism.

Sometimes the interviewer will be running behind schedule. Don't be upset, be sympathetic. He might be under pressure to interview a lot of candidates and to quickly fill a demanding position. So be sure to come to your interview with good reading material to keep yourself occupied. This will help increase your patience and ease your tenseness.

The Interview

The very beginning of the interview is the most important part because it determines the rapport for the rest of it. Those first few moments are especially crucial. Do you smile when you meet? Do you establish enough eye contact, but not too much? Do you walk into the office with a self-asssured and confident stride? Do you shake hands firmly? Do you make small talk easily without being garrulous? It is human nature to judge people by that first impression, so make sure it is a good one. But most of all, try to be yourself.

Often the interviewer will begin, after the small talk, by proceeding to tell you about the company, the division, the department, or perhaps, the position. Because of your detailed research, the information about the company will be repetitive for you and the interviewer would probably like nothing better than to avoid this regurgitation of the company biography. So if you can do so tactfully, indicate to the interviewer that you are very familiar with the firm. If he/she seems intent on providing you with background information, despite your hints, then acquiesce. But be sure to remain attentive. If you can manage to generate a brief discussion of the company or the industry at this point, without being forceful, great. It will help to further build rapport, underscore your interests and increase your impact.

Soon (if it didn't begin that way) the interviewer will begin the questions. This period of the interview falls into one of two categories (or somewhere in between): either a structured interview, where the interviewer has a prescribed set of questions to ask; or an unstructured interview, where the interviewer will ask only leading questions to get you to talk about yourself, your experiences and your goals. Try to sense as quickly as possible which direction the interview wishes to proceed and follow along in the

Some Favorite
Interview Questions

Tell me about yourself...

Why did you leave your last job?

What excites you in your current job?

What are your career goals?

Where would you like to be in 5 years?

What are your greatest strengths?

What are your greatest weaknesses?

Why do you wish to work for this firm?

Where else are you seeking employment?

Why should we hire you?

direction he/she seems to be leading. This will make the interviewer feel more relaxed and in control of the situation.

Many of the questions will be similiar to the ones that you were expecting and you will have prepared answers. Remember to keep attuned to the interviewer and make the length of your answers appropriate to the situation. If you are really unsure as to how detailed a response the interviewer is seeking, then ask. Query if he/she would prefer more details of a particular aspect.

As the interview progresses, the interviewer will probably mention what he/she considers to be the most important responsibilities of the position. If applicable, draw parallels between your experience and the demands of the position as seen by the interviewer. Describe your past experience in the same manner that you did on your resume: emphasizing results and achievements and not merely describing activities. If you listen carefully (listening is a very important part of the interviewing process) the interviewer might very well mention or imply the skills in terms of what the interviewer is seeking. But don't exaggerate. Be on the level.

Try not to cover too much ground during the first interview. This interview is often the toughest, with many candidates being screened out. If you are interviewing for a very competitive position, you will have to make an impression that will last. Focus on a few of your greatest strengths that are relevant to the position. Develop these points carefully, state them again in other words, and then try to summarize them briefly at the end of the interview.

Often the interviewer will pause towards the end and ask if you have any questions? Particularly in a structured interview, this might be the one chance to really show your knowledge of and interest in the firm. Have prepared a list of specific questions that are of real interest to you. Let your questions subtly show your research and your extensive knowledge of the firm's activities. It is wise to have an extensive list of questions, as several of them may have already been answered during the interview.

Do not allow your opportunity to ask questions become an interrogation. Avoid bringing your list of questions to the interview. And ask questions that you are fairly certain the interviewer can answer (remember how you feel when you cannot answer a question during an interview).

Even if you are unable to determine the salary range beforehand, do not ask about it during the first interview. You can always ask about it later. Above all, don't ask about fringe benefits until you have been offered a position. (Then be sure to get all the details.) You should be able to determine the company's policy on fringe benefits relatively easily before the interview.

Try not to be negative about anything during the interview. (Particularly any past employer or any previous job.) Be cheerful. Everyone likes to work with someone who seems to be happy.

Don't let a tough question throw you off base. If you don't know the answer to a question, say so simply-do not apologize. Just smile. Nobody can answer every question--particularly some of the questions that are asked in job interviews.

Before your first interview, you may have been able to determine how many interviews the employer usually has for positions at your level. (Of course it may differ quite a bit within one firm.) Usually you can count on at least three or four interviews, although some firms, such as some of the professional partnerships, are well-known to give a minimum of six interviews for all professional positions.

You're Fired!!

- You are not the first and you will not be last to go through this traumatic experience. Thousands of professionals are fired every week.

- Being fired is not a reflection on you as a person. It is usually a reflection of your company's staffing needs and its perception of your recent job performance.

- Share the fact with your relatives and friends. Being fired is not something of which to be ashamed.

- Don't start your job search with a flurry of unplanned activity. Start by choosing a strategy and working out a plan.

- Now is not the time for major changes in your life. If possible, remain in the same career and in the same geographical location, at least until you have been working again for a while. On the other hand, if the only industry for which you are trained is leaving, or is severely depressed in your area, then you should give prompt consideration to moving or switching careers.

- Register for unemployment compensation immediately. A thorough job search could take months. After all, your employers have been contributing to unemployment insurance specifically for you ever since your first job. Don't be surprised to find other professionals collecting unemployment compensation also. Unemployment compensation is for everybody who is between jobs.

- Be prepared to answer the question during job interviews of why you think you were fired. Avoid mentioning you were fired while arranging interviews. Try especially hard not to speak negatively of your past employer and not to sound particularly worried about your current, temporarily-unemployed status.

- Do not spend much time reflecting on why you were fired or how you might have avoided it. Look ahead. Think positively. And be sure to follow a careful plan during your job search.

Depending on what information you are able to obtain you might want to vary your strategy quite a bit from interview to interview. For instance if the first interview is a screening interview then try to have a few of your strengths really stand out. On the other hand, if later interviews are primarily with people who are in a position to veto your hiring, but not to push it forward (and few people are weeded out at these stages), then you should primarily focus on building rapport as opposed to reiterating and developing your key strengths.

If it looks as though your skills and background do not match the position your interviewer was hoping to fill, ask him or her if there is another division or subsidiary that perhaps could profit from your talents.

After The Interview

Write a follow-up letter immediately after the interview, while the interview is still fresh in the interviewer's mind. Then, if you have not heard from the interviewer within seven days, call him/her to stress your continued interest in the firm and the position and to request a second interview.

A parting word of advice. Again and again during your job search you will be rejected. You will be rejected when you apply for interviews. You will be rejected after interviews. For every job you finally receive you will probably have received a multitude of rejections. Don't let these rejections slow you down. Keep reminding yourself that the sooner you go out and get started on your job search and get those rejections flowing in, the closer you will be to obtaining the better job.

RESUMES AND COVER LETTERS

RESUMES AND COVER LETTERS

THIS SECTION CONTAINS:

1.Resume Preparation

2.Resume Format

3.Resume Content

4.Should You Hire A Resume Writer?

5.Sample Resumes

6.Cover Letter Preparation

7.General Model for a Cover Letter.

8.Sample Cover Letters

9.General Model for a Follow-up Letter.

10.Listings of area resume and career counseling services.

RESUMES/OVERVIEW

When filling a position, a recruiter will often have 100 plus applicants, but time to interview only the 5 or 10 most promising ones. So he or she will have to reject most applicants after a brief skimming of their resume.

Unless you have phoned and talked to the recruiter - which you should do whenever you can - you will be chosen or rejected for an interview entirely on the basis of your resume and cover letter. So your resume must be outstanding. (But remember - a resume is not a substitution for a job search campaign. YOU must seek a job. Your resume is only one tool.)

RESUME PREPARATION

One page, usually.

Unless you have an unusually strong background with many years of experience and a large diversity of outstanding achievements, prepare a one page resume. Recruiters dislike long resumes.

8 1/2 x 11 Size

Recruiters often get resumes in batches of hundreds. If your resume is on small size paper it is likely to get lost in the pile. If oversized it's likely to get crumpled at the edges, and won't fit in their files.

Typesetting

Modern photocomposition typesetting gives you the clearest, sharpest image, a wide variety of type styles and effects such as italics, bold facing, and book like justified margins. Your original will be on a piece of photographic paper, or you don't have photocomposition. Typesetting is the best resume preparation process, but the most expensive.

Word Processing

The most flexible way to get your resume typed is on a good quality word processor. With word processing, you can make changes almost instantly because your resume will be stored on magnetic disk and the machine will do all the re-typing automatically. A word processing service will usually offer you a variety of type styles in both regular and proportional spacing. You can have bold facing for emphasis, justified margins, and clear, sharp copies.

Typing

Household typewriters and office typewriters with nylon or other cloth ribbons are NOT good for typing the resume you will have printed. If you can't get word processing or typesetting, hire a professional with a high quality office typewriter with a plastic ribbon (usually called a "carbon ribbon").

Printing

Find the best quality offset printing process available. DO NOT make your copies on an office photocopier. Only the personnel office may see the resume you mail. Everyone else may see only a copy of it. Copies of copies quickly become unreadable. Some professionally maintained, extra-high-quality photocopiers are of adequate quality, if you are in a rush. But top quality offset printing is best.

Proofread Your Resume

Whether you typed it yourself or had it written, typed, or typeset. Mistakes on resumes can be embarrassing. Particularly when something obvious such as your name is misspelled. No matter how much you paid someone else to type or write or typeset your resume YOU lose if there is a mistake. So proofread as carefully as possible. Get a friend to help you. Read your draft aloud as your friend checks the proof copy. Then have your friend read aloud while you check. Next, read it letter by letter to check spelling and punctuation.

If you are having it typed or typeset by a resume service or a printer, and you can't bring a friend or take the time during the day to proof it, pay for it and take it home. Proof it there and bring it back later to get it corrected and printed.

RESUME FORMAT

(See samples)

Basic Data

Your name, phone number, and a complete address should be at the top of your resume. (If you are a university student, you should also show your home address and phone number.)

**Separate your education
and work experience**

In general, list your experience first. If you have recently graduated, list your education first, unless your experience is more important than your education. (For example if you have just graduated from a teaching school, have some business experience and are applying for a job in business you would list your business experience first.) If you have two or more years of college, you don't need to list high schools.

Reverse chronological order

To a recruiter your last job and your latest schooling are the most important. So put the last first and list the rest going back in time.

Show dates and locations

Put the dates of your employment and education on the left of the page. Put the names of the companies you worked for and the schools you attended a few spaces to the right of the dates. Put the city and state or city and country where you studied or worked to the right of the page.

Avoid sentences and large blocks of type

Your resume will be scanned, not read. Short, concise phrases are much more effective than long-winded sentences. Keep everything easy to find. Avoid paragraphs longer than 6 lines. Never go 10 or more lines in a paragraph. If you have more than 6 lines of information about one job or school, put it in two or more paragraphs.

RESUME CONTENT

Be factual

In many companies inaccurate information on a resume or other application material will get you fired as soon as the inaccuracy is discovered. Protect yourself.

Be positive

You are selling your skills and accomplishments in your resume. If you achieved something, say so. Put it in the best possible light. Don't hold back or be modest, no one else will. But don't exaggerate to the point of misrepresentation.

Be brief

Write down the important (and pertinent) things you have done, but do it in as few words as possible. The shorter your resume is the more carefully it will be examined.

Work experience

Emphasize continued experience in a particular type of function or continued interest in a particular industry. De-emphasize irrelevant positions. Delete positions that you held for less than four months. (Unless you are a very recent college grad or still in school.)

Stress your results

Elaborate on how you contributed to your past employers. Did you increase sales, reduce costs, improve a product, implement a new program? Were you promoted?

Mention relevant skills and responsibilities

Be specific. Slant your past accomplishments toward the type of position that you hope to obtain. Example: Do you hope to supervise people? Then state how many people, performing what function, you have supervised.

Education

Keep it brief if you have more than two years of career experience. Elaborate more if you have less experience. Mention degrees received and any honors or special awards. Note individual courses or research projects that might be relevant for employers. For instance if you are a liberal arts major, be sure to mention courses in such areas as: accounting, statistics, computer programming, or mathematics.

Job objective?

Leave it out. Even if you are certain of exactly the type of job that you desire, the inclusion of a job objective might eliminate you from consideration for other positions that a recruiter feels are a better match for your qualifications.

Personal data

Keep it very brief. Two lines maximum. A one-word mention of commonly practiced activities such as golf, skiing, sailing, chess, bridge, tennis etc. can prove to be a good way to open up a conversation during an interview. Do not include your age, weight, height, etc.

SHOULD YOU HIRE A RESUME WRITER?

Advantages to writing it yourself: If you write reasonably well, there are some advantages to writing your resume yourself. To write it well you will have to review your experience and figure out how to explain your accomplishments in clear, brief phrases. This will help you when you explain your work to interviewers.

If you write your resume, everything in it will be in your own words - it will sound like you. It will say what you want it to say. And you will be much more familiar with the contents. If you are a good writer, know yourself well and have a good idea of what parts of your background employers are looking for, you may be able to write your own resume better than anyone else can. If you write your resume yourself you should have someone who can be objective (preferably not a close relative) review it with you.

When should you have your resume professionally written?

If you have difficulty writing in Resume Style (which is quite unlike normal written language). If you are unsure of which parts of your background you should emphasize, or if you think your resume would make you case better if it did not follow the standard form outlined here or in a book on resumes.

There are two reasons even some professional resume writers we know have had their resumes written with the help of fellow professionals. First, when they need the help of someone who can be objective about their background, and second, when they want an experienced sounding board to help focus their thoughts.

If you decide to hire a resume writer

The best way to choose a writer is by reputation - the recommendation of a friend, a personnel director, your school placement officer or someone else knowledgeable in the field.

You should ask, "If I'm not satisfied with what you write, will you go over it with me and change it?"

You should ask, "How long has the person who will write my resume been writing resumes?"

There is no sure relation between price and quality, except that you are unlikely to get a good writer for less than $50 for an uncomplicated resume and you shouldn't have to pay more than $300 unless your experience is very extensive or complicated. There will be additional charges for printing.

Few resume services will give you a firm price over the phone, simply because some people's resumes are too complicated and take too long to do at any predetermined price. Some services will quote you a price that applies to almost all of their customers. Be sure to do some comparative shopping. Obtain a firm price before you engage their services and find out how expensive minor changes will be.

COVER LETTERS

Always mail a cover letter with your resume. In a cover letter you can show an interest in the company that you can't show in a resume. You can point out one or two skills or accomplishments the company can put to good use.

Make it personal

The more personal you can get the better. If someone known to the person you are writing has recommended you contact the company, get permission to include that name in the letter. If you have the name of a person to send the letter to, make sure you have the name spelled correctly and address it directly to that person. Be sure to put the person's name and title on both the letter and envelope. This will ensure that your letter will get through to the proper person, even if a new person now occupies this position. But even if you are addressing it to the "Personnel Director" or the "Hiring Partner," send a letter.

Type cover letters in full. Don't try the cheap and easy ways like photocopying the body of your letter and typing in the inside address and salutation. You will give the impression that you are mailing to a multitude of companies and have no particular interest in any one. Have your letters fully typed and signed with a pen.

Phone

Precede or follow your mailing with a phone call.

Bring extra copies of your resume to the interview

If the person interviewing you doesn't have your resume, be prepared. Carry copies of your own. Even if you have already forwarded your resume be sure to take extra copies to the interview, as someone other than the interviewer(s) might now have the first copy you sent.

RESUME AND CAREER COUNSELING SERVICES OF THE DISTRICT OF COLUMBIA

ALTERNATIVE BUSINESS SYSTEMS
2021 L Street, N.W.,
Suite 250,
Washington, DC 20006.
202/887-0771.
Contact Barbara Katz, Owner. Appointment requested. Founded 1977. General business services offered to firms with emergency overload situations, firms who do not have enough personnel and individuals. Services commonly provided include: Internships; Printing Services; Resume Writing and Preparation; Mailings of Job Searches; and other Word Processing functions.

THE PERSONNEL INSTITUTE
1000 Connecticut Avenue, N.W.,
Washington, DC 20036.
202/223-4911.
Contact Dr. William E. Stuart, President. Employment consultants. No appointment required. Founded 1963. Equipped to perform psychological testing and staffing studies. The Personnel Insitute has an ongoing Outplacement Division as well as an Executive Search Department. Specializes in the areas of: Computer Hardware and Software; Engineering; MIS/EDP; Manufacturing; Minorities; Technical and Scientific; Veterans; Women. Positions commonly filled include: Aerospace Engineer; Bank Officer/Manager; Biologist; Biomedical Engineer; Computer Programmer; EDP Specialist; Economist; Electrical Engineer; Financial Analyst; Goverment Relations Specialist; Industrial Designer; Industrial Engineer; MIS Specialist; Marketing Specialist; Mechanical Engineer; Operations/Production Specialist; Physicist; Quality Control Supervisor; Systems Analyst; Washington Representative. Company pays fee. Number of placements per year: 201-500.

RESUME AND CAREER COUNSELING SERVICES OF MARYLAND

ACTION RESUMES
195 Grosvenor Lane
Severna Park, MD 21146
Contact Don Frazier, Owner.
301/544-0355.
Appointment requested. Founded 1975. Services commonly provided include: Resume Writing and Preparation.

M & S STAFF CONSULTING, LTD.
8750 Georgia Avenue
Suite E-122
Silver Spring, MD 20910
301/565-3900.

Contact Mr. Robert L. McDermott, President. Employment agency; temporary help service. Appointment requested. Founded 1974. Services commonly provided include: Resume Writing and Preparation.

PTS
5457 Twin Knolls Road
Suite 201
Columbia, MD 21045
301/730-0583.
Contact Barney Bohanan. Appointment requested. Founded 1975. Services commonly provided include: Resume Writing and Preparation; Bulk Mailings; Typing Term Papers. Any type of Secretarial Services.

THE RESUME PLACE
310 Frederick Road
Baltimore, MD 21228
301/744-4324.
Contact Wendy S. Enelow, General Manager. Appointment requested. Founded 1973. Services commonly provided include: Resume Writing and Preparation; Typesetting; Word Processing; Printing; Cover Letters; Individual Career Counseling. Also includes: General Business Services; Proofreading; Graphics/Illustrations; Mailing List Management. Student discounts offered.

SAMUEL R. BLATE ASSOCIATES
10331 Watkins Mill Drive
Gaithersburg, MD 20879-2935
301/840-2248
Contact Samuel R. Blate, President. Appointment required (flexible hours). Founded 1978. Specializes in Writing, Rewriting, and Editing a variety of material. Services provided include: Interview Preparation; Personal Counseling; Resume and Cover Letter Writing/Preparation.

RESUME AND CAREER COUNSELING SERVICES OF VIRGINIA

ACTION RESUMES/RUTKALS RESUMES
HC-38 Box 1012
Winchester, VA 22601
703/888-3790.
Contact Mike Rutkals, Resume Writer. Appointment required. Founded 1978. Extensive, skilled, patient interviewing uncovers the best in all applicants, producing an honest resume which will almost unconsciously get the best job for the person. Embossed papers, metal type, carbon ribbon for a striking image. Services commonly provided include: Career Assessment; Educational Counseling; Individual Career Counseling; Interview Preparation; Resume Writing/Preparation; Word Processing. Special groups served include: Adolescents; College Graduates; Elderly; Ex-Offenders; Handicapped; MBA Graduates; Minorities; Professional; Spanish-speaking Immigrants; Veterans; Women. Will decrease fee for those in need.

ERICH NORD ASSOCIATES
6801 Whittier Avenue, #304
McLean, VA 22101
703/556-9505.
Contact Joan Wikstrom, Principal. Appointment required. Founded 1981. Licensed, professional counseling offered to the general population. Holistic approach combined with personnel and teaching experience provides pragmatic atmosphere in which the client can consider new behaviors. Services commonly provided include: Career Assessment; Educational Counseling; Group Counseling; Individual Counseling; Interview Preparation; Personal Counseling; Psychological Counseling; Resume Writing/Preparation. Special groups served include: College Graduates; Elderly; Ex-Offenders; MBA Graduates; Military; Minorities; Professionals; Retirees; Veterans; Women.

CHRONOLOGICAL RESUME

(Prepared on photo typesetter.)

NATHAN JAMES FREDERICK, III

10012 Ocean View Park
Los Angeles, California 90012
213/744-8112

**business
experience**

1978 to present   **PACIFIC COMPUTER LEASING**   **Los Angeles, CA**

Manager of Debt Placement
- Responsible for developing and maintaining bank and institutional debt sources.
- Structured leases for maximum tax advantages.
- Have documented and closed $120,000,000 of secured loans.
- Work closely with investment bankers and bank and institutional funding sources.

1971-1978   **PRIME COMPUTER, INC.**   **Natick, MA**

Customer Finance Marketing Manager, North America
- Responsible for the profitable management of finance lease and tax exempt installment programs in the United States and Mexico used by government and business.
- Implementation of the programs through field based customer financing representatives. Insured financing arrangements met FASB requirements for sale recognition by vendor.
- Made certain pricing and documentation were suitable for sale of portfolio to funding institutions. Typical transaction exceeded $750,000.

1968-1971   **COPPERBOTTOM INFORMATION SYSTEMS**   **Philadelphia, PA**

11 70-5 71   Manager of Marketing Proposal Analysis   **Atlanta, GA**
- Advised field sales force in the initial stages of proposals with emphasis on the financial aspects of operating and finance leases, installment sales, and multi-party transactions.

1 70-11 70   Sectional Revenue Manager   **Winston-Salem, NC**
- Achieved planned lease purchase revenue mix, by appropriate pricing policies and financial agreements with customers.

6 68-1 70   Sales Finance   **Baltimore, MD**
- Implemented and administered Copperbottom's finance lease program. Educated field sales personnel in financial plans. Handled administration of equipment add-ons, replacements, handled contract amendments.

1962-1968   **BAYBANK, N.A.**   **Portland, OR**
- Branch Manager responsible for all aspects of the day-to-day operation of a branch bank.

**education
1956-1960**   **BABSON COLLEGE**   **Wellesley, MA**
- Bachelor of Science in Business Administration with a major in financial management, minor in mathematics.

languages   Fluent in Spanish.

references   References will be supplied upon request.

CHRONOLOGICAL RESUME

(Prepared on photo typesetter.)

KENNETH WANG
412 Country Club Lane
Albany. New York 12207
518/371-4387

EXPERIENCE

1977-Present   THE CENTER COMPANY. Albany. NY

Systems Analyst, design systems for the manufacturing unit. Specifically, physical inventory, program specifications, studies of lease buy decisions, selection of hardware for the IBM 9999. 1010. and Alpha Communications, and supervise the outside contractors and inside users. Wrote On Site Computer Terminal Operators Manual. Modelled product mix problems with the LAPSP (Logistical Alternative Product Synthesis Programming).

As *Industrial Engineer* from February 1979 to February 1980. computerized system design. Evaluated manufacturing operations operator efficiency productivity index and budget allocations. Analyzed material waste and recommended solutions.

ADDITIONAL EXPERIENCE

1975-1976   *Graduate Research Assistant* at New York State Institute of Technology.

1970-1972   *Graduate Teaching Assistant* at Salem State University.

EDUCATION

1974-1976   NEW YORK STATE INSTITUTE OF TECHNOLOGY. Albany. NY
M.S. in Operations Research. G.P.A.: 3.6. Graduate courses included Advanced Location and Queueing Theories. Forecasting. Inventory and Material Flow Systems. Linear and Nonlinear Determination Models, Engineering Economics and Integer Programming.

1972-1974   M.S. in Information and Computer Sciences. G.P.A.: 3.8. Curriculum included Digital Computer Organization & Programming. Information Structure & Process. Mathematical Logic. Computer Systems. Logic Design and Switching Theory.

1970-1972   SALEM STATE UNIVERSITY. Salem. OR
M.A. in Mathematics. G.P.A.: 3.6.

1963-1967   ALI. KOREA UNIVERSITY. Seoul. Korea
B.S. in Engineering.

AFFILIATIONS

Member of the American Institute of Computer Programmers. Association for Computing Machinery and the Operations Research Society of America.

PERSONAL

Married. three dependents. Able to relocate.

CHRONOLOGICAL RESUME

(Prepared on photo typesetter.)

KATHERINE ELIZABETH BRETTENER
2011 Hill Top View Way
San Francisco, California 94105
415/532-4731

EXPERIENCE

ULTRASHEEN STONE JEWELER   San Francisco, California
1976-Present
Senior/Designer
Created ultrasheen stone jewelry for exhibits at Rotunda Gallery, Sak's Fifth Avenue, New York;
San Regret Gallery, Los Angeles (1980); Institute of Contemporary Art, San Francisco (1979);
Weatherway Gallery, and Smith Street Shop, Seattle, Washington (1978).

AMERICAN ARTISTIC FOUNDATION   San Francisco, California
1975
Organizational Assistant
Gathered material for presentation of Art Day Catalog at the American Artistic Foundation.
Accepted by juried committee to present work in Art Day Catalog.

DIABLO PHOTO STUDIO   San Francisco, California
1974
Promotional Assistant
Did public relations work for industrial and commercial photographers. Sought corporate accounts
for on-location product photography.

GALILEO GALLERY   Seattle, Washington
1973
Retail Sales Representative
Assisted in art displays and sold merchandise.

EDUCATION

UNIVERSITY OF CALIFORNIA, Berkeley   Berkeley, California
Awarded PhD. Degree in Existential Philosophy in 1978.

STANFORD UNIVERSITY   Stanford, California
Awarded Bachelor of Arts Degree in Art History in 1974. Curriculum emphasis in Modern
European Period.

BACKGROUND

Will travel. Enjoy all aspects of performing and creative art, tennis, and yoga.

References available upon request.

CHRONOLOGICAL RESUME

(Prepared on word processor.)

JAMES WASHINGTON WHITE, JR.

U.S. Address:
486 East 77th Street
New York, New York 10021
(212) 212-2121

Jamaican Address:
Room 1234
Playboy, Jamaica
Doctor's Beach, Jamaica
(809) 326-1312

experience
1974-present   PLAYBOY, JAMAICA LTD.   DOCTOR'S BEACH, JAMAICA
Resident Engineer for this publicly owned resort
with main offices in Chicago, Illinois responsibilities include:

Maintain electrical generating and distribution
equipment.

Supervise an eight-member staff in maintenance of
refrigeration equipment, power and light generators,
water purification plant, and general construction
machinery.

1972-1974   NIGRIL BEACH HOTEL   NIGRIL BEACH, JAMAICA
Resident Engineer for a privately-held resort,
assigned total responsibility for facility generating
equipment.

Directed maintenance, operation and repair of diesel
generating equipment.

1970-1972   Directed overhaul of turbo generating equipment in
two Mid-Western localities and assisted in overhaul
of a turbo generating unit in Mexico.

1965-1970   CAPITAL CITY ELECTRIC   WASHINGTON, D.C.
Service Engineer for the power generation service
division of this regional power company, supervised
the overhaul, maintenance and repair of large generators and associated auxiliary equipment.

other
experience   A Night File Supervisor for Columbia Mutual Life
Insurance Company (1963-1965) and an Apprentice
Welder at the Potomac Naval Shipyard from 1961-1962.

Volunteer Co-ordinator Washington D.C. NAACP 1969;
Activities Co-chairman 1968

education
1962-1965   FRANKLIN INSTITUTE   BALTIMORE, MARYLAND
Awarded a degree of Associate of Engineering.
Concentration in Mechanical Power Engineering
Technology.

personal   Willing to travel and relocate.
Interested in sailing, scuba diving, deep sea fishing.

References available upon request.

CHRONOLOGICAL RESUME

(Prepared on word processor.)

JOAN M. MORRISON
43 Hilltop Drive
Chicago, Illinois 60612
(312) 312-3123 (home)
(312) 423-4234 (work)

**RELATED
EXPERIENCE
1972-Present**
GREAT LAKES PUBLISHING CO.,CHICAGO, ILLINOIS
Operations Supervisor (1976-Present) in the
Engineering Division of this major trade publishing
house, responsible for maintaining on line computerized
customer files, title files, accounts receivable,
inventory and sales files.

Organize department activities, establish priorities
and train personnel. Provide corporate accounting with
monthly reports of sales, earned income from journals,
samples, inventory levels/value and sales tax data.
Divisional sales average $3 Million annually.

Senior Customer Service Representative (1974-1976)
in the Construction Division, answered customer service
inquiries regarding orders and accounts receivable,
issued return and shortage credits and expedited
special sales orders for direct mail and sales to trade
schools.

Customer Service Representative (1972-1973), International Division. Same duties as for Construction
Division except sales were to retail stores and
universities in Europe.

1970-1972
B. DALTON, BOOKSELLER, SALT LAKE CITY, UTAH
Assistant Manager of this retail branch of a major
domestic book seller, maintained all paperback
inventories at necessary levels, deposited receipts
daily and created window displays.

**EDUCATION
1966-1970**
UNIVERSITY OF MAINE, ORONO, MAINE
Awarded a degree of Bachelor of Arts in French
Literature.

LANGUAGES
Fluent in French. Able to write in French, German
and Spanish.

PERSONAL
Willing to travel and relocate, particularly in
Europe.

References available upon request.

CHRONOLOGICAL RESUME

(Prepared on photo typesetter.)

THOMAS L. HAMLER, JR.

414 Loland Street
Greenwich, Connecticut 06830
203/548-2319

**BUSINESS
EXPERIENCE**

1979-Present   *Venture Developer,* New York Community Economic Development Assistance Corporation. Planning and negotiation of manufacturing and commercial ventures involving Community Development Corporations, private entrepreneurs, financial and government institutions. Projects completed or in process include start-ups, joint ventures, turnarounds and real estate enterprises valued in excess of $170 million.

1977   *Real Estate Developer,* Southwestern Connecticut Development Corporation. Planned major redevelopment projects in the Stamford and Bridgeport areas, including 160,000 square feet of new and recycled office space, and two new supermarkets; negotiated for acquisition of industrial properties for manufacturing joint ventures.

1976-1977   *Project Manager,* State Crossing Industrial Park, a joint development of the Economic Development and Industrial Corporation of New York and the Regional Industrial Fund of Connecticut. Planned and coordinated execution of site acquisition, preparation and revenue bond financing for a major computer manufacturer; packaged SBA loans and industrial revenue bonds for industrial firms.

1975-1976   *Research Analyst,* Federal Reserve Bank of New York. Analyzed trends in capital market behavior and business investment; studied MESBICs and other sources of venture capital for small businesses.

1972-1975   *Consultant,* Connecticut House Ways and Means Committee. Investigated state purchase of service contracts with private providers.

1970-1972   *Associate,* Means, Thompson & Simpson Construction Consultants, Inc., New York, NY. Advised major commercial construction firms principally on industrial park development.

EDUCATION   Master of Business Administration, Columbia, 1974.

Bachelor of Arts, Yale University, 1970.

American Institute of Banking, "Commercial Lending Practices."

PERSONAL   Little League Baseball Coach. Married, two sons.

FUNCTIONAL RESUME

(Prepared on photo typesetter.)

JOHN SINGLETON COPLEY
420 Boylston Street
Pittsburgh, Pennsylvania 15234
412/323-3491

Solid background in plate making, separations, color matching, background definition, printing, mechanicals, color corrections, and supervision of personnel. A highly motivated manager, adept problem-solver and effective communicator. Proven ability to:

- Create Commercial Graphics
- Produce Embossing Drawings
- Color Separate
- Analyze Consumer Acceptance

- Meet Graphic Deadlines
- Control Quality
- Resolve Printing Problems
- Expedite Printing Operations

Qualifications

Printing — Black and white and color. Can judge acceptability of color reproduction by comparing it with original. Can make four or five color corrections on all media. Have long developed ability to restyle already reproduced four-color art work. Can create perfect tone for black and white match fill-ins for resume cover letters.

Customer Relations — Work well with customers to assure specifications are met and customers are satisfied. Can guide work through entire production process and strike a balance between technical printing capabilities and need for customer approval.

Management — Schedule work to meet deadlines. Direct staff in production procedures. Control budgets, maintain quality control from inception of project through final approval for printing.

Specialties Make silk screen overlays and overlays for a multitude of processes. Velo bind, GBC bind, perfect bind. Gold leaf embossing, silver inlay stamping. Have knowledge to prepare posters, flyers, business cards and personalized stationery.

Personnel Supervision — Foster an atmosphere that encourages highly talented artists to balance high level creativity with a maximum of production. Have managed a group of over 20 photographers, developers, plate etchers, checkers and artists. Met or beat production deadlines. Am continually instructing new employees, apprentices and students in both artistry and technical operations.

Experience

Assistant Production Manager. Artsign Digraphics, Erie, PA (1952-Present) Part time.
Professor of Graphic Arts, Pennsylvania College of Fine Arts, Pittsburgh, PA (1950-Present)

Education

Massachusetts Conservatory of Art PhD 1950

GENERAL MODEL
FOR A COVER LETTER

Your
Address

Date

Contact Person Name
Title
Company
Address

Dear Mr.(Ms.) _____ :

    Immediately explain why your background makes
you the best candidate for the position that you
are applying for. Keep the first paragraph short
and hard-hitting.

    Detail what you could contribute to this com-
pany. Show how your qualifications will benefit
this firm. Remember to keep this letter short;
few recruiters will read a cover letter longer
than a half-a-page.

    Describe your interest in the corporation.
Subtly emphasize your knowledge about this firm
(the result of your research effort) and your
familiarity with the industry. It is common
courtesy to act extremely eager to work for any
company that you interview.

    In the closing paragraph you should specifi-
cally request an interview. Include your phone
number and the hours when you can best be reached.
Alternatively, you might prefer to mention that
you will follow-up with a phone call (to arrange
an interview at a mutually convenient time) within
the next several days.

               Sincerely yours,

               (signature)

               Full Name (typed)

Enc. Resume

COVER LETTER

49 Smith Park Circle
Houston, Texas 77031

October 5, 19___

Mr. Clinton P. Thomas
Vice President and Director of Personnel
Riverbay Fire Insurance Group
Riverbay Plaza
Houston, Texas 77035

Dear Mr. Thomas:

I am the career oriented individual who can successfully provide technical direction and training to pension analysts in connection with FKLE system.

My major and most recent background is directly involved in the administration of pension and profit sharing plans with TRMZ. Furthermore, my extensive experience both as a Group Pension Pre-Scale Underwriter and as a Pension Underwriter involves data processing knowledge and over- all pension administration.

A prime function of mine is decision making with reference to group pension business. You specifically seek an individual who can recommend changes and/or new procedures of plan administration and maintenance plus assistance in development of pension administration kits for use by the field force at Riverbay. I feel that I possess the ability to fulfill your need dramatically.

I would welcome the practical opportunity to work directly with general agents and plan trustees in qualifying, revising and requalifying pension and profit sharing plans required by TRMZ. You will note in my resume my background in working with others in both an advisory and shirt-sleeve capacity.

I look forward to hearing from you.

Sincerely,

Samuel A. Waters

Enc. Resume

COVER LETTER

1015 Commonwealth Avenue
Apartment 16
Boston, Massachusetts 02145

February 15, 19__

Mr. Clark T. Johnson
Vice-President/Human Resources
Boston City Bank Corporation
110 Milk Street
Boston, Massachusetts 02114

Dear Mr. Johnson:

Having majored in Mathematics at Boston University, where I also worked as a Research Assistant, I am confident that I would make a very successful Research Trainee in your Economics Research Department.

In addition to my strong background in mathematics, I also offer significant business experience, having worked in a data processing firm, a bookstore, and a restaurant. I am sure that my courses in statistics and computer programming would prove particularly useful in the position of Research Trainee.

I am attracted to City Bank by your recent rapid growth and the superior reputation of your Economic Research Department. After studying different commercial banks, I have concluded that City Bank will be in a strong competitive position to benefit from upcoming changes in the industry, such as the phasing out of Regulation Q.

I would like to interview with you at your earliest convenience. I am best reached between 3 and 5 p.m. at 277-1483.

Sincerely yours,

Steven M. Phillips

Enc. Resume

COVER LETTER

1012 Winding Hill Road
Newark, New Jersey 07101

December 10, 19__

Mr. Daniel Wentworth
Personnel Manager
Mitchell & Brothers Engineering Services, Inc.
Central Park Square Building
New York, New York 10019

Dear Mr. Wentworth:

My diversity as well as my depth of engineering experience
in the wastewater treatment field could prove to be a
particularly strong asset for Mitchell & Brothers given
the firm's current and continued commitment to being a
pioneering innovator in the engineering and construction
of wastewater treatment facilities.

I offer an extensive background in investigating, reporting
and designing multimillion dollar wastewater treatment
facilities, pumping facilities and sewer lines in New Jersey
and in Puerto Rico. In addition I have experience in
coordinating engineering services during construction
of sewers and pumping facilities in Hawaii.

One of my basic strengths is my ability to act as liason
for diverse engineering and non-engineering individuals and
groups to keep a project on schedule and in line with
funding constraints.

I have come to a point in my career where I desire to
expand into areas where I might utilize over 8 years of
solid engineering experience. These areas include hazardous
waste treatment, industrial wastewater and water treatment,
and water supply.

I will be glad to furnish any additional information you
desire. You may reach me during the day at 201/576-1100.
I look forward to hearing from you.

Sincerely,

John T. Lent

Enc. Resume

GENERAL MODEL
FOR A FOLLOW-UP LETTER

```
                                      Your
                                      Address

                                      Date


Contact Person Name
Title
Company
Address

Dear Mr.(Ms.) _____:

    Remind the interviewer of the position for
which you were interviewed, as well as the date.
Thank him (her) for the interview.

    Confirm your interest in the opening and the
organization.  Use specifics to emphasize both
that you have researched the firm in detail and
considered how you would fit into the company and
the position.

    Like in your cover letter, emphasize one or
two of your strongest qualifications and slant
them toward the various points that the inter-
viewer considered the most important for the posi-
tion.  Keep the letter brief, a half-page is
plenty.

    If appropriate, close with a suggestion for
further action, such as a desire to have addi-
tional interviews.  Mention your phone number and
the hours that you can best be reached.  Alter-
natively, you may prefer to mention that you will
follow-up with a phone call in several days.

                          Sincerely yours,

                          (signature)

                          Your Full Name (typed)
                          Phone number (if not in text)
```

JOBS IN EACH INDUSTRY

JOBS IN EACH INDUSTRY

The following chapter includes descriptions of many of the most common occupations, with an emphasis on those that have especially strong growth outlooks for the 1990's. For each position, you will find a brief description of what the position entails, the background or qualifications you would need for entering and advancing in that occupation, the salary expectations for various levels within the occupational category, and a forecast of the job's growth potential for the 1990's.

ACCOUNTANT/AUDITOR

DESCRIPTION:

Accountants prepare and analyze financial reports that furnish important financial information. Four major fields are public, management, government accounting, and internal auditing. Public accountants have their own businesses or work for accounting firms. Management accountants, also called industrial or private accountants, handle the financial records of their company. Government accountants examine the records of government agencies and audit private businesses and individuals whose dealings are subject to government regulation. Accountants often concentrate on one phase of accounting. For example, many public accountants may specialize in auditing, tax, or estate planning. Others specialize in management consulting and give advice on a variety of matters. Management accountants provide the financial information executives need to make sound business decisions. They may work in areas such as taxation, budgeting, costs, or investments. Internal auditing, a specialization within management accounting, is rapidly growing in importance. Internal auditors examine and ensure efficient and economical operation. Government accountants are often Internal Revenue Service agents or are involved in financial management and budget administration.

About 60 percent of all accountants do management accounting. An additional 25 percent are engaged in public accounting through independent firms. Other accountants work for government, and some teach in colleges and universities. Accountants and auditors are found in all business, industrial, and governmental organizations.

BACKGROUND AND QUALIFICATIONS:

Although many graduates of business schools are successful, most public accounting and business firms require applicants for accountant and internal auditor positions to have at least a BA in Accounting or a closely related field. Many employers prefer those with a Master's degree in Accounting. Most large employers prefer applicants who are familiar with computers and their applications in accounting and internal auditing.

Previous experience in accounting can help an applicant get a job. Many colleges offer students an opportunity to gain experience through summer or part-time internship programs conducted by public accounting firms. Such training is invaluable in gaining permanent employment in the field.

Professional recognition through certification or licensing also is extremely valuable. Anyone working as a Certified Public Accountant (CPA) must hold a certificate issued by a state board of accountancy. All states use the four-part Uniform CPA Exam, prepared by the American Institute of Certified Public Accountants, to establish certification. The CPA exam is very rigorous, and candidates are not required to pass all four parts at once. Most states require applicants to have some public accounting experience for a CPA certificate, and those with BA's often need two years of experience. New trends require the candidate to have a BA plus 30 additional semester hours.

The Institute of Internal Auditors confers the Certified Internal Auditor (CIA) certificate upon graduates from accredited colleges and universities who have completed three years internal auditing and who have passed a four-part exam. The National Association of Accountants (NAA) confers the Certificate in Management Accounting (CMA) upon candidates who pass a series of uniform exams and meet specific educational and professional standards. A growing number of states require both CPA's and licensed public accountants to complete a certain number of hours of continuing education before licenses can be renewed. Increasingly, accountants are studying computer programming so they can adapt accounting procedures to data processing.

Junior public accountants usually start by assisting with auditing work for several clients. They may advance to intermediate positions with greater responsibility in one or two years, and to senior positions within another few years. Those who deal successfully with top industry executives often become supervisors, managers, or partners, or transfer to executive positions in private firms. Beginning management accountants often start as ledger accountants, junior internal auditors, or as trainees for technical accounting positions. They may advance to chief plant accountant, chief cost accountant, budget director, or manager of internal auditing. Some become controllers, treasurers, financial vice-presidents, or corporation presidents.

EARNINGS:

Starting: with BA, average $21,200; with MA, average $25,600. Entire career: Range is roughly $20,000 to $70,000.

OUTLOOK:

Employment of accountants and auditors is expected to grow much faster than the average for all occupations through the year 2000 due to the key role these workers play in the management of all types of businesses. Although increased demand will generate many new jobs, most openings will result from the need to replace workers who leave the occupation or retire. While accountants and auditors tend to leave the profession at a lower rate than members of most other occupations, replacement needs will be substantial because the occupation is large.

Accountants rarely lose their jobs when other workers are laid off during hard economic times. Financial information must be developed and tax reports prepared regardless of the state of the economy.

ACTUARY

DESCRIPTION:

Actuaries design insurance and pension plans that can be maintained on a sound financial basis. They assemble and analyze statistics to calculate probabilities of death, sickness, injury, disability, unemployment, retirement, and property loss from accident, theft, fire, and other hazards. Actuaries use this information to determine the expected insured loss. The actuary calculates premium rates and determines policy contract provision for each type of insurance offered. Most actuaries specialize in either life and health insurance, or property and liability (casualty) insurance; a growing number specialize in pension plans. About two-thirds of all actuaries work for private insurance companies, the majority in life insurance. Consulting firms and rating bureaus employ about one-fifth of all actuaries. Other actuaries work for private organizations administering independent pension and welfare plans.

BACKGROUND AND EXPERIENCE:

A good educational background for a beginning job in a large life or casualty insurance company is a Bachelor's degree in Mathematics or Statistics; a degree in Actuarial Science is preferred. Courses in accounting, computer science, economics, and insurance also are useful. Of equal importance, however, is the need to pass one or more of the exams offered by professional actuarial societies. Three societies sponsor programs leading to full professional status in the specialty. The Society of Actuaries gives nine actuarial exams for the life and health insurance, and pension fields; The Casualty Actuarial Society gives 10 exams for the property and liability fields; and the American Society of Pension Actuaries gives nine exams covering the pension field.

Actuaries are encouraged to complete the entire series of exams as soon as possible; completion generally takes from five to ten years. Actuaries who complete five exams in either the life insurance segment of the pension series, or seven exams in the casualty series are awarded "associate" membership in their society. Those who have passed an entire series receive full membership and the title "Fellow".

Beginning actuaries often rotate among different jobs to learn various actuarial operations and to become familiar with different phases of insurance work. At first, their work may be routine, such as preparing tabulations for actuarial tables or reports. As they gain experience, they may supervise clerks, prepare correspondence and reports, and do research. Advancement to more responsible positions such as assistant, associate, or chief actuary depends largely on job performance and the number of actuarial exams passed. Many actuaries, because of their broad knowledge of insurance and related fields, are selected for administrative positions in other company activities, particularly in underwriting, accounting, or data processing. Many advance to top executive positions.

EARNINGS:

New college graduates entering the life insurance field without having passed any exams average $19,000 to $24,000. After the completion of the first exam, the average is $21,000 to $25,000, and with two exams passed, the average is $23,000 to $26,000. Each exam passed usually earns an approximate $1,000 increase. Associates average $32,000 to $45,000. Beginning fellows average $44,000 to $55,000 and fellows with several years experience average more than $60,000.

OUTLOOK:

Employment of actuaries is expected to grow much faster than the average for all occupations through the year 2000. Most job openings, however, are expected to arise each year to replace actuaries who transfer to other occupations, or retire. Job opportunities should be favorable for college graduates who have passed at least two actuarial exams while still in school and have a strong mathematical and statistical background.

ADMINISTRATOR

DESCRIPTION:

Administrators perform a wide variety of office paperwork tasks. These tasks might range from preparing a summary of sales activity to filing and retrieving information. A lower-level administrator might serve primarily as a typist, office machine operator, or secretary, being closely supervised by an office superior. An upper-level administrator might supervise the work of many office workers and be responsible for a broad range of office duties that support an organization's activities.

BACKGROUND AND QUALIFICATIONS:

Because of the broad range of duties and responsibilities of administrators at different levels or within different organizations, the actual job and its requisite background and experience may vary greatly from one firm to the next, and from one position to the next. However, all but the highest managerial levels of administrative work require strong office skills such as fast and accurate typing and the ability to prepare business correspondence. In larger organizations with more complex office tasks, a college background is becoming an increasingly valuable asset. Also, experience or familiarity with computers, word processors, or data processing equipment greatly improves an applicant's employability and chances for promotion.

EARNINGS:

Pay varies widely depending upon the company and position. A position requiring only a high school diploma and no typing skills may pay $12,000 per year, while an entry-level position requiring a college degree, fast typing skills, and the ability to take shorthand may pay $18,000 per year.

OUTLOOK:

Despite the nearly universal use of computer and word processing automation in the office, administrative positions are still expected to offer above average growth. Also, with many new entrants to the job market trying to obtain junior managerial jobs and similar posts, Administrative positions are likely to be less competitive than many other types of jobs. Administrators are found in all industries, but especially in Banking, Insurance, Utilities, and other companies with a high volume of paperwork.

ADVERTISING WORKER

DESCRIPTION:

There are several different occupations commonly associated with the field of advertising. Advertising Managers direct the advertising program of the business for which they work. They determine the size of the advertising budget, the type of ad and the media to use, and what advertising agency, if any, to employ. Managers who decide to employ an agency work closely with the advertising agencies to develop advertising programs for client firms and individuals. Copywriters develop the text and headlines to be used in the ads. Media Directors negotiate contracts for advertising for advertising space or air time. Production Managers and their assistants arrange to have the ad printed for publication, filmed for television, or recorded for radio.

BACKGROUND AND QUALIFICATIONS:

Most employers prefer college graduates. Some employers seek persons with degrees in advertising with heavy emphasis on marketing, business, and journalism; others prefer graduates with a liberal arts background; some employers place little emphasis on the type of degree. Opportunities for advancement in this field generally are excellent for creative, talented, and hard-working people. For example, copywriters and account executives may advance to more responsible work in their specialties, or to managerial jobs if they demonstrate ability in dealing with clients. Some especially capable employees may become partners in an existing agency, or they may establish their own agency.

EARNINGS:

In 1986, the lowest 10 percent of advertising workers earned $17,700 or less, while the top 10 percent earned over $52,500. Salaries between $75,000 and $100,000 are not uncommon. Many earn bonuses equal to 10 percent or more of their regular salaries. Salary levels vary substantially depending upon the level of managerial responsibility, length of service, and size and location of the firm.

OUTLOOK:

Employment of advertising managers is expected to increase faster than the average for all occupations through the year 2000 as increasingly intense domestic and foreign competition in products and services offered consumers requires greater marketing and promotional efforts. In addition to rapid growth, many job openings will occur each year to replace managers who move into the top positions or retire. However, the ample supply of experienced professional and technical personnel and recent college graduates seeking these management positions may result in substantial job competition.

ARCHITECT

DESCRIPTION:

Architects provide a wide variety of professional services to individuals, organizations, corporations, or government agencies planning a building project. Architects are involved in all phases of development of a building or project, from the initial discussion of general ideas through completion of construction. Their duties require a variety of skills, including design, engineering, managerial, and supervisory.

The architect and client first discuss the purposes, requirements, and cost of a project. The architect then prepares schematic drawings that show the scale and the mechanical and structural relationships of the building. If the schematic drawings are accepted, the architect develops a final design showing the floor plans and the structural details of the project.

Architects also specify the building materials and, in some cases, the interior furnishings. In all cases, the architect must ensure that the structure's design and specifications conform to local and state building codes, zoning laws, fire regulations, and other ordinances. After all drawings are completed, the architect assists the client in selecting a contractor and negotiating the construction contract. As construction proceeds, the architect visits the building site from time to time to ensure that the contractor is following the design using the specified materials.

Besides designing structures, architects may also help in selecting building sites, preparing cost and land-use studies, and long-range planning for site development. When working on large projects or for large architectural firms, architects often specialize in one phase of work, such as designing or administering construction contracts. This often requires working with engineers, urban planners, landscape architects, and others.

Most architects work for architectural firms or for builders, real estate firms, or other businesses that have large construction programs. Some work for governmental agencies. Although found in many areas, a large proportion of architects are employed in seven cities: Boston, Chicago, Los Angeles, New York, Philadelphia, San Francisco, and Washington, DC.

BACKGROUND AND QUALIFICATIONS:

Every state requires individuals to be licensed before they may call themselves architects or contract for providing architectural services. To qualify for the licensing exam, a person must have either a Bachelor of Architecture degree followed by three years of acceptable practical experience in an architect's office, or a Master of Architecture degree followed by two years of experience. As a substitute for formal training, most states accept additional experience (usually 12 years) and successful completion of a qualifying test for admission to the licensing examination. Many architectural school graduates work in the field although they are not licensed. However, a Registered Architect is required to take legal responsibility for all work. New graduates usually begin as drafters for architectural firms, where they prepare architectural drawings and make models of structures under the direction of a Registered Architect. After several years of experience, they may advance to Chief or Senior Drafter responsible for all major details of a set of working drawings, and for supervising other drafters. Others may work as Designers, Construction Contract Administrators, or Specification Writers who prepare documents that specify the building materials, their method of installation, the quality of finishes, required tests, and many other related details.

EARNINGS:

The median annual earnings for salaried architects who worked full time were about $30,000 in 1986. The middle 50 percent earned between $21,700 and $37,600. The top 10 percent earned more than $51,000 and the lowest 10 percent, less than $16,200.

Architects who are partners in well-established architectural firms or solo practitioners generally earn much more than their salaried employees, but their income may fluctuate due to changing business conditions. Architects may have difficulty getting established in their own practices and may go through a period when their expenses are greater than their income.

OUTLOOK:

Employment of architects is expected to rise faster than the average for all occupations through the year 2000, although growth in employment will be slower than in recent years. However, demand for architects is highly dependent upon the level of construction, particularly of non-residential structures such as office buildings and shopping centers. Although rapid growth in this area is expected, construction is sensitive to cyclical changes in the economy. During recessions or slow periods for construction, architects will face competition for job openings or clients, and layoffs may occur.

ATTORNEY

DESCRIPTION:

Certain activities are common to nearly every attorney's work. Probably the most fundamental is interpretation of the law. Every attorney, whether representing the defendant in a murder trial, or the plaintiff in a lawsuit, combines an understanding of the relevant laws with knowledge of the facts in the case, to determine how the first affects the second. Based on this determination, the attorney decides what action would best serve the interests of the client.

A significant number specialize in one branch of law, such as corporate, criminal, labor, patent, real estate, tax, admiralty, probate, or international law. Communications lawyers, for example, may represent radio and television stations in their dealings with the Federal Communications Commission in such matters as preparing and filing license renewal applications, employment reports, and other documents required by the FCC on a regular basis. Lawyers representing public utilities before state and federal regulatory agencies handle matters involving utility rates. They develop strategy, arguments, and testimony; prepare cases for presentation; and argue the case. These attorneys also inform clients about changes in regulations and give advice about the legality of certain actions.

A single client may employ a lawyer full time. Known as House Counsel, this lawyer usually advises a company about legal questions that arise from business activities. Such questions might involve patents, governments regulations, a business contract with another company, or a collective bargaining agreement with a union.

Some attorneys use their legal background in administrative or managerial positions in various departments of large corporations. A transfer from a corporation's legal department to another department is often viewed as a way to gain administrative experience and rise in the ranks of management. People may also use their legal background as journalists, management consultants, financial analysts, insurance claim adjusters, real estate appraisers, lobbyists, tax collectors, probation officers, and credit investigators.

BACKGROUND AND QUALIFICATIONS:

To practice law in the courts of any state, a person must be admitted to its bar. Applicants for admission to the bar must pass a written examination; however, a few states drop this requirement for graduates from its own law schools. Lawyers who have been admitted to the bar in one state may be admitted in another without taking an examination if they meet the state's standard of good moral character and have a specified period of legal experience. Federal courts and agencies set their own qualifications for those practicing before them. To qualify for the bar examination in most states, an applicant must complete at least three years of college, and graduate from a law school approved by the American Bar Association

EARNINGS:

Beginning attorneys in private industry averaged nearly $31,000 in 1986. In the Federal Government, annual starting salaries for attorneys in 1987 were about $22,500 or $27,200, depending upon academic and personal qualifications. Factors affecting the salaries offered to new graduates include:

Academic record; type, size, and location of employers; and the desired specialized educational background. The field of law makes a difference, too. Patent lawyers, for example, generally are among the highest paid attorneys.

Salaries of experienced attorneys also vary widely according to the type, size, and location of the employers. The average salary of the most experienced lawyers in private industry in 1986 was over $101,000. General attorneys in the Federal Government averaged around $46,000 a year in 1986; the relatively small number of patent attorneys in the Federal Government averaged around $55,400.

OUTLOOK:

Rapid growth in the nation's requirements for lawyers is expected to bring job openings into rough balance with the relatively stable number of law school graduates each year and result in an easing of competition for jobs through the year 2000. During the 1970's, the annual number of law school graduates more than doubled, even outpacing the rapid growth of jobs. Although graduates with superior academic records from well-regarded law schools continued to enjoy excellent opportunities, most graduates encountered increasingly keen competition for jobs. Growth in the yearly number of law school graduates has tapered off during the 1980's, but, nevertheless, the number remains at a level high enough to tax the economy's capacity to absorb them. The number of law school graduates is expected to continue to remain near its present level through the year 2000, allowing employment growth to bring the job market for lawyers back into balance.

Employment of lawyers has grown very rapidly since the early 1970's, and is expected to continue to grow much faster than the average for all occupations through the year 2000. Increased population and growing business activity help sustain the strong growth in demand for attorneys. This demand also will be spurred by growth of legal action in such areas as employee benefits, consumer protection, the environment, and safety, and an anticipated increase in the use of legal services by middle-income groups through legal clinics and prepaid legal service programs.

Turnover of jobs in this occupation is low because its members are well paid and enjoy considerable social status, and a substantial educational investment is required for entry. Nevertheless, most job openings will stem from the need to replace lawyers who transfer to other occupations or retire.

BANK OFFICER/MANAGER

DESCRIPTION:

Because banks offer a broad range of services, a wide choice of careers is available. Loan Officers may handle installment, commercial, real estate, or agricultural loans. To evaluate loan applications properly, officers need to be familiar with economics, production, distribution, merchandising, and commercial law, as well as having a knowledge of business operations and financial analysis. Bank officers in trust management must have knowledge of financial planning and investment for investment research for estate and trust administration. Operations Officers plan, coordinate, and control the work flow, update systems, and strive for administrative efficiency. Careers in bank operations include Electronic Data Processing Manager and other positions involving internal and customer services. A Correspondent Bank Officer is responsible for relations with other banks; a Branch Manager, for all functions of a branch office; and an International Officer, for advising customers with financial dealings abroad. A working knowledge of a foreign country's financial system, trade relations, and economic conditions is beneficial to those interested in international banking. Other career fields for bank officers are auditing, economics, personnel administration, public relations, and operations research.

BACKGROUND AND QUALIFICATIONS:

Bank officers and management positions generally are filled by management trainees, and occasionally by promoting outstanding bank clerks and tellers. A Business Administration degree with concentrations in finance or a liberal arts curriculum, including accounting, economics, commercial law, political science, or statistics, serves as excellent preparation for officer trainee positions. In large banks that have special training programs, promotions may occur more quickly. For a senior officer position, however, an employee usually needs many years of experience. Although experience, ability, and leadership are emphasized for promotion, advancement may be accelerated by special study. The American Bankers Association (ABA) offers courses, publications, and other training aids to officers in every phase of banking. The American Institute of Banking, an arm of the ABA, has long filled the same educational need among bank support personnel.

EARNINGS:

The median salary of financial manager was $30,400 in 1986. The lowest 10 percent earned $17,100 or less, while the top 10 percent earned over $52,000. The salary level depends upon the size and location of the firm, and is likely to be higher in large institutions and cities. Many financial managers in private industry receive additional compensation in the form of bonuses, which also vary substantially by size of firm.

OUTLOOK:

Employment of financial managers is expected to increase about as fast as the average for all occupations through the year 2000. Expanding automation - such as use of computers for electronic funds transmission and for data and information processing - may make financial managers more productive. However, the growing need for skilled financial management in the face of increasing domestic and foreign competition, changing laws regarding taxes and other financial matters, and greater emphasis on accurate reporting of financial data should spur demand for financial managers. New jobs will also be created by the increasing variety and complexity of services - including financial planning - offered by financial institutions. However, most job openings will result from the need to replace those who transfer to other fields or retire.

BIOCHEMIST

DESCRIPTION:

Biochemists study the chemical composition and behavior of living things. They often study the effects of food, hormones, or drugs on various organisms. The methods and techniques of biochemists are applied in areas such as medicine and agriculture. More than three out of four biochemists work in basic and applied research activities. Some biochemists combine research with teaching in colleges and universities. A few work in industrial production and testing activities. About one-half of all biochemists work for colleges or universities, and about one-fourth for private industry, primarily in companies manufacturing drugs, insecticides, and cosmetics. Some biochemists work for non-profit research institutes and foundations; others for federal, state, and local government agencies. A few self-employed biochemists are consultants to industry and government.

BACKGROUND AND QUALIFICATIONS:

The minimum educational requirement for many beginning jobs as a biochemist, especially in research and teaching, is an advanced degree. A PhD is a virtual necessity for persons who hope to contribute significantly to biochemical research and advance to many management or administrative jobs. A BS in Biochemistry, Biology, or Chemistry may qualify some persons for entry jobs as research assistants or technicians. Graduates with advanced degrees may begin their careers as teachers or researchers in colleges or universities. In private industry, most begin in research jobs, and with experience may advance to positions in which they plan and supervise research. New graduates with a BA or BS often start work as research assistants or technicians. These jobs in private industry often involve testing and analysis.

EARNINGS:

According to the College Placement Council, beginning salary offers in private industry in 1986 averaged $19,000 a year for bachelor's degree recipients in biochemistry.

In the Federal Government in 1987, biological scientists having a BS could begin at $14,822 to $22,458, depending on their college records. Those having an MS could start at $18,358 to $22,458. Those with PhD could begin at $27,172 to $32,567 a year. Biological scientists in the Federal Government averaged $37,200 a year in 1986.

OUTLOOK:

Employment of biochemists is expected to increase about as fast as the average for all occupations through the year 2000. Most growth will be in private industry, primarily in genetic and biotechnical research and in production - using newly developed biological methods. Efforts to preserve the environment should also result in growth.

Biochemists are less likely to lose their jobs during recessions than those in many other occupations since most are employed on long-term research projects or in agriculture, activities which are not much affected by economic fluctuations.

BLUE-COLLAR WORKER SUPERVISOR

DESCRIPTION:

Supervisors direct the activities of other employees and frequently ensure that millions of dollars worth of equipment and materials are used properly and efficiently. While blue-collar worker supervisors are most commonly known as foremen or forewomen, they also have many other titles. In the textile industry, they are referred to as second hands; on ships, they are known as boatswains, and in the construction industry, they are often called overseers, strawbosses, or gang leaders. Supervisors make work schedules and keep production and employee records. They must use judgement in planning and must allow for unforeseen problems such as absent workers, or machine breakdowns. Teaching employees safe work habits and enforcing safety rules and regulations are among other supervisory responsibilities. Supervisors also may demonstrate timesaving or laborsaving techniques to workers, and train new employees. Worker supervisors tell their subordinates about company plans and policies; recommend good workers for wage increases, awards, or promotions; and deal with poor workers by issuing warnings or recommending that they be fired. In companies where employees belong to labor unions, supervisors meet with union representatives to discuss work problems and grievances. They must know the provisions of labor-management contracts and run their operations according to these agreements.

BACKGROUND AND QUALIFICATIONS:

When choosing supervisors, employers generally look for experience, skill, and leadership qualities. Most supervisors rise through the ranks; however, a growing number of employers are hiring trainees with a college background. This practice is most prevalent in industries with highly technical production processes, such as the chemical, oil, and electronics industries. Employers generally prefer backgrounds in business administration, industrial relations, mathematics, engineering, or science. The trainees undergo on-the-job training until they are able to accept supervisory responsibilities.

Outstanding supervisors may move up to higher management positions. In manufacturing, for example, they may advance to jobs such as department head or plant manager. Some supervisors, particularly in the construction industry, use the experience and skills they gain to go into business for themselves.

EARNINGS:

Median weekly earnings for blue-collar worker supervisors were about $485 in 1986. The middle 50 percent earned between $350 and $630. The lowest 10 percent earned less than $210, and the highest 10 percent earned over $790. Supervisors receive a salary determined by the wage rates of the highest paid workers they supervise. For example, most companies keep wages of supervisors about 10 to 30 percent higher than those of their subordinates. Some supervisors receive overtime pay.

OUTLOOK:

Employment of blue-collar worker supervisors is expected to increase more slowly than the average for all occupation through the year 2000. Although rising incomes will stimulate demand for goods such as air-conditioners, home entertainment equipment, personal computers, and automobiles, employment in manufacturing industries will decline, due in part to increasing foreign competition. The production-related occupations in manufacturing, including blue-collar worker supervisors, will be the ones most adversely affected. Offsetting the decline in the number of supervisors in manufacturing, however, will be an increase in jobs in non-manufacturing industries, especially in the trade and service sectors.

In addition to the jobs resulting in increased demand for supervisors, many openings will arise from the need to replace workers who leave the occupation. Supervisors have a relatively strong attachment to the occupation, but because the occupation is so large, turnover results in a large number of openings. Because blue-collar worker supervisors are so important to the successful operation of a firm, they are often protected from layoffs during a recession. Supervisors in the construction industry, however, may experience periodic layoffs when construction activity declines.

BUYER/MERCHANDISE MANAGER

DESCRIPTION:

All merchandise sold in a retail store appears in that store on the decision of a buyer. Although all buyers seek to satisfy their stores' customers and sell at a profit, the type and variety of goods they purchase depends on the store where they work. A buyer for a small clothing store, for example, may purchase its complete stock of merchandise. Buyers who work for larger retail businesses often handle a few related lines of goods, such as men's wear, ladies' sportswear, or children's toys, among many others. Some, known as foreign buyers, purchase merchandise outside the United States. Buyers must be familiar with the manufacturers and distributors who handle the merchandise they need. They also must keep informed about changes in existing products and the development of new ones. Merchandise Managers plan and coordinate buying and selling activities for large and medium-sized stores. They divide the budget among buyers, decide how much merchandise to stock, and assign each buyer to purchase certain goods. Merchandise Managers may review buying decisions to ensure that needed categories of goods are in stock, and help buyers to set general pricing guidelines.

Some buyers represent large stores or chains in cities where many manufacturers are located. The duties of these "market representatives" vary by employer; some purchase goods, while others supply information and arrange for store buyers to meet with manufacturer's representatives when they are in the area. New technology has altered the buyers' role in retail chain stores. Cash registers connected to a computer, known as point-of-sale terminals, allow retail chains to maintain centralized, up-to-the-minute inventory records. With these records, a single garden furniture buyer, for example, can purchase lawn chairs and picnic tables for the entire chain.

BACKGROUND AND QUALIFICATIONS:

Because familiarity with the merchandise and with the retailing business itself is such a central element in the buyer's job, prior retailing experience sometimes provides sufficient preparation. More and more, however, employers prefer applicants who have a college degree. Most employers accept college grads in any field of study and train them on the job. In many stores, beginners who are candidates for buying jobs start out in executive training programs. These programs last from six to eight months, and combine classroom instruction in merchandising and purchasing with short rotations in various store jobs. This training introduces the new worker to store operations and policies, and provides the fundamentals of merchandising and management. The trainee's first job is likely to be that of Assistant Buyer. The duties include supervising sales workers, checking invoices on material received, and keeping account of stock on hand. Assistant Buyers gradually assume purchasing responsibilities, depending upon their individual abilities and the size of the department where they work. Training as an Assistant Buyer usually lasts at least one year. After years of working as a Buyer, those who show exceptional ability may advance to Merchandise Manager. A few find promotion to top executive jobs such as general merchandise manager for a retail store or chain.

EARNINGS:

Median annual earnings of buyers were $20,700 in 1986. Most buyers earned between $14,600 and $29,000 a year. The lowest 10 percent averaged less than $11,400, while the top 10 percent earned more than $41,300. A buyer's income depends upon the amount and type of product purchased, the employer's sales volume and, to some extent, the buyer's seniority. Buyers for large wholesale distributors and for mass merchandisers such as discount or large chain department stores ar among the most highly paid.

Buyers often earn cash bonuses based on their performance and may receive discounts on merchandise bought from the employer. In addition, many firms have incentive plans, such as profit sharing and stock options.

OUTLOOK:

Employment of buyers is expected to grow more slowly than the average for all occupations though the year 2000 as more wholesale and retail trade establishments automate and centralize their purchasing departments. Productivity gains resulting from the increased use of computers to control inventory, maintain records, and reorder merchandise will be the principal factor restraining employment growth. Most job openings, therefore, will result from replacement needs, which occur as experienced buyers transfer to other occupations in sales or management, change careers, or stop working altogether.

The number of qualified jobseekers will continue to exceed the number of openings because merchandising attracts many college graduates. Prospects are likely to be best for qualified applicants who enjoy the competitive, fast-paced nature of merchandising.

CHEMIST

DESCRIPTION:

Chemists search for and put into practical use new knowledge about substances. Their research has resulted in the development of a tremendous variety of synthetic materials, such as nylon and polyester fabrics. Nearly one-half of all chemists work in research and development. In basic research, chemists investigate the properties and composition of matter and the laws that govern the combination of elements. Basic research often has practical uses. In research and development, new products are created or improved.

Nearly one-eighth of all chemists work in production and inspection. In production, chemists prepare instructions (batch sheets) for plant workers that specify the kind and amount of ingredients to use and the exact mixing time for each stage in the process. At each step, samples are tested for quality control to meet industry and government standards. Other chemists work as Marketing or Sales Representatives because of their technical knowledge of the products sold. A number of chemists teach in colleges and universities. Some chemists are consultants to private industry and government agencies. Chemists often specialize in one of several subfields of chemistry; Analytical Chemists determine the structure, composition, and nature of substances, and develop new techniques; Organic Chemists at one time studied only the chemistry of living things, but their area has been broadened to include all carbon compounds; Inorganic Chemists study non-carbon compounds; Physical Chemists study energy transformations to find new and better energy sources.

BACKGROUND AND QUALIFICATIONS:

A BA with a major in Chemistry or a related discipline is sufficient for many entry-level jobs as a chemist. However, graduate training is required for many research jobs and most college teaching jobs require a PhD. Beginning chemists with a Master's Degree can usually go into applied research. The PhD is generally required for basic research, for teaching in colleges and universities, and for advancement to many administrative positions.

EARNINGS:

According to the College Placement Council, chemists with a bachelor's degree were offered starting salaries averaging $23,400 a year in 1986; those with a master's degree, $28,000; and those with a PhD, $36,400.

According to the American Chemical Society, median salaries of their members with a bachelor's degree were $33,000 a year in 1986; with a master's degree, $37,900; with a PhD, $47,800.

In a Bureau of Labor Statistics survey, chemists in private industry averaged $22,500 a year in 1986 at the most junior level, and $74,600 at senior supervisory levels. Experienced midlevel chemists with no supervisory responsibilities averaged $41,500.

Depending on a person's college record, the annual starting salary in the Federal Government in early 1987 for an inexperienced chemist with a bachelor's degree was between $14,800 and $18,350. Those who had two years of graduate study began at $22,450 a year, and with a PhD, $27,170 to $32,570. The average salary for all chemists in the Federal Government in 1986 was $38,600 a year.

OUTLOOK:

Employment of chemists is expected to grow more slowly than the average for all occupations through the year 2000.

CLAIM REPRESENTATIVE

DESCRIPTION:

The people who investigate insurance claims, negotiate settlements with policy holders, and authorize payments are known as claim representatives - a group that includes claim adjusters and claim examiners. When a casualty insurance company receives a claim, the claim adjuster determines whether the policy covers it and the amount of the loss. Adjusters use reports, physical evidence, and testimony of witnesses in investigating a claim. When their company is liable, they negotiate with the claimant and settle the case. Some adjusters work with all lines of insurance. Others specialize in claims from fire, marine loss, automobile damage, workers' compensation loss, or product liability. A growing number of casualty companies employ special adjusters to settle small claims. These workers, generally called Inside Adjusters or Telephone Adjusters, contact claimants by telephone or mail and have the policy holder send repair costs, medical bills, and other statements to the company. In life insurance companies, the counterpart of the claim adjuster is the claim examiner, who investigates questionable claims or those exceeding a specified amount. They may check claim applications for completeness and accuracy, interview medical specialists, consult policy files to verify information on a claim, or calculate benefit payments. Generally, examiners are authorized to investigate and approve payment on all claims up to a certain limit; larger claims are referred to a senior examiner.

BACKGROUND AND QUALIFICATIONS:

No specific field of college study is recommended. Although courses in insurance, economics, or other business subjects are helpful, a major in most college fields is adequate preparation. Most large insurance companies provide beginning claim adjusters and examiners with on-the-job training and home study courses. Claim representatives are encouraged to take courses designed to enhance their professional skills. For example, the Insurance Institute of America offers a six semester study program leading to an Associate's Degree in Claims Adjusting, upon successful completion of six exams. A professional Certificate in Insurance Adjusting also is available from the College of Insurance in New York City. The Life Office Management Association (LOMA), in cooperation with the International Claim Association, offers a claims education program for life and health examiners. The program is part of the LOMA Institute Insurance Education Program leading to the professional designation FLMI (Fellow, Life Management Institute) upon successful completion of eight written exams. Beginning adjusters and examiners work on small claims under the supervision of an experienced employee. As they learn more about claim investigation and settlement, they are assigned claims that are either higher in loss value or more complex. Trainees are promoted as they demonstrate competence in handling assignments and as they progress in their course work. Employees who show unusual competence in claims work or outstanding administrative skills may be promoted to department supervisor in a field office, or to a managerial position in the home office. Qualified adjusters and examiners sometimes transfer to other departments, such as underwriting or sales.

EARNINGS:

According to a survey of property and liability insurance companies, claim examiners earned a median annual salary of $29,100 in 1986; claim supervisors, $32,300; and claim managers, $41,300.

OUTLOOK:

Employment of claim representatives is expected to grow faster than the average for all occupations as the increasing volume of insurance sales results in more insurance claims. Shifts in the age distribution of the population will result in a large increase in the number of people who assume career and family responsibilities. People in this group have the greatest need for life and health insurance, and protection for homes, automobiles, and other possessions. A growing demand for insurance coverage for working women is also expected. New or expanding businesses will need protection for new plants and equipment and for insurance covering their employees' health and safety. Opportunities should be particularly good for claim representatives who specialize in complex business insurance such as marine cargo, workers' compensation, and product and pollution liability insurance.

COMMERCIAL ARTIST

DESCRIPTION:

A team of commercial artists with varying skills and specializations often creates the artwork in newspapers and magazines, and on billboards, brochures, and catalogs. This team is supervised by an Art Director, whose main function is to develop a theme or idea for an ad or advertising campaign. After the Art Director has determined the main elements of an ad or design, he or she will turn the project over to two specialists for further refinement. The Sketch Artist, also called a Renderer, does a rough drawing of any pictures required. The Layout Artist, who is concerned with graphics rather than art work, constructs or arranges the illustrations or photographs, plans the typography, and picks colors for the ad.

Other commercial artists, usually with less experience, are needed to turn out the finished products. Letterers put together headlines and other words on the ad. Mechanical Artists paste up an Engraver's guide of the ad. Paste-Up Artists and other less experienced employees do more routine work such as cutting mats, assembling booklets, or running errands.

Advertising artists create the concepts and artwork for a wide variety of items. These include direct mail advertising, catalogs, counter displays, slides, and filmstrips. They also design or lay out newspapers, magazines, and advertising circulars. Some commercial artists specialize in producing fashion illustrations, greeting cards, or book illustrations, or in making technical drawings for industry.

BACKGROUND AND QUALIFICATIONS:

Persons can prepare for a career in commercial art by attending either a 2- or 4-year trade school, community college, college, or university offering a program in commercial art.

EARNINGS:

Median earnings for salaried commercial graphic artists who usually work full time were about $20,000 a year in 1986. The middle 50 percent earned between $15,200 and $26,000 a year.

Earnings for self-employed visual artists vary widely. Those struggling to gain experience and a reputation may be forced to charge what amounts to less than the minimum wage for their work. Well-established freelancers and fine artists are able to make a very comfortable living. Self-employed artists do not receive fringe benefits such as paid holidays, sick leave, health insurance, or pension benefits.

OUTLOOK:

The graphic arts fields have a glamorous and exciting image. Because formal entry qualifications are few, many people with a love for drawing and creative ability qualify for entry. As a result, competition for both salaried jobs and freelance work is keen. Freelance work may be hard to come by, especially at first, and many freelancers earn very little until they acquire experience and establish a good reputation.

DATA PROCESSING SPECIALIST

DESCRIPTION:

The main function of a data processing specialist is to type data from documents such as checks, bills, and invoices quickly and accurately, and enter this information into a computer system. This is done with a variety of typewriter-like equipment. Many specialists use a machine that converts the information they type to magnetic impulses on tapes or disks. The information is then read into the computer from the tape or disk. Some specialists operate on-line terminals of the main computer system that transmit and receive data. Although brands and models of computer terminals and data entry equipment differ somewhat, their operation and keyboards are similar.

Some specialists working from terminals use data from the computer to produce business, scientific, and technical reports. In some offices, specialists also operate computer peripheral equipment such as printers and tape readers, and act as Tape Librarians.

BACKGROUND AND QUALIFICATIONS:

Employers usually require a high school education and the ability to key data in at a certain speed. Applicants are often tested for speed and accuracy. Some employers prefer applicants with experience or training in the operation of data entry equipment, and Console Operators are often required to have a college education. In some firms, other clerical workers such as tabulating and bookkeeping machine operators may be transferred to jobs as data processing specialists. Training in the use of data entry and similar keyboard equipment is available in high schools or private business schools.

EARNINGS:

In 1986, median annual earnings of full-time data processing specialists were $14,400. The middle 50 percent earned between $11,600 and $18,300. The bottom 10 percent earned less than $9,700, while the top 10 percent earned more than $23,100 a year. Specialists in the transportation and utilities industries and manufacturing had higher average earnings than those in trade and the financial and service industries. Outlook: the employment of data processing specialists is expected to decline through the year 2000. Despite this decline, many openings, including part-time ones, will occur each year, due to the need to replace workers who transfer to other occupations or leave the labor force. Related occupations include secretaries, typists, receptionists, and typesetters and compositors.

DIETITIAN/NUTRITIONIST

DESCRIPTION:

Dietitians, sometimes called nutritionists, are professionals trained in applying the principles of nutrition to food selection and meal preparation. They counsel individuals and groups; set up and supervise food service systems for institutions such as hospitals, prisons, and schools; and promote sound eating habits through education and administration. Dietitians also work on education and research.

Clinical Dietitians provide nutritional services for patients in hospitals, nursing homes, clinics, or doctors' offices. They assess patients' nutritional needs, develop and implement nutrition programs, and evaluate and report the results. Clinical dietitians, sometimes called therapeutic dietitians, confer with doctors and nurses about each patient in order to coordinate nutritional intake with other treatments-medications in particular.

Community Dietitians counsel individuals and groups on sound nutrition practices to prevent disease and to promote good health. Employed in such places as home health agencies, health maintenance organizations, and human service agencies that provide group and home-delivered meals, their job is to establish nutritional care plans, and communicate the principles of good nutrition in a way individuals and their families can understand.

Research dietitians are usually employed in academic medical centers or educational institutions, although some work in community programs. Using established research methods and analytical techniques, they conduct studies in areas that range from basic science to practical applications. Research dietitians may examine changes in the way the body uses food over the course of a lifetime, for example, or study the interaction of drugs and diet. They may investigate nutritional needs of persons with particular diseases, behavior modification, as it relates to diet and nutrition, or applied topics such as food service systems and equipment.

BACKGROUND/QUALIFICATIONS

The basic educational requirement for this field is a bachelor's degree with a major in foods and nutrition or institution management. To qualify for professional credentials as a Registered Dietitian, the American Dietetic Association (ADA) recommends one of the following educational paths: Completion of a four-year coordinated undergraduate program which includes 900 to 1,000 hours of clinical experience; completion of a bachelor's degree from an approved program plus an accredited dietetic internship; completion of a bachelor's or master's degree from an approved program and six month's approved work experience.

EARNINGS:

Entry-level salaries of dietitians in hospitals averaged $20,400 a year in 1986. Outlook: Employment of dietitians is expected to grow faster than the average for all occupations through the year 2000.

DRAFTSPERSON

DESCRIPTION:

Drafters prepare detailed drawings based on rough sketches, specifications, and calculations made by scientists, engineers, architects, and designers. Final drawings contain a detailed view of the object from all sides as well as specifications for materials to be used, procedures to be followed, and other information needed to carry out the job. There are two methods by which these drawings are prepared. In the traditional method, drafters sit at drawing boards and use compasses, dividers, protractors, triangles, and other drafting devices to prepare the drawing manually. In the new method, drafters use computer-aided drafting (CAD) systems. They sit at computer work stations and may make the drawing on a videoscreen. In some cases, the design may never be placed on paper. It may be stored electronically and, in some factories, may be used to guide automatic machinery. These systems free drafters from much routine drafting work and permit many variations of a design to be prepared easily. CAD systems allow a design to be viewed from various angles and perspectives not usually available with more traditional drafting methods so that design work can be better, faster, and more thorough. In addition to drafting equipment and CAD systems, drafters use technical handbooks, tables, and calculators in preparing drawings and related specifications.

BACKGROUND/REQUIREMENTS

It is preferred that applicants have two years of post-high school training in technical institutes, junior and community colleges, or extension divisions of universities. Some persons receive training in the Armed Forces. Training for a career in drafting should include courses in mathematics, physical science, mechanical drawing, and drafting. Courses in shop practices and shop skills are also helpful, since most higher level drafting jobs require knowledge of manufacturing or construction methods. Many technical schools offer courses in structural design, architectural drawing, and engineering or industrial technology. Beginners usually start as junior drafters doing routine work under close supervision. After gaining experience, they do more difficult work with less supervision and may advance to senior drafter or supervisor. With appropriate college, they may become engineers, designers, or architects.

EARNINGS:

Median annual earnings of drafters who work year round, full time were about $21,400 in 1986; the middle 50 percent earned between $16,500 and $29,000 annually.

OUTLOOK:

Little change in employment of drafters is expected to occur through the year 2000. Related occupations include architects, engineering technicians, engineers, landscape architects, photogrammetrists, and surveyors.

ECONOMIST

DESCRIPTION:

Economists study the way a society uses scarce resources such as land, labor, raw materials, and machinery to produce goods and services. They analyze the costs and benefits of distributing and using resources in a particular way. Their research might focus on such topics as energy costs, inflation, business cycles, unemployment, tax policy, farm prices, and many other areas.

Being able to present economic and statistical concepts in a meaningful way is particularly important for economists whose research is policy directed. Economists who work for business firms may be asked to provide management with information on which decisions such as the marketing or pricing of company products are made; to look at the advisability of adding new lines of merchandise, opening new branches, or diversifying the company's operations; to analyze the effects of changes in the tax laws; or to prepare economic or business forecasts. Business economists working for firms that carry on operations abroad may be asked to prepare forecasts of foreign economic conditions. About three of every four economists work in private industry, including manufacturing firms, banks, insurance companies, securities and investment companies, economic research firms and management consulting firms. Some run their own consulting businesses. A number of economists combine a full-time job in government, business or an academic institution with part-time or consulting work in another setting.

BACKGROUND AND QUALIFICATIONS:

A Bachelors degree in Economics is sufficient for many beginning research, administrative, management trainee, and business sales jobs. However, graduate training is increasingly necessary for advancement to more responsible positions as economists. In government research organizations and consulting firms, economists who have Master's degrees can usually qualify for more responsible research and administrative positions. A PhD may be necessary of top positions in some organizations. Experienced business economists may advance to managerial or executive positions in banks, industrial concerns, trade associations, and other organizations where they formulate practical business and administrative policy.

EARNINGS:

According to a 1986 salary survey by the College Placement Council, persons with a bachelor's degree in economics received an average starting salary of about $22,400 a year; in marketing and distribution, about $19,300.

Median annual earnings of full-time economists were about $36,000 in 1986. According to a survey by the National Association of Business Economists, however, median base salary for business economists was $54,000. Economists in general administration and international economics commanded the highest salaries, while those in market research and econometrics received the lowest. The highest paid business economists were in the securities and investment, retail and wholesale trade and insurance industries; the lowest paid were in the education, non-profit research organizations and real estate industries.

OUTLOOK:

Employment of economists is expected to grow faster than the average for all occupations through the year 2000. Most job openings, however, will result from the need to replace experienced economists who transfer to other occupations, retire, or leave the labor force for other reasons.

ENGINEER

DESCRIPTION:

Engineers apply the theories and principles of science and mathematics to practical technical problems. Often, their work is the link between a scientific discovery and its useful application. Engineers design machinery, products, systems, and processes for efficient and economical performance. Engineering is a highly specialized field and the work and engineer does depends greatly upon the industry in which he/she is employed. The following descriptions outline the basic specialties and their respective employment outlooks.

Aerospace Engineer

Aerospace Engineers design, develop, test, and help produce commercial and military aircraft, missiles, spacecraft, and related systems. They play an important role in advancing the state of the technology in commercial aviation, defense and space exploration. Aerospace Engineers often specialize in an area of work like structural design, navigational guidance and control, instrumentation and communication, or production methods. They also may specialize in one type of aerospace product, such as passenger planes, helicopters, satellites, or rockets. **Outlook:** Employment of aerospace engineers is expected to grow more slowly than average for all occupations through the year 2000. During the 1980's, their employment grew very rapidly. However, because of Defense Department expenditures for military aircraft, missiles and other aerospace systems are not expected to grow much.

Chemical Engineer

Chemical Engineers are involved in many phases of the production of chemicals and chemical products; They design equipment and chemical plants as well as determining methods of manufacturing these products. Often, they design and develop chemical processes such as those used to remove chemical contaminants from waste materials. Because the duties of the chemical engineer cuts across many fields, these professionals must have knowledge of chemistry, physics, and mechanical and electrical engineering. This branch of engineering is so diversified and complex that chemical engineers frequently specialize in a particular operation such as oxidation or polymerization. Others specialize in a particular area such as pollution control or the production of a specific product like plastics or rubber.**Outlook:** Employment of chemical engineers is expected to grow about as fast as the average for all occupations through the year 2000.

Civil Engineer

Civil Engineers, who work in the oldest branch of the engineering profession, design and supervise the construction of roads, harbors, airports, tunnels, bridges, water supply and sewage systems, and buildings. Major specialties within Civil Engineering are structural, hydraulic, environmental/sanitary, transportation, urban planning, and soil mechanics. Many Civil Engineers are in supervisory or administrative positions ranging from supervisor of a construction site, to city engineer, to top level executive. Others teach in colleges and universities, or work as consultants. Outlook: Employment of civil engineers is expected to increase faster than the average for all occupations through the year 2000.

Electrical Engineer

Electrical Engineers design, develop, test and supervise the manufacture of electrical and electronic equipment. Electrical equipment includes power-generating and transmission equipment used by electrical utilities, electric motors, machinery controls, and lighting and wiring in buildings, automobiles, and aircraft. Electronic equipment includes radar, computers, communications equipment, and consumer goods such as television sets and stereos. Electrical Engineers also design and operate facilities for generating and distributing electrical power. Electrical Engineers generally specialize in a major area, such as integrated circuits, computers, electrical equipment manufacturing, communications, or power distributing equipment, or in a subdivision of these areas, microwave communication or aviation electronic systems, for example. Electrical Engineers design new products, specify their uses, and write performance requirements and maintenance schedules. **Outlook:** The outlook for electrical engineers is estimated to be good through the year 2000.

Industrial Engineer

Industrial Engineers determine the most effective ways for an organization to use the basic factors of production--people, machines and materials. They are more concerned with people and methods of business organization than are engineers in other specialties, who generally are concerned more with particular products or processes, such as metals, power or mechanics. To solve organizational, production, and related problems most efficiently, Industrial Engineers design data processing systems and apply mathematical concepts. They also develop management control systems to aid in financial planning and cost analysis, design production planning and control systems to coordinate activities and control product quality, and design or improve systems for the physical distribution of goods and services. Industrial engineers also conduct plant location surveys, where they look for the best combination of sources of raw materials, transportation, and taxes, and develop wage and salary administration positions and job evaluation programs. Many industrial engineers move into managerial positions because the work is closely related. **Outlook:** Employment opportunities for industrial engineers are expected to be good; their employment is expected to grow faster than the average for all occupations through the year 2000. Most job openings, however, will result from the need to replace industrial engineers who transfer to other occupations or leave the labor force.

Metallurgical Engineer

Metallurgical Engineers develop new types of metals with characteristics that are tailored for specific requirements, such as heat resistance, lightweight strength, or high malleability. They also develop methods to process and convert metals into useful products. Most of these engineers generally work in one of three major branches of metallurgy: extractive or chemical, physical, or mechanical. Extractive metallurgists are concerned with extracting metals from ores, and refining and alloying them to obtain useful materials. Physical metallurgists deal with the nature, structure, and physical properties of metals and their alloys, and with the methods of converting refined metals into final products. Mechanical metallurgists develop methods to work and shape materials, such as casting, forging, rolling, and drawing. **Outlook:** Employment of metallurgical, ceramic, and materials engineers is expected to grow more rapidly than the average for all occupations through the year 2000.

Mining Engineer

Mining engineers find, extract, and prepare minerals for manufacturing industries to use. They design open pit and underground mines, supervise the construction of mine shafts and tunnels in underground operations, and devise methods for transporting minerals to processing plants. Mining Engineers are responsible for the economical and efficient operation of mines and mine safety, including ventilation, water supply, power, communications, and equipment maintenance. Some Mining Engineers work with geologists and metallurgical engineers to locate and appraise new ore deposits. Others develop new mining equipment or direct mineral processing operations, which involve separating minerals from the dirt, rock, and other materials they are mixed with. Mining Engineers frequently specialize in the mining of one specific mineral such as coal or copper. With increased emphasis on protecting the environment, many Mining Engineers have been working to solve problems related to mined land reclamation, and water and air pollution. **Outlook:** The employment outlook for mining engineers is expected to remain constant through the year 2000, due to expected low growth in demand for coal, metals, and other minerals.

Petroleum Engineer

Petroleum Engineers are mainly involved in exploring and drilling for oil and gas. They work to achieve the maximum profitable recovery of oil and gas from a petroleum reservoir by determining and developing the best and most efficient methods. Since only a small proportion of the oil and gas in a reservoir will flow out under natural forces, Petroleum Engineers develop and use various artificial recovery methods, such as flooding the oil field with water to force the oil to the surface. Even when using the best recovery methods, about half the oil is still left in the ground. Petroleum Engineers' research and development efforts to increase the proportion of oil recovered in each reservoir can make a significant contribution to increasing available energy resources. **Outlook:** Employment of petroleum engineers is expected to grow more slowly than the average for all occupations through the year 2000. With the drop in oil prices, domestic petroleum companies have curtailed exploration, resulting in poor employment opportunities.

BACKGROUND AND QUALIFICATIONS:

A bachelor's degree in engineering from an accredited engineering program is generally acceptable for beginning engineering jobs. College graduates trained in one of the natural sciences or mathematics also may qualify for some beginning jobs. Most engineering degrees may be obtained in branches such as electrical, mechanical, or civil engineering. College graduates with a degree in science or mathematics and experienced engineering technicians may also qualify for some engineering jobs, especially in engineering specialties in high demand. Graduate training is essential for engineering faculty positions but is not required for the majority of entry level engineering jobs. All 50 states require licensing for engineers whose work may affect life, health, or property, or who offer their services to the public. Beginning engineering graduates usually work under the supervision of experienced engineers, and in larger companies, may receive seminar or classroom training. As engineers advance in knowledge, they may become technical specialists, supervisors, or managers or administrators within the field of engineering. Some engineers obtain advanced degrees in business administration to improve their growth opportunities, while others obtain law degrees and become patent attorneys.

EARNINGS:

Average starting salaries for engineers by category are: Petroleum Engineer, $33,000; Chemical Engineer, $29,256; Electrical Engineer, $28,368; Mechanical Engineer, $27,864; Metallurgical Engineer, $27,864; Aeronautical Engineer, $27,780; Industrial Engineer, $27,048; Mining Engineer, $25,956; Civil Engineer, $24,132. Those engineers in the private industry in 1986 averaged $27,866 at the most junior level, while those at senior managerial levels averaged $79,021.

FINANCIAL ANALYST

DESCRIPTION:

A financial analyst prepares the financial reports required by the firm to conduct its operations and satisfy tax and regulatory requirements. Financial analysts also oversee the flow of cash and financial instruments and develop information to assess the present and future financial status of the firm.

BACKGROUND AND QUALIFICATIONS:

A bachelor's degree in accounting or finance is suitable academic preparation for a financial manager. An MBA degree in addition to a bachelor's degree in any field is acceptable to many employers.

EARNINGS:

The median annual salary of financial managers was $30,400 in 1986. The lowest 10% earned $17,000 or less, while the top 10% earned over $52,000. The salary level depends upon the size and location of the firm, and is likely to be higher in large institutions and cities. Many financial analysts in private industry receive additional compensation in the form of bonuses, which also vary substantially by size of firm.

OUTLOOK:

Employment of financial managers is expected to increase about as fast as the average for all occupations through the year 2000.

FOOD TECHNOLOGIST

DESCRIPTION:

A food technologist studies the chemical, physical and biological nature of food to learn how to safely process, preserve, package, distribute, and store it. Some develop new products, while others insure quality standards. They are, like Animal scientists, Dairy scientists, Horticulturists, Soil scientists, Animal and plant breeders, entomologists, and agriculturalists, classified generally as Agricultural Scientists by the U.S. Department of Labor.

BACKGROUND AND QUALIFICATIONS:

Educational requirements for the agricultural scientist depend a great deal upon the area and type of work performed. A Ph.D degree in agricultural science is usually required for college teaching, independent research, and for advancement to many administrative and management jobs. A bachelor's degree is sufficient for some sales, production management, inspection, and other nonresearch jobs, but, in some cases, promotions may be limited. Degrees in some related sciences such as biology, chemistry, or physics or in related engineering specialties also may be acceptable for some agricultural science jobs.

OUTLOOK:

Employment of agricultural scientists is expected to grow about as fast as the average for all occupations through the year 2000.

EARNINGS:

According to the College Placement Council, starting salary offers for agricultural scientists with a bachelor's degree averaged $19,200 a year in 1986. In the Federal Government in 1987, an agricultural scientist with a bachelor's degree started at $14,822 or $18,358 a year, depending on their college records.

FORESTER

DESCRIPTION:

Foresters plan and supervise the growing, protection and harvesting of trees. They plot forest areas, approximate the amount of standing timber and future growth, and manage timber sales. Some foresters also protect the trees from fire, harmful insects, and disease. Some foresters also protect wildlife and manage watersheds; develop and supervise campgrounds, parks, and grazing lands; and do research. Foresters in extension work provide information to forest owners and to the general public.

BACKGROUND AND QUALIFICATIONS:

A bachelor's degree in forestry is the minimum educational requirement for professional careers in forestry. In 1986, 55 colleges and universities offered bachelor's or higher degrees in forestry; 47 of these were accredited by the Society of American Foresters.

OUTLOOK:

Employment of foresters and conservation scientists is expected to grow more slowly than the average for all occupations through the year 2000.

EARNINGS:

Most graduates entering the Federal Government as foresters, range managers, or soil conservationists in 1987 with a bachelor's degree started at $14,800 a year. Those with a master's degree could start at $22,500. Holders of doctorates could begin at $27,500, or, in research positions, at $32,600.

GEOGRAPHER

DESCRIPTION:

Geographers study the interrelationship of humans and the environment. Economic geographers deal with the geographic distribution of an area's economic activities. Political geographers are concerned with the relationship of geography to political phenomena. Physical geographers study physical processes in the earth and its atmosphere. Urban geographers study cities and metropolitan areas, while regional geographers specialize in the physical, climatic, economic, political and cultural characteristics of a particular region or area. Medical geographers study the effect of the environment on health.

BACKGROUND AND QUALIFICATIONS:

The minimum educational requirement for entry-level positions is a BA or BS degree in Geography. However, a Masters degree is increasingly required for many entry level positions. Applicants for entry level jobs would find it helpful to have training in a specialty such as cartography, photogrammerty, remote sensing data interpretation, statistical analysis including computer science, or environmental analysis. To advance to a senior research position in private industry and perhaps gain a spot in management, a geographer would probably be required to have an advanced degree.

EARNINGS:

Starting salaries in government and industry average $16,000 to $20,000. Those with a Master's degree start at about $22,500, and while many of those with a PhD start at about $27,200, some can start as high as $32,600.

OUTLOOK:

Average growth throughout the 1990's.

GEOLOGISTS AND GEOPHYSISICTS

DESCRIPTION:

Geologists study the structure, composition and history of the earth's crust. By examining surface rocks and drilling to recover rock cores, they determine the types and distribution of rocks beneath the earth's surface. They also identify rocks and minerals, conduct geological surveys, draw maps, take measurements, and record data. Geological research helps to determine the structure and history of the earth, and may result in significant advances, such as in the ability to predict earthquakes. An important application of geologists' work is locating oil and other natural and mineral resources. Geologists usually specialize in one or a combination of general areas: earth materials, earth processes, and earth history.

Geophysicists study the composition and physical aspects of the earth and its electric, magnetic and gravitational fields. Geophysicists usually specialize in one of three general phases of the science -- solid earth, fluid earth, and upper atmosphere. Some may also study other planets.

BACKGROUND AND QUALIFICATIONS:

A Bachelor's degree in geology or geophysics is adequate for entry into some lower level geology jobs, but better jobs with good advancement potential usually require at least a master's degree in geology or geophysics. Persons with strong backgrounds in physics, mathematics, or computer science also may qualify for some geophysics jobs. A PhD is essential for most research positions.

EARNINGS:

Surveys by the College Placement Council indicate that graduates with bachelor's degrees in physical and earth sciences received an average starting offer of $19,200 a year in 1986.

In the Federal Government in early 1987, geologists and geophysicists having a bachelor's degree could begin at $14,822 or $18,358 a year, depending on college records; those having a master's degree, at $27,172 or $32,567. In 1986, the average salary for geologists in the federal government was about $37,500, and for geophysicists, $40,900.

OUTLOOK:

Employment of geologists and geophysicists is expected to grow more slowly than the average for all occupations through the year 2000, mainly due to the reduction in energy exploration by oil companies.

HOTEL MANAGER/ASSISTANT MANAGER

DESCRIPTION:

Hotel managers are responsible for operating their establishments profitably and satisfying guests. They determine room rates and credit policy, direct the operation of the food service operation, and manage the housekeeping, accounting, security, and maintenance departments of the hotel. Handling problems and coping with the unexpected are important parts of the job. A small hotel or motel requires only a limited staff, and the manager may have to fill various front office duties, such as taking reservations or assigning rooms. When management is combined with ownership, these activities may expand to include all aspects of the business.

General managers of large hotels usually have several assistants or department heads who manage various parts of the operation. Because hotel restaurant and cocktail lounges are important to the success of the entire establishment, they are almost always operated by managers with experience in the restaurant field. Other areas that are usually handled separately include advertising, rental of banquet and meeting facilities, marketing and sales, personnel and accounting. Large hotel and motel chains often centralize some activities, such as purchasing and advertising, so that individual hotels in the chain may not need managers for these departments. Managers who work for chains may be assigned to organize a newly-built or purchased hotel, or to reorganize an existing hotel or motel that is not operating successfully.

BACKGROUND AND QUALIFICATIONS:

Experience is the most important consideration in selecting hotel managers. However, employers are increasingly emphasizing college education. A BA in Hotel/Restaurant Administration provides particularly strong preparation for a career in hotel management. Most hotels promote employees who have proven their ability, usually front office clerks, to Assistant Manager, and eventually to General Manager. Hotel and motel chains may offer better employment opportunities because employees can transfer to another hotel or motel in the chain, or to the central office if an opening occurs.

EARNINGS:

In 1986, annual salaries of assistant hotel managers averaged an estimated $34,500, according to a survey conducted by the American Hotel and Motel Association. Assistants employed by large hotels, with 600 or more rooms, averaged an estimated $45,500 that year, while those in small hotels of 200 or fewer, averaged $21,100. Salaries of assistant managers also vary according to responsibilities. For example, food and beverage managers averaged $42,000, whereas front office managers averaged $24,700. The manager's level of experience is also an important factor.

In 1986, salaries of general managers averaged an estimated $63,900, ranging from an average of about $38,400 in hotels and motels with less than 200 rooms to more than $87,000 in hotels with 600 rooms or more.

OUTLOOK:

Employment of salaried hotel managers is expected to grow much faster than the average for all occupations through the year 2000 as more large hotels and motels are built.

INDUSTRIAL DESIGNER

DESCRIPTION:

Industrial Designers combine artistic talent with a knowledge of marketing, materials, and methods of production to improve the appearance and functional design of products so that they compete favorably with similar goods on the market. Although most Industrial Designers are engaged in product design, others are involved in different facets of design. To create favorable public images for companies and for government service, some designers develop trademarks or symbols that appear on the firm's products, advertising, brochures, and stationery. Some design containers and packages that both protect and promote their contents. Others prepare small display exhibits or the entire layout for industrial fairs. Some design the interior layout of special purpose commercial buildings such as restaurants and supermarkets.

Corporate Designers usually work only on products made by their employer. This may involve filling day-to-day design needs of the company, or long-range planning of new products. Independent consultants who serve more than one industrial firm often plan and design a great variety of products. Most designers work for large manufacturing companies designing either consumer or industrial products, or for design consulting firms. Others do freelance work, or are on the staffs of architectural and interior design firms.

BACKGROUND AND QUALIFICATIONS:

The normal requirement for entering this field of work involves completing a course of study in industrial design at an art school, university, or technical college. Most large manufacturing firms hire only industrial designers who have a Bachelor's degree in the field. Beginning industrial designers frequently do simple assignments. As they gain experience, they may work on their own, and many become supervisors with major responsibility for the design of a product or group of products. Those who have an established reputation and the necessary funds may start their own consulting firms.

EARNINGS:

Median annual earnings of experienced full-time designers were almost $25,000 in 1986. The middle 50 percent earned between $16,800 and $34,400 a year. The bottom 10 percent earned less than $15,200, and the top percent earned more than $46,500. Earnings of self-employed designers vary greatly, depending on their talent and business ability, but generally are higher than those of salaried designers.

OUTLOOK:

Employment in design occupations is expected to grow faster than the average for all occupations through the year 2000. Continued emphasis on product quality and safety, on design of new products for businesses and offices, and on high-technology products in medicine and transportation should expand the demand for industrial designers.

INSURANCE AGENT/BROKER

DESCRIPTION:

Agents and brokers usually sell one or more of the three basic types of insurance: life, casualty, and health. Underwriters offer various policies that, besides providing health benefits, may also provide retirement income, funds for education, or other benefits. Casualty Insurance Agents sell policies that protect individual policyholders from financial losses resulting from automobile accidents, fire, or theft. They also sell industrial or commercial lines, such as workers' compensation, products liability, or medical malpractice insurance. Health insurance policies offer protection against the high costs of hospital and medical care, or loss of income due to illness or injury. Many agents also offer securities, such as mutual fund shares or variable annuities.

An insurance agent may be either an insurance company employee or an independent who is authorized to represent one or more insurance companies. Brokers are not under exclusive contract with any single company; instead, they place policies directly with the company that best meets a company's needs.

Insurance agents spend most of their time discussing insurance needs with prospective and existing clients. Some time must be spent in office work to prepare reports, maintain records, plan insurance programs that are tailored to prospects' needs, and draw up lists of prospective customers. Specialists in group policies may help an employer's accountant set up a system of payroll deductions for employees covered by the policy.

BACKGROUND AND QUALIFICATIONS:

All insurance agents and most insurance brokers must obtain a license in the state where they plan to sell insurance. In most states, licenses are issued only to applicants who pass written examinations covering insurance fundamentals and the state insurance laws. Agents who plan to sell mutual fund shares and other securities also must be licensed by the state. New agents usually receive training at the agencies where they will work, and frequently at the insurance company's home office. Beginners sometimes attend company-sponsored classes to prepare for the examination. Others study on their own and accompany experienced sales workers when they call on prospective clients.

EARNINGS:

Beginners in this field are often guaranteed a moderate salary while they learn the business and build a clientele. In 1986, many large companies paid new agents a median salary of about $1,400 a month during this training period, which usually lasts about six months. Life insurance agents with about five to nine years of experience had a median income of about $47,000 in 1986; those with ten years or more of experience had a median income of $70,000. The size of the commission depends on the types and amount of insurance sold, and whether the transaction is a new policy or a renewal.

OUTLOOK:

Employment of insurance agents and brokers is expected to grow about as fast as the average for all occupations through the year 2000. Turnover is high because many beginners are able to establish a sufficiently large clientele in this highly competitive business. Most individuals and businesses consider insurance a necessity, regardless of economic conditions. Therefore, agents are not likely to face unemployment because of a recession.

MANAGER

DESCRIPTION:

Managers supervise employees and are accountable for the overall success of the operation which they direct. The scope and nature of a manager's responsibilities depend greatly upon the position and the size of his or her organization.

A Department Manager at a retail store, for example, may actually spend most of his or her time waiting on customers, and his or her managerial duties may be limited to scheduling employees' work shifts to properly staff the department, or to training new employees in such simple tasks as operating the check-out terminal, processing credit card purchases, and displaying merchandise.

A Branch Manager, even in a small store or service operation, might have considerably broader duties and responsibilities. He or she might, in addition to supervising and training employees, be responsible for hiring and firing decisions. He or she might have a limited ability to purchase items, and might have some control over a local advertising budget. He or she might also deal with local suppliers of goods and services. Some organizations, however, prefer to delegate rather limited responsibility to Branch managers, and instead rely upon a strong network of Regional Managers who travel from branch to branch, making key operating decisions.

Factories or service firms with extensive processing requirements employ Operations and Production Managers. While these managers typically supervise many people, their primary responsibility is the overall success of the operation, which may be dependent upon equipment, raw material, purchased goods, or outside vendors. The Operations Manager at a bank, for example, remains heavily dependent upon data processing equipment, and usually will have an extensive background in this area. The Production manager at a petroleum refinery, for another example, remains heavily dependent upon a large variety of specialized equipment, and will usually have a background in engineering or chemistry.

The General Manager is responsible for the overall day-to-day operations of the firm or operating unit. He or she must be acquainted with each part of the operation. In a small store, the General Manager may spend most of his or her time performing nonmanagerial tasks such as making purchases, or even waiting on customers. In a large corporation, on the other hand, the General Manager (who is often the Executive Vice President) will spend much of his or her time meeting with key executives in each department to ensure that company operations are being conducted successfully.

BACKGROUND AND QUALIFICATIONS:

The educational background of managers and top executives varies as widely as the nature of their diverse responsibilities. Most general managers and top executives have a bachelor's degree in liberal arts or business administration. Graduate and professional degrees are common. Many managers in administrative, marketing, financial, and manufacturing activities have a master's degree in business administration. Larger firms usually have some form of management training program, usually open to recent college graduates. While such programs are usually competitive, they generally offer an excellent opportunity to quickly familiarize oneself with many different aspects of a firm's business. Also, such programs are often open to a broad range of candidates, including both candidates with a BS in business administration, and liberal arts graduates as well.

EARNINGS:

The estimated median annual salary of general managers and top executives was around $34,000 in 1986. Many earned well over $52,000. Salary levels vary substantially depending upon the level of managerial responsibility, length of service, and type, size, and location of the firm.

A college graduate entering a Management Trainee program or position can expect to begin at approximately $300 per week. Some Branch Managers may earn up to $20,000 to $30,000 per year. Some firms prefer to pay managers relatively low salaries, but offer profit-sharing or similar incentive bonus-type plans to compensate.

OUTLOOK:

Employment of general managers and top executives is expected to grow about as fast as the average for all occupations through the year 2000.

MANUFACTURERS' SALES WORKERS

DESCRIPTION:

Most manufacturers employ sales workers to market their products to other businesses, mainly to other producers, wholesalers, and retailers. Manufacturers also sell directly to institutions such as schools, hospitals, and libraries. The sales workers who represent a manufacturer to prospective buyers are usually called manufacturers' representatives, although the job title may vary by product line.

Manufacturers' sales workers visit prospective buyers to inform them about the products they sell, analyze the buyer's needs, suggest how their products can meet these needs, and take orders. Sales workers visit firms in their territory, using an approach adapted to their line of merchandise. Sometimes sales workers promote their company's products at trade shows and conferences.

Manufacturers' sales workers spend most of their time visiting prospective customers. They also prepare reports on sales prospects or customers' credit ratings, plan their work schedules, draw up lists of prospects, contact the firm to schedule appointments, handle correspondence, and study literature about their products.

BACKGROUND AND QUALIFICATIONS:

Although a college degree is increasingly desirable for a job as a manufacturer's sales worker, many employers hire individuals without a degree who have previous sales experience. Most entrants to this occupation, even those with college degrees, transfer from other occupations, but some are recent graduates. Entrants are older, on the average, than entrants to other occupations. Sales representatives who have good sales records and leadership ability may advance to sales supervisor, branch manager, or district manager. Those with managerial ability eventually may advance to sales manager or other executive positions; many top executives in industry started as sales representatives. Some people eventually go into business for themselves as independent representatives, while others find opportunities in advertising and marketing research.

EARNINGS:

Manufacturers' sales workers may be paid under different types of compensation plans. Some manufacturers pay experienced sales workers a straight commission, based on the dollar amount of their sales; others pay a fixed salary. Median earnings of full-time manufacturers' sales workers were about $25,600 in 1986.

OUTLOOK:

Little or no change in employment is expected in the occupation through the year 2000. Increased reliance on electronic ordering systems and a trend toward increased utilization of wholesale distribution channels will limit future employment growth.

PERSONNEL AND LABOR RELATIONS SPECIALIST

DESCRIPTION:

Personnel and labor relations specialists provide the necessary link between management and employees which helps management make effective use of employees' skills, and helps employees find satisfaction in their jobs and working conditions. Personnel specialists interview, select, and recommend applicants to fill job openings. They handle wage and salary administration, training and career development, and employee benefits. Labor Relations Specialists usually deal in union-management relations, and people who specialize in this field work primarily in unionized businesses and government agencies. They help management officials prepare for collective bargaining sessions, participate in contract negotiations with the union, and handle day-to-day matters of labor relations agreements.

In a small company, personnel work consists mostly of interviewing and hiring, and one person usually handles all phases. By contrast, a large organization needs an entire staff, which might include Recruiters, Interviewers, Counselors, Job Analysts, Wage and Salary Analysts, Education and Training Specialists, as well as technical and clerical workers. Personnel work often begins with the Personnel Recruiter or Employment Interviewer who travels around the country, often to college campuses, in the search for promising job applicants. These specialists talk to applicants, and then select and recommend those who appear qualified to fill vacancies. They often administer tests to applicants and interpret the results. Job Analysts and Salary & Wage Administrators examine detailed information on jobs, including job qualifications and worker characteristics, in order to prepare manuals and other materials for these courses, and look into new methods of training. They also counsel employees participating in training opportunities, which may include on-the-job, apprentice, supervisory, or management training.

Employee Benefits Supervisors and other Personnel Specialists handle the employer's benefits programs, which often includes health insurance, life insurance, disability insurance, and pension plans. These specialist also coordinate a wide range of employee services, including cafeterias and snack bars, health rooms, recreational facilities, newsletters and communications, and counseling for work-related personal problems. Counseling employees who are reaching retirement age is a particularly important part of the job. Labor Relations Specialists give advice on labor management relations. Nearly three out of four work in private industry, for manufacturers, banks, insurance companies, airlines, department stores, and virtually every other business concern.

BACKGROUND AND QUALIFICATIONS:

The educational backgrounds of personnel, training, and labor relations specialists and managers vary considerably due to the diversity of duties and level of responsibility. While some employers look for graduates with degrees in Personnel Administration or Industrial and Labor Relations, others prefer graduates with a general business background. Still others feel that a well-rounded liberal arts education is the best preparation. A college degree in Personnel Administration, Political Science, or Public Administration can be an asset in looking for personnel work with a government agency. Graduate study in industrial or labor relations is often required for work in labor relations. Although a law degree is often required for entry-level jobs, most of the people who are responsible for contract negotiations are lawyers, and a combination of industrial relations courses and a law degree is becoming highly desirable.

New Personnel Specialists usually enter formal or on-the-job training programs to learn how to classify jobs, interview applicants, or administer employee benefits. Next, new workers are assigned to specific areas in the employee relations department to gain experience. Later, they may advance within their own company, transfer to another employer, or move from personnel to labor relations work. Workers in the middle ranks of a large organization often transfer to a top job in a smaller company. Employees with exceptional ability may be promoted to executive positions, such as Director of Personnel, or Director of Labor Relations.

EARNINGS:

Beginning Personnel/Labor Relations Specialists earned an average of $14,800 per year in 1987. Those with a superior academic record or an additional year of specialized experience started at $18,400 per year. Holders of a master's degree started at $22,500, and those with a doctorate in a personnel field earned $27,200.

OUTLOOK:

The number of jobs in this field is projected to increase through the year 2000, although most job openings will be due to replacement needs. The job market is likely to remain competitive in view of the abundant supply of college graduates and experienced workers with suitable qualifications.

PHYSICIST

DESCRIPTION:

Through systematic observation and experimentation, Physicists describe the structure of the universe and the interaction of matter and energy in fundamental terms. Physicists develop theories that describe the fundamental forces and laws of nature. The majority of Physicists work in research and development. Some do basic research to increase scientific knowledge. Some engineering-oriented Physicists do applied research and help develop new products. Many Physicists teach and do research in colleges and universities. A small number work in inspection, quality control, and other production-related jobs in industry, while others do consulting work.

Most Physicists specialize in one or more branches of the science. A growing number of Physicists are specializing in fields that combine physics and a related science. Furthermore, the practical applications of a Physicist's work have become increasingly merged with engineering. Private industry employs more than one half of all Physicists, primarily in companies manufacturing chemicals, electrical equipment, and aircraft and missiles. Many others work in hospitals, commercial laboratories, and independent research organizations.

BACKGROUND AND QUALIFICATIONS:

Graduate training in physics or a closely related field is almost essential for most entry-level jobs in physics, and for advancement into all types of work. A PhD is normally required for faculty status at colleges and universities, and for industrial or government jobs administering research and development programs. Those with a Master's Degree qualify for many research jobs in private industry and in the Federal Government. In colleges and universities, some teach and assist in research while studying for their PhD degrees. Those with a BA may qualify for some applied research and development positions in private industry and in government, and some holding Bachelor's degrees are employed as research assistants in colleges and universities while studying for advanced degrees. Many also work in engineering and other scientific fields. Physicists often begin their careers performing routine laboratory tasks. After gaining some experience, they are assigned more complex tasks and may advance to work as project leaders or research directors. Some work in top management jobs. Physicists who develop new products sometimes form their own companies or join new firms to exploit their own ideas.

EARNINGS:

Starting salaries in private industry averaged about $31,200 a year in 1986 for those with a Master's degree, and $42,500 for those with a PhD, according to an American Institute of Physics survey. Average earnings for all Physicists in the Federal Government in 1986 were $45,600 a year.

OUTLOOK:

Physicists with a PhD should experience good employment opportunities by the late 1990s. The employment of Physicists is expected to improve as retirements increase. Related industries: engineers, chemistry, geology, and geophysics.

PUBLIC RELATIONS WORKER

DESCRIPTION:

Public Relations workers aid businesses, government, universities, and other organizations build and maintain a positive public image. They apply their talents and skills in a variety of different areas, including press, community, or consumer relations, political campaigning, interest-group representation, fund-raising, or employee recruitment. Public relations is more than "telling the employer's story", however. Understanding the attitudes and concerns of customers, employees, and various other public groups, and effectively communicating this information to management to help formulate policy is an important part of the job.

Public Relations staffs in very large firms may number 200 or more, but in most firms the staff is much smaller. The Director of Public Relations, who is often a vice-president of the company, may develop overall plans and policies with a top management executive. In addition, large Public Relations departments employ writers, research workers, and other specialists who prepare material for the different media, stockholders, and other groups the company wishes to reach.

Manufacturing firms, public utilities, transportation companies, insurance companies, and trade and professional associations employ many

Public Relations workers. A sizeable number work for government agencies, schools, colleges, museums, and other educational, religious, human service, and other organizations. The rapidly expanding health field also offers opportunities for Public Relations work. A number of workers are employed by Public Relations consulting firms which furnish services to clients for a fee. Others work for advertising agencies.

BACKGROUND AND QUALIFICATIONS:

A college education combined with Public Relations experience is excellent preparation for Public Relations work. Although most beginners in the field have a college degree in communications, public relations, or journalism, some employers prefer a background in a field related to the firm's business. Other firms want college graduates who have worked for the news media. In fact, many editors, reporters, and workers in closely related fields enter Public Relations work. Some companies, particularly those with large Public Relations staffs, have formal training programs for new workers. In other firms, new employers work under the guidance of experienced staff members.

Promotion to supervisory jobs may come as workers demonstrate their ability to handle more demanding and creative assignments. Some experienced Public Relations workers start their own consulting firms. The Public Relations Society accredits Public Relations Officers who have at least five years of experience in the field and have passed a comprehensive six-hour examination.

EARNINGS:

Median earnings for public relations workers who were not self-employed were $26,900 in 1986. The middle 50 percent earned between $19,700 and $41,200 annually; the lowest 10 percent earned less than $14,400; and the top 10 percent earned more than $51,500. In the Federal Government, persons with a bachelor's generally started at $18,400 a year in 1987; those with a master's degree generally started at $22,500 per year.

OUTLOOK:

Employment of public relations workers is expected to increase much faster than the average for all occupations through the year 2000.

PURCHASING AGENT

DESCRIPTION:

Purchasing Agents, also called Industrial Buyers, obtain goods and services of the quality required at the lowest possible cost, and see that adequate supplies are always available. Agents who work for manufacturing firms buy machinery, raw materials, product components, services, and maintenance and repair supplies; those working for government agencies may purchase such items as office supplies, furniture, business machines, or vehicles, to name some.

Purchasing Agents usually specialize in one or more specific groups of commodities. Agents are assigned to sections, headed by Assistant Purchasing Managers, who are responsible for a group of related commodities. In smaller organizations, Purchasing Agents generally are assigned certain categories of goods. About half of all purchasing agents work for manufacturing firms.

BACKGROUND AND QUALIFICATIONS:

Most large organizations now require a college degree, and many prefer applicants who have an MBA degree. Familiarity with the computer and its uses is desirable in understanding the systems aspect of the purchasing profession. Following the initial training period, Junior Purchasing Agents usually are given the responsibility for purchasing standard and catalog items. As they gain experience and develop expertise in their assigned areas, they may be promoted to Purchasing Agent and then Senior Purchasing Agent. Continuing education is essential for Purchasing Agents who want to advance their careers. Purchasing Agents are encouraged to participate in frequent seminars offered by professional societies, and to take courses in the field at local colleges and universities.

The recognized mark of experience and professional competence is the designation Certified Purchasing Manager (CPM). This designation is conferred by the National Association of Purchasing Management, Inc. upon candidates who have passed four examinations and who meet educational and professional experience requirements.

EARNINGS:

Median annual earnings for purchasing agents were slightly over $23,200 in 1986. The middle 50 percent earned between $17,000 and $21,000. The bottom 10 percent earned less than $13,400, and the top 10 percent earned more than $42,400.

OUTLOOK:

Employment of purchasing agents and managers is expected to increase more slowly than the average for all occupations during the 1990's. Computerization of purchasing coupled with an increased reliance on a smaller number of suppliers should boost the productivity of purchasing personnel.

QUALITY CONTROL SUPERVISOR:

DESCRIPTION:

A quality control supervisor may either be involved in the spot checking of items being manufactured or processed, or in assuring that the proper processes are being followed. A quality control system involves selection and training of personnel, product design, the establishment of specifications, procedures and tests, the design and maintenance of facilities and equipment, the selection of materials, and recordkeeping. In an effective quality control system, all these aspects are evaluated on a regular basis, and modified and improved when appropriate.

BACKGROUND AND QUALIFICATIONS:

While some quality control positions involved with the supervision of the production of simpler items might require little background besides on-the-job training, many require a specialized degree in engineering, chemistry, or biology. While all manufacturing firms require some degree of quality control, this is especially important in the chemistry, food and drug industries. Some drug manufacturers for example, may assign one out of six production workers to quality assurance functions alone.

EARNINGS:

Earnings by quality control workers vary widely, depending upon the industry. An entry level position in the food, drug, or chemical industry, for example, requires a BA in Chemistry or Biology, and brought a starting salary in 1986 in the $300-400 per week range.

OUTLOOK:

Also varies greatly, depending upon the industry.

REPORTER/EDITOR:

DESCRIPTION:

Newspaper Reporters gather information on current events and use it to write stories for daily or weekly newspapers. Large dailies frequently assign teams of reporters to investigate social, economic, or political conditions, and reporters are often assigned to "beats", such as police stations, courthouses, or governmental agencies, to gather news originating in these places. General Assignment Reporters write local news stories on a wide range of topics, from public meetings to human interest stories.

Reporters with a specialized background or interest in a particular area write, interpret, and analyze the news in fields such as medicine, politics, foreign affairs, sports, fashion, art, theater, consumer affairs, travel, finance, social events, science, education, business, labor, religion, and other areas. Critics review literary, artistic, and musical works and performances while editorial writers present viewpoints on topics of interest. Reporters on small newspapers cover all aspects of local news, and also may take photographs, write headlines, lay out pages, and write editorials. On some small weeklies, they may also solicit advertisements, sell subscriptions, and perform general office work. Reporters must be highly motivated, and are expected to work long hours.

BACKGROUND AND QUALIFICATIONS:

Most newspapers will only consider applicants with a degree in journalism, which includes training in the liberal arts in addition to professional training in journalism. Others prefer applicants who have a bachelor's degree in one of the liberal arts and a master's degree in journalism. Experience as a part-time "stringer" is very helpful in finding full time employment as a Reporter.

Most beginning Reporters start on weekly or small daily newspapers, with a small number of outstanding journalism graduates finding work with large daily newspapers, although this is a rare exception. Large dailies generally look for at least three years of reporting experience, acquired on smaller newspapers.

Beginning Reporters are assigned duties such as reporting on civic and community meetings, summarizing speeches, writing obituaries, interviewing important community leaders or visitors, and covering police, government, or courthouse proceedings. As they gain experience, they may report on more important events, cover an assigned beat, or specialize in a particular field. Newspaper Reporters may advance to large daily newspapers or state and national newswire services. However, competition for such positions is fierce, and news executives are flooded with applications from highly qualified reporters every year. Some experienced Reporters become columnists, correspondents, editorial writers, editors, or top executives; these people represent the top of the field, and competition for them is extremely keen. Other reporters transfer to related fields, such as public relations, writing for magazines, or preparing copy for radio or television news programs.

EARNINGS:

Reporters working for daily newspapers having contracts negotiated by the Newspaper Guild had starting salaries ranging from about $9,400 to nearly $47,000 a year in 1986. The majority started at between $15,600 and $23,400 a year.

Experienced reporters averaged about $31,200 annually in 1986, according to figures provided by The Newspaper Guild. Virtually all experienced reporters earned over $20,800 a year, while the top contractual salary was $48,300 a year. A number of top reporters on big city dailies earned even more, on the basis of merit. Benefits may vary widely according to length of service and the size and location of the employer. Most reporters, however, receive benefits such as paid vacations, and group insurance and pension plans.

OUTLOOK:

Employment of reporters and correspondents is expected to grow through the year 2000, primarily due to the anticipated increase in the number of smalltown and suburban daily and weekly newspapers.

SECURITIES AND FINANCIAL SERVICES SALES REPRESENTATIVES

DESCRIPTION:

Securities Sales Representatives: Most investors, whether they are individuals with a few hundred dollars or large institutions with millions to invest, use securities sales representatives when buying or selling stocks, bonds, shares in mutual funds, or other financial products. Securities sales representatives also provide many related services for their customers. Depending on a customer's knowledge of the market, they may explain the meaning of stock market terms and trading practices; offer financial counseling; devise an individual financial portfolio including securities, corporate and municipal bonds, life insurance, annuities, and other investments; and offer advice on the purchase or sale of particular securities.

Financial Services Sales Representatives: Financial services sales representatives call on various businesses to solicit applications for loans and new deposit accounts for banks or savings and loan associations. They also locate and contact prospective customers to present their bank's financial services and to ascertain the customer's banking needs. At most small and medium-sized banks, branch managers and commercial loan officers are responsible for marketing the bank's financial services. As banks offer more and increasingly complex financial services, for example, securities brokerage and financial planning-the job of financial services sales representatives will assume greater importance.

BACKGROUND AND QUALIFICATIONS:

A college education is becoming increasingly important, as securities sales representatives must be well informed about economic conditions and trends. Although employer seldom require specialized academic training, courses in business administration, economics, and finance are helpful. Securities sales representatives must meet State licensing requirements, which generally include passing an examination, and, in some cases, furnishing a personal bond. In addition, sales representatives must register as representatives of their firm according to regulations of the securities exchanges where they do business or the National Association of Securities Dealers, Inc. (NASD). Before beginners can qualify as registered representatives, they must pass the General Securities Registered Representative Examination.

Banks and other credit institutions prefer to hire college graduates for financial services sales jobs. A business administration degree with a specialization in finance or a liberal arts degree including courses in accounting, economics, and marketing serves as excellent preparation for this job. Financial services sales representatives learn through on-the-job training under the supervision of bank officers. Outstanding performance can lead to promotion to managerial positions.

EARNINGS:

According to the Securities Industry Association, average annual earnings of beginning securities sales representatives were $37,000 in 1986. Financial services sales representatives are paid a salary; some receive bonuses if they meet certain established goals. Average earnings of financial services sales representatives are substantially less than those of securities sales representatives.

OUTLOOK:

The demand for securities sales representatives fluctuates as the economy expands and contracts. Employment of securities sales representatives is expected to expand as economic growth, rising personal incomes, and greater inherited wealth increase the funds available for investment. Employment of financial services sales representatives is also expected to increase through the year 2000, as banks and credit institutions expand the financial services they offer, and issue more loans for personal and commercial use.

STATISTICIAN

DESCRIPTION:

Statisticians devise, carry out, and interpret the numerical results of surveys and experiments. In doing so, they apply their knowledge of statistical methods to a particular subject area, such as economics, human behavior, the natural sciences, or engineering. They may use statistical techniques to predict population growth or economic conditions, develop quality control tests for manufactured products, or help business managers and government officials make decisions and evaluate the results of new programs. Over half of all Statisticians are in private industry, primarily in manufacturing, finance, and insurance firms.

BACKGROUND AND QUALIFICATIONS:

A bachelor's degree in statistics or mathematics is the minimum educational requirement for many beginning jobs in statistics. For other entry-level jobs in the field, however, a BA with a major in an applied field of study such as economics or a natural science, and a minor in statistics is preferable. A graduate degree in mathematics or statistics is essential for college and university teaching. Most mathematics statisticians have at least a BA in mathematics and an advanced degree in statistics.

Beginning statisticians who have a BA often spend their time performing routine work under the supervision of an experienced Statistician. Through experience, they may advance to positions of greater technical and supervisory responsibility. However, opportunities for promotion are best for those with advanced degrees.

EARNINGS:

In the Federal Government in 1987, the average starting salary of statisticians who had a bachelor's degree and no experience was $14,800 or $18,400 a year, depending on their grades. Beginning statisticians with a master's degree averaged $22,500 or $27,200. Those with a PhD began at $27,200 or $32,600. The average annual salary for statisticians in the Federal Government was about $39,400 in 1986.

OUTLOOK:

Employment opportunities for persons who combine training in statistics with knowledge of computer science or a field of application - such as biology, economics or engineering - are generally expected to be favorable through the year 2000.

SYSTEMS ANALYST

DESCRIPTION:

Systems analysts plan efficient methods of processing data and handling the results. Analysts use various techniques, such as cost accounting, sampling, and mathematical model building to analyze a problem and devise a new system. The problems that Systems Analysts solve range from monitoring nuclear fission in a powerplant to forecasting sales for an appliance manufacturing firm. Because the work is so varied and complex, Analysts usually specialize in either business or scientific and engineering applications. Most Systems Analysts work in manufacturing firms, banks, insurance companies, and data processing service organizations. In addition, large numbers work for wholesale and retail businesses and government agencies.

BACKGROUND AND QUALIFICATIONS:

College graduates are almost always sought for the position of Systems Analyst. For some of the more complex positions, persons with graduate degrees are preferred. Employers usually seek Analysts with a background in accounting, business management, or economics for work in a business environment, while a background in the physical sciences, mathematics, or engineering is preferred for work in scientifically oriented organizations. A growing number of employers seek applicants who have a degree in Computer Science, Information Systems, or Data Processing. Regardless of the college major, employers seek those who are familiar with programming languages.

In order to advance, Systems Analysts must continue their technical education. Technological advances come so rapidly in the computer field that continuous study is necessary to keep computer skills up to date. Training usually takes the form of one- and two-week courses offered by employers and software vendors. Additional training may come from professional development seminars offered by professional computing societies. An indication of experience and professional competence is the Certificate in Data Processing (CDP). This designation is conferred by the Institute for Certification of Computer Professionals, and is granted to candidates who have five years experience and have passed a five-part examination.

EARNINGS:

Median annual earnings of systems analysts who worked full time in 1986 were about $32,800. In the Federal Government, the entrance salary for recent college graduates with a bachelor's degree was about $14,800 a year in

1987. Salaries tend to be highest in mining and public utilities and lowest in finance, insurance, and real estate.

OUTLOOK:

The demand for systems analysts is expected to rise through the year 2000, as advances in technology lead to new applications for computers. Factory and office automation, advances in telecommunications technology, and scientific research are just a few areas where use of computers will expand.

TECHNICAL WRITER/EDITOR

DESCRIPTION:

Technical Writers and Technical Editors research, write, and edit technical materials, and also may produce publications and audiovisual materials. To ensure that their work is accurate, Technical Writers must be expert in the subject area in which they are writing. Editors are also responsible for the accuracy of material on which they work. Some organizations use job titles other than Technical Writer/Editor, such as Staff Writer, Publications Engineer, Communications Specialist, Publications Engineer, Communications Specialist, Industrial Writer, Industrial Materials Developer, and others.

Technical Writers set out either to instruct or inform, and in many instances they do both. They prepare manuals, catalogs, parts lists, and instructional materials needed by sales representatives who sell machinery or scientific equipment and by the technicians who install, maintain, and service it. Technical Writers are often part of a team, working closely with scientists, engineers, accountants, and others. Technical Editors take the material Technical Writers products and further polish it for final publication and use. Many writers and editors work for large firms in the electronics, aviation, aerospace, ordinance, chemical, pharmaceutical, and computer manufacturing industries. Firms in the energy, communications, and computer software fields also employ many Technical Writers, and research laboratories employ significant numbers.

BACKGROUND AND QUALIFICATIONS:

Employers seek people whose educational background, work experience, and personal pursuits indicate they possess both writing skills and appropriate scientific knowledge. Knowledge of graphics and other aspects of publication production may be helpful in landing a job in the field. An understanding of current trends in communication technology is an asset, and familiarity with computer operations and terminology is increasingly important. Many employers prefer candidates with a degree in science or engineering, plus a minor in English, journalism, or technical communications. Other employers emphasize writing ability and look for candidates whose major field of study was journalism, English, or the liberal arts. Depending on their line of business, these employees almost always require course work or practical experience in a specific subject as well, computer science, for example.

People with a solid background in science or engineering are at an advantage in competing for such jobs. Those with BA's or MA's in Technical Writing are often preferred over candidates with little or no technical background. Beginning Technical Writers often assist experienced writers by doing library research and preparing drafts of reports. Experienced Technical Writers in companies with large writing staffs may eventually move to the job of Technical Editor, or shift to an administrative position in the publication or technical information departments. The top job is usually that of Publications Manager (and other titles), who normally supervises all of the people directly involved in producing the company's technical documents. The manager supervises not only the Technical Writers and Editors, but also staff members responsible for illustrations, photography, reproduction, and distribution.

EARNINGS:

In 1986, beginning salaries for writers and editorial assistants ranged from $18,400 to $29,300 annually, according to surveys by the Executive Compensation Service. Salaries for technical writers ranged from $19,300 to $37,800. Experienced editors generally earned between $20,900 and $39,000; supervisory editors, $28,600 to $42,600 a year.

OUTLOOK:

Through the year 200, the outlook for writing and editing jobs is expected to continue to be keenly competitive. With the increasing complexity of industrial and scientific equipment, more users will depend on the technical writer's ability to prepare precise but simple explanations and instructions.

UNDERWRITER

DESCRIPTION:

Underwriters appraise and select the risks their company will insure. Underwriters decide whether their insurance company will accept risks after analyzing information in insurance applications, reports from loss control consultants, medical reports, and actuarial studies. Most Underwriters specialize in one of the three major categories of insurance: life, casualty, and health. They further specialize in group or individual policies.

BACKGROUND AND QUALIFICATIONS:

For beginning underwriters, most large insurance companies seek college graduates with degrees in liberal arts or business administration. Underwriter Trainees begin by evaluating routine applicants under the close supervision of an experienced risk appraiser. Continuing education is a necessity if the Underwriter expects to advance to senior level positions. Insurance companies generally place great emphasis on completion of one or more of the many recognized independent study programs. Many companies pay tuition and the cost of books for those who successfully complete Underwriting courses; some offer salary increases as an additional incentive. Independent study programs are available through the American Institute of Property and Liability Underwriters, the Health Insurance Association of America, and the Life Office Management Association.

As Underwriters gain experience, they can qualify as a "Fellow" of the Academy of Life Underwriters by passing a series of examinations and completing a research paper on a topic in the field. Exams are given by the Institute of Home Office Underwriters and the Home Office Life Underwriters Association. Designation as "Fellow" is recognized as a mark of achievement in the underwriting field. Experienced Underwriters who complete a course of study may advance to Chief Underwriter or Underwriting Manager. Some Underwriting Managers are promoted to senior managerial positions after several years.

EARNINGS:

According to a survey of property and liability insurance companies, personal lines (noncommercial) underwriters earned a median salary of $21,300 a year in 1986, while commercial lines underwriters earned $23,600 a year. Senior personal and commercial lines underwriters received a median salary of $28,600.

OUTLOOK:

Employment of underwriters is expected to rise faster than the average for all occupations through the year 2000 as insurance sales continue to expand. Most job openings, however, are expected to result from the need to replace underwriters who transfer to other occupations or stop working altogether.

PRIMARY WASHINGTON EMPLOYERS

For more information on accounting opportunities in Greater Washington, look for the following professional and trade organizations in Chapter 8, beginning on page 265:

American Institute of Certified Public Accountants
The EDP Auditors Association
Institute of Internal Auditors
National Association of Accountants
National Society of Public Accountants

District of Columbia

ARTHUR ANDERSEN & CO.
1666 K Street NW 5th Floor
Washington DC 20006
202/862-3100
Contact George L. Sill, Director of Professional Personnel for accounting and tax positions. Contact Kathryn D. Griffin, Director of Consulting Recruiting for consulting positions. Contact Fred J. Weir, Director of Administration for all other positions. One of the eight largest professional service organizations in the world, operating offices in more than 40 countries. Operating under two strategic business units: Audit and Tax, and Management Information Consulting (Andersen Consulting.) The Audit Division offers assignments in a wide range of businesses and industries; company offers a highly recognized professional development program in all phases of the industry. The Tax Division offers assignments involving consultation and compliance in all areas of taxation, including income, estate, trust, and gift taxation, with client assignments providing exposure to a wide range of businesses and industries. Andersen Consulting offers opportunities for both entry-level and experienced personnel in providing professional systems and consulting services to clients, and consulting services to a wide range of businesses and industries. Corporate headquarters location: Chicago, IL.

COOPERS & LYBRAND
1800 M Street NW
Washington DC 20036
202/822-4191
Contact Recruitment Specialist. One of the "Big Eight" certified public accounting firms, providing a broad range of services in the areas of accounting and auditing, taxation, management consulting and actuarial, and benefits and compensation consulting. Operates almost 90 offices in the United States; 350 offices in 90 foreign locations. Common positions include: Accountant; Actuary; Computer Programmer; Economist; Financial Analyst; Statistician; Systems Analyst. Principal educational backgrounds sought: Accounting; Business Administration; Computer Science; Economics; Finance. Company benefits include: medical insurance; dental insurance; pension plan; life insurance; disability coverage; limited tuition assistance; profit sharing; savings plan. Divisional headquarters location. Corporate headquarters location: New York, NY. Operations at this facility include: administration; service.

ERNST & YOUNG
1225 Connecticut Avenue NW
Washington DC 20036
202/862-6000
Contact Tom Wagner, Partner. Provides auditing, accounting, tax, and management consulting services, as one of the 'Big Eight' CPA firms. Offices are located in most major United States metropolitan areas and in numerous international locations. Corporate headquarters location: Cleveland, OH.

GRANT THORNTON
1850 M Street NW, #300
Washington DC 20036
202/296-7800
Contact Personnel Department. An accounting firm.

LAVENTHOL & HORWATH
1101 17th Street NW Suite 1200
Washington DC 20036
202/296-2250
Contact Personnel Department. An accounting firm.

KENNETH LEVENTHAL & CO.
2000 K Street NW Suite 750
Washington DC 20006
202/775-1880
Contact Joe King, Managing Partner. An accounting firm.

MITCHELL/TITUS & CO.
1825 K Street NW Suite 1115
Washington DC 20006
202/293-5713, 5714, 5715
Contact Jackie E. Winson, Personnel. An accounting firm. Common position: Accountant. Principal educational background sought: Accounting. Company benefits include: medical insurance; pension plan; life insurance; tuition assistance; disability coverage; employee discounts. Corporate headquarters location: New York, NY.

PRICE WATERHOUSE
1801 K Street NW
Washington DC 20006
202/785-6406
Contact Robert L. Drake, Director/Human Resources. An international certified public accounting firm with nearly 400 offices, about 100 in the United States. Professional employment reaches 28,000 in 98 countries worldwide. Services include accounting and auditing, tax consulting, and all areas of management consulting. National office: New York, NY.

REGARDIE BROOKS & LEWIS, CPA'S
7101 Wisconsin Avenue
Washington DC 20814
202/654-9000
Contact Personnel. An accounting firm.

Maryland

ARTHUR ANDERSEN
201 North Charles Street
Baltimore MD 21201
301/727-5800
Contact Personnel. An accounting firm.

PAUL BROWNER, CHARTERED
932 Hungerford Drive, Suite 17
Rockville MD 20850
301/340-3340
Contact Paul Browner, President. An accounting firm.

CLIFTON GUNDERSON & CO.
412 The Exchange Building
1122 Kenilworth
Towson MD 21204
301/337-3830
Contact Mr. Terry Hancock, Partner in Charge. An accounting firm.

COOPERS & LYBRAND
217 East Redwood Street
Baltimore MD 21201
301/783-7653
Contact Joseph A. Crumbling, Human Resources Manager. An accounting firm. Common positions include: Accountant. Principal educational background sought: Accounting. Company benefits include: medical, dental, and life insurance; pension plan; tuition assistance; disability coverage; savings plan. Corporate headquarters location: New York, NY.

ERNST & YOUNG & CO.
100 South Charles Street
Baltimore MD 21201
301/539-4500
Contact Recruiting Director. An accounting firm.

FAW CUSSON & CO.
17 South Washington Street
P.O. Box 1168
Easton MD 21601
301/822-0045
Contact John Keen, Partner. An accounting firm.

GRANT THORTON
2 Hopkins Plaza, Suite 700
Baltimore MD 21201
301/685-4000
Contact Darlene Smith, Personnel. A national accounting firm.

KAMANITZ UHLFELDER PERMISON
1515 Reistertown Road
Baltimore MD 21208
301/484-8700
Contact Personnel Department. An accounting firm.

LESTER, GREEN AND COMPANY
8601 Georgia Avenue Suite 610
Silver Springs MD 20910
301/585-0099
Contact Norman Lester, Personnel. An accounting firm.

PEAT MARWICK MAIN & COMPANY
111 South Calvert Street
Baltimore MD 21202
301/783-8300
Contact Judith Burns, Office Administrator. An accounting firm. Common positions at this facility include: Accountant; Administrator; Attorney; Economist; Biomedical Engineer; Financial Analyst; Marketing Specialist; Personnel & Labor Relations Specialist; Statistician; Health Care Specialist; Tax Specialist. Principal educational backgrounds sought: Accounting; Biology; Business Administration; Chemistry; Communications; Computer Science; Economics; Engineering; Finance; Marketing; Mathematics; Health Care; Tax; Law; Real Estate; Tax Management; Information Technologies. Company benefits include: medical insurance; dental insurance; pension plan; life insurance; disability coverage; savings plan; 401 K. Corporate headquarters location: New York, NY. Operations at this facility: service.

PEAT MARWICK MAIN/COLUMBIA
5565 Sterret Place
Columbia MD 21044
301/997-0330
Contact Personnel Department. An accounting firm.

PRICE WATERHOUSE
7 St. Paul Street, Suite 1700
Baltmore MD 21202
301/625-8328
Contact Thomas Kovell, Human Resources Manager. An accounting firm. Common positions include: Accountant; Computer Programmer. Principal educational backgrounds sought: Accounting; Computer Science; Liberal Arts. Company benefits include: medical, dental and life insurance; pension plan; disability coverage; savings plan. Corporate headquarters located in New York, NY. Operations at this facility include: regional headquarters; administration; service; sales.

STEGMAN & COMPANY, P.A.
36 South Charles Street, Suite 2200
Baltimore MD 21201
301/685-1700
Contact William Clark, Director. An accounting firm. Common positions include: Accountant. Principal educational backgrounds sought: Accounting.

ADVERTISING/PUBLIC RELATIONS

For more information on advertising/public relations opportunities in Greater Washington, look for the following professional and trade organizations in Chapter 8, beginning on page 265:

American Advertising Federation
American Association of Advertising Agencies
American Marketing Association
Business-Professional Advertising Association
Public Relations Society of America
Television Bureau of Advertising

District of Columbia

GOLDBERG MARCHESANO KOHLMAN INC.
927 15th Street NW
Washington DC 20005
202/789-2000
Contact Sandy Socrates, V.P. Operations. A full service advertising agency. Common positions include: Accountant; Account Executive; Art Director; Broadcast Manager; Creative Director; Buyer (Media); Commercial Artist; Executive Assistant; Mechanical Artist; Operations/Production Specialist; Receptionist; Traffic Specialist; Word Processor. Principal educational backgrounds sought: Accounting; Art/Design; Business Administration; Communications; Computer Science; Liberal Arts; Marketing. Company benefits include: medical, dental, and life insurance; disability coverage. Corporate headquarters location. Operations at this facility include: administration; service.

PORTER NOVELLI INC.
1001 30th Street NW, Suite 2000
Washington DC 20007
202/342-7000
Contact Brenda Shierman, Personnel. An advertising agency.

Maryland

WEITZMAN DYM & ASSOCIATES
7474 Greenway Center Drive #1100
Greenbelt MD 20770
301/345-8200
Contact Elner Gant, Personnel Director. An advertising agency.

APPAREL & TEXTILE MANUFACTURING

For more information on apparel and textile opportunities in Greater Washington, look for the following professional and trade organizations in Chapter 8, beginning on page 265:

American Apparel Manufacturers Association
American Textile Manufacturers Institute
National Apparel Distributors
Northern Textile Association
Textile Research Institute

Maryland

JOS. A. BANK CLOTHIERS
25 Crossroads Drive
Owings Mills MD 21117
301/837-1700
Contact Catherine F. Wood, Employment Coordinator. A manufacturer and retailer of traditionally tailored men's and women's clothing. Common positions include: Accountant; Blue-Collar Worker Supervisor; Buyer; Computer Programmer; Customer Service Representative; Department Manager; Operations/Production Manager; Personnel & Labor Relations Specialist; Sales Representative. Principal educational backgrounds sought: Accounting; Business Administration; Communications; Computer Science; Marketing. Company benefits include: medical, dental, and life insurance; tuition assistance; disability coverage; employee discounts; 401K retirement plan. Corporate headquarters location. Operations at this facility include: regional headquarters; manufacturing. New York Stock Exchange.

CLAIRE FROCK COMPANY INC.
201 Poplar Street
Thurmont MD 21788
301/271-7377
Contact Jerry Moore, Personnel Department. Manufactures women's sportswear, pantsuits, and dresses. Corporate headquarters location.

MISTY MANUFACTURING COMPANY
1407 Parker Road
Baltimore MD 21227
301/242-8200
Contact Cathy Stanson, Personnel Director. Produces women's and men's rainwear. Corporate headquarters location: New York, NY.

MOTHER GOOSE COMPANY
191 Shaeffer Avenue
Westminster MD 21157
301/848-3300
Contact Bernie Krals, Controller. Manufactures a nationally-distributed line of children's shoes. Primary customers include department stores, retail chains, independent retailers. A subsidiary of Kessler Shoe Manufacturing Company. Corporate headquarters location. Operations include: research; manufacturing; sales; administration; retailing. Common positions include: Accountant; Business & Systems Analyst; Field Sales Supervisor; Field Sales Representative; Retail Store Managers. Principal educational backgrounds sought: Business Administration; Marketing; Computer Science. Company benefits include: medical insurance; life insurance; tuition assistance; profit sharing; bonus; employee discounts.

ARTS / ENTERTAINMENT / LEISURE

For more information on arts/entertainment opportunities in Greater Washington, look for the following professional and trade organizations in Chapter 8, beginning on page 265:

American Association of Zoological Parks & Aquariums
American Federation of Musicians

American Federation of Television and Radio Artists
National Endowment for the Arts
Theatre Communications Group

<u>District of Columbia</u>

AMERICAN FILM INSTITUTE
John F. Kennedy Center
Washington DC 20566
202/828-4060
Contact Personnel Department. An organiztion whose operations include a school, magazine publication, and the preservation of films.

RINGLING BROTHERS/
BARNUM & BAILEY CIRCUS
3201 New Mexico Ave.
Washington DC 20016
202/529-9100
Contact Mary Ann Ottenberg, Administration. Headquarters of the well known circus company.

BANK/SAVINGS & LOAN

For more information on banking opportunities in Greater Washington, look for the following professional and trade organizations in Chapter 8, beginning on page 265:

American Bankers Association
Bank Administration Institute
Independent Bankers Association of America
Institute of Financial Education
National Council of Savings Institutions

<u>District of Columbia</u>

AMERICAN SECURITY BANK NA
1501 Pennsylvania Avenue NW
Washington DC 20013
202/624-4000
Contact Personnel Department. The principal commercial banking subsidiary of American Security Corporation, a bank holding company engaged in commercial, international, and mortgage banking, as well as offering trust, insurance, and travel services. Corporate headquarters location.

BOARD OF GOVERNORS OF THE
FEDERAL RESERVE SYSTEM
20th & C Streets NW
Washington DC 20551
202/452-3880
Contact Kathy Warehime, Recruitment Planning & Placement Manager. The primary function of the Board of Governors of the Federal Reserve System is the setting of monetary policy to foster stable

economic conditions and long-term economic growth. The Board makes policy through the Federal Open Market Committee, which consists of the seven members of the Board, the president of the New York Federal Reserve Bank, and four of the presidents of the other 11 District banks, who serve in rotation. In addition, the Board has broad supervisory and regulatory responsibilities over the activities of the Federal Reserve Banks, its member banks, bank holding companies, and other financial institutions. It sets margin requirements on credit purchases in the stock market and oversees certain, international banking activities. Through its Division of Consumer and Community Affairs, the Board carries out its responsibilities for protecting consumers' rights in borrowing transactions and implements laws to help communities meet their credit needs. Headquarters location. Common positions include: Attorney; Computer Scientist; Economist; EDP Auditor; Financial Analyst; Technical Writer/Editor. Principal educational backgrounds sought: Computer Science; Economics; Finance; Mathematics; Law. Company benefits include: medical insurance; dental insurance; pension plan; life insurance; tuition assistance; disability coverage; employee discounts; savings plan; Thrift/IRA/401K's.

CITIZENS BANK OF WASHINGTON NA
11th & G Streets NW
Suite 307
Washington DC 20005
202/626-0272
Contact Mary Guarnieri, Director of Human Resources. Provides a full range of banking services. Common positions include: Accountant; Administrator; Bank Officer/Manager; Credit Manager; Customer Service Representative; Branch Manager; Operations/Production Manager; Teller; Proof Operator; Secretary; Loan Officer. Principal educational backgrounds sought: Business Administration; Economics; Finance. Company benefits include: medical insurance; dental insurance; pension plan; life insurance; tuition assistance; disability coverage; Corporate headquarters location. Parent company is Citizens Bank of Maryland. Corporate headquarters location.

COMPTROLLER OF THE CURRENCY
490 L'Enfant Plaza SW
Washington DC 20219
202/447-1543
Contact Rebecca Minton, National Recruitment Coordinator. The Office of the Comptroller of the Currency is a federal regulatory agency with supervisory responsibility for the country's national banks. The key figure in fulfilling the OCC's regulatory mission is the national bank examiner, a highly trained financial professional. Candidates with backgrounds in finance, banking, economics and business administration are encouraged to apply. Company benefits include a compressed work schedule with alternate Fridays off; a choice of group health plans; and dental, vision, life, travel accident, and long-term disability insurance.

CRESTAR BANK/
GREATER WASHINGTON REGION
New York Avenue NW
Washington DC 20005
202/879-6170
Contact Patricia O. Lohr, Senior Vice-President. The northern region of Crestar Bank. The company has $10.5 billion in assets. Common positions Bank Officer/Manager; Credit Manager; Customer Service Representative; Financial Analyst; Branch Manager; Department Manager; Management Trainee; Personnel & Labor Relations Specialist; Sales Representative. Principal educational backgrounds sought: Accounting; Business Administration; Economics; Finance; Liberal Arts; Marketing. Company benefits include: medical, dental, and life insurance; pension plan; tuition assistance; disability coverage; profit sharing; savings plan. Corporate headquarters location: Richmond, VA. Parent company is Crestar Financial Corp. Operations at this facility include: regional headquarters.

DISTRICT OF COLUMBIA NATIONAL BANK
1801 K Street NW, Suite 250
Washington DC 20006
202/955-8710
Contact Dolores Gomes, Assistant Vice-President/Personnel. Operates a metropolitan bank with seven local branch offices. Corporate headquarters location.

EXPORT-IMPORT BANK OF THE UNITED STATES
Room 1005
811 Vermont Avenue NW
Washington DC 20571
202/566-8869
Contact Carol Miller, Personnel Management Specialist. An agency of the federal government, the bank provides assistance to American exporters through loans, guarantees, and insurance programs. Headquarters location. Common positions include: Accountant; Economist; Financial Analyst. Principal educational backgrounds sought: Accounting; Economics; Finance. Company benefits include: medical and life insurance; pension plan.

THE NATIONAL BANK OF WASHINGTON
4340 Connecticut Avenue NW
Washington DC 20008
202/537-2027
Contact Patricia Johnson, Vice-President for Employment. Multiple area locations. Washington DC's oldest and third largest bank, with assets of more than $1 billion. Corporate headquarters location.

SECURITY NATIONAL BANK
1130 Connecticut Avenue NW
Washington DC 20036
202/331-5600
Contact Tripp Jones, Personnel Officer. A full service commercial bank with nine area banking locations. Corporate headquarters location.

UNITED NATIONAL BANK
3940 Minnesota Avenue NE
Washington DC 20019
202/452-5800
Contact Personnel Director. A commercial bank.

Maryland

THE BANK OF BALTIMORE
201 West Centre Street
Baltimore MD 21201
301/783-6866
Contact Employment Manager. A regional commercial bank with 50+ branches. Corporate headquarters are located in Baltimore and regional headquarters in Bethesda, MD. Parent company: Baltimore Bancorp (a holding company). Common positions at this facility include: Accountant; Administrator; Bank Officer/Manager; Computer Programmer; Credit Manager; Customer Service Representative; Financial Analyst; Branch Manager; Department Manager; Management Trainee; Personnel & Labor Relations Specialist; Sales Representative; Systems Analyst. Principal educationsl backgrounds sought: Accounting; Business Administration; Computer Science; Finance. Company

benefits include: medical insurance; dental insurance; pension plan; life insurance; tuition assistance; disability coverage. New York Stock Exchange.

CARROLLTON BANK
P.O. Box 1391
Baltimore MD 21203
301/837-9800
Contact Lilian Kennedy, Personnel Director. Operates a full-service commercial bank. Corporate headquarters location.

CITIZENS BANK & TRUST OF MARYLAND
6200 Baltimore Boulevard
Riverdale MD 20737
301/699-7025
Contact Debbie Funkhouser, Human Resources Manager. A full-service commercial bank, offering checking and savings accounts, NOW accounts, Christmas clubs, certificates of deposit, All-Savers certificates, IRA and Keough accounts, safe-deposit boxes, travelers checks, personal money orders, credit cards, and commercial, construction, mortgage, consumer and check credit loans, and money market investment services. Also offers trust services, automatic deposit services, and stock and other securities transactions services. Operates more than 70 branches. Common positions include: Administrator; Bank Officer/Manager; Computer Programmer; Credit Manager; Branch Manager; Management Trainee; Public Relations Worker. Principal educational backgrounds sought: Accounting; Business Administration; Computer Science; Finance; Marketing; Mathematics. Company benefits include: medical, dental, and life insurance; pension plan; tuition assistance; disability coverage; profit sharing; savings plan. Corporate headquarters location. Operations at this facility include: regional headquarters.

CITIZENS NATIONAL BANK
390 Main Street
Laurel MD 20707
301/725-3100
Contact Barbara Ireland, Vice President/Personnel. Operates a full-service commercial bank, with sixteen area branch offices. Corporate headquarters location.

CITIZENS SAVINGS & LOAN ASSOCIATION
8487 Fenton Street
Silver Springs MD 20910
301/565-8945
Contact Louise Shupe, Personnel Director. Operates a full-service savings and loan association, with 16 offices serving Montgomery, Frederick, Howard, and Prince George's counties. Assets exceed $225 million. Corporate headquarters location.

CRESTAR BANK MD
7500 Wisconsin Avenue
Bethesda MD 20814
301/951-3000
Contact Manager. Operates a full-service commercial bank, with ten area branches. Corporate headquarters location.

THE EQUITABLE TRUST COMPANY
320 Main Street
Laurel MD 20707
301/547-4000
Contact Bill Gardner, Office Manager. Provides a range of banking and trust services.

FARM CREDIT BANK OF BALTIMORE

P.O. Box 1555
Baltimore MD 21203
301/628-5500

Contact Employment Manager. Agricultural lender. Common positions include: Accountant; Computer Programmer; Systems Analyst. Principal educational backgrounds sought: Accounting; Business Administration; Computer Science; Economics; Finance; Agriculture. Company benefits include: medical, dental, and life insurance; pension plan; tuition assistance; disability coverage; profit sharing. Corporate headquarters location. Operations at this facility include: divisional headquarters; administration.

FIRST AMERICAN BANK OF MARYLAND

8401 Colesville Road
Silver Springs MD 20910
301/565-7172

Contact Nila C. Bobila, Human Resources Officer. Operates a full-service commercial bank with 34 branches; a major subsidiary of First American Bankshares (Washington, DC). Assets exceed $922 million. Corporate headquarters location. Common positions include: Bank Officer/Manager; Credit Manager; Customer Service Representative; Branch Manager; Department Manager; Management Trainee. Principal educational backgrounds sought: Business Administration; Communications; Economics; Finance; Marketing. Company benefits include: medical insurance; dental insurance; pension plan; life insurance; tuition assistance; disability coverage; profit sharing; savings plan.

FIRST NATIONAL BANK OF MARYLAND

110 Paca Street-8th Floor
Baltimore MD 21201
301/244-4000

Contact Brian King, Personnel Director. A full-service commercial bank, offering a complete range of banking services. Several area locations. Corporate headquarters location.

FIRST NATIONAL BANK OF SOUTHERN MARYLAND

14700 Main Street
P.O. Box 60
Upper Marlboro MD 20772
301/627-6000

Contact Kathy Martin, Personnel Director. Operates a full-service commercial bank with 11 area branch offices. Corporate headquarters location.

MADISON NATIONAL BANK

10000 B Derekwood Lane
Lanham MD 20706
202/452-5500

Contact Human Resources Department. Offers complete commercial banking services, excluding trust services, through eight offices in Washington DC. Corporate headquarters location.

MARYLAND FEDERAL SAVINGS & LOAN ASSOCIATION

3505 Hamilton Street
Hyattsville MD 20782
301/779-1200 ext 269, 270

Contact Helen M. Dolan, Sr. Vice President. Operates an area savings bank with 15 branch offices. Corporate headquarters location.

MERCANTILE BANKSHARES CORPORATION
750 Old Hammonds Ferry Road
Linthicum MD 21090
301/347-8260
Contact Coleen M. Burke, Vice President. A bank holding company controlling eleven Maryland general commercial banks (including the Mercantile Safe Deposit & Trust, Bank of Southern Maryland, Potomac Valley Bank, and others), as well as other operations in mortgage banking, commercial and consumer financing, and insurance. Operates, through subsidiaries, more than eighty branch banking offices throughout Maryland. Common positions include: Accountant; Administrator; Bank Officer/Manager; Computer Programmer; Customer Service Representative; Financial Analyst; Management Trainee; Systems Analyst. Principal educational backgrounds sought: Accounting; Business Administration; Computer Science; Economics; Finance; Liberal Arts. Company benefits include: medical, dental and life insurance; pension plan; tuition assistance; disability coverage; profit sharing; savings plan; employee stock option plan. Corporate headquarters location: Baltimore, MD.

MNC FINANCIAL
225 North Calvert Street
Baltimore MD 21202
301/244-6960
Contact Employment Office. A diversified full-service regional institution which delivers a broad range of commercial and consumer banking services in Maryland, the District of Columbia, Delaware, Pennsylvania and Virginia. MNC Financial is the corporate parent of Maryland National Bank, Maryland Bank NA (MBNA), and MNC Affiliates Group. With $17 billion assets, MNC ranks as the 35th largest largest U.S. bank holding company.

NCNB BANK OF MARYLAND
P.O. Box 1316
Baltimore MD 21203
301/385-8612
Contact Linda Sokolowski, Personnel Manager. Operates a full-service commercial bank. Common positions include: Accountant; Bank Officer/Manager; Credit Manager; Customer Service Representative; Branch Manager; Department Manager; Marketing Specialist. Principal educational backgrounds sought: Accounting; Business Administration; Finance. Company benefits include: medical, dental, and life insurance; pension plan; tuition assistance; disability coverage; employee discounts; savings plan. Corporate headquarters located in Charlotte, NC (North Carolina National Bank). Operations at this facility include: administration. New York Stock Exchange.

SOVRAN FINANCIAL CORPORATION
6610 Rockledge Drive,
Bethesda MD 20817
301/270-7170
Contact Philip E. Cawley, Employment Manager. Sovran Financial Corporation, one of the Mid Atlantic's leading financial institutions. Offers a wide range of banking services through over 80 locations. Common positions include: Accountant; Bank Officer/Manager; Computer Programmer; Credit Manager; Customer Service Representative; Financial Analyst; Branch Manager; Management Trainee; Marketing Specialist. Principal educational backgrounds sought: Business Administration; Computer Science; Finance. Company benefits include: medical, dental and life insurance; pension plan; tuition assistance; disability coverage; profit sharing; employee discounts; savings plan. Regional headquarters location.

Northern Virginia

CENTRAL FIDELITY BANK
1021 East Cary Street
P.O. Box 27602
Richmond VA 23261
804/697-7204
Contact Bill Leedon, V.P. Human Resources. A full-service banking institution. Common positions include: Bank Officer/Manager; Financial Analyst. Principal educational backgrounds sought: Accounting; Business Administration; Computer Science; Finance; Marketing. Company benefits include: medical insurance; dental insurance; life insurance; pension plan; tuition assistance; disability coverage; profit sharing; employee discounts; savings plan. Corporate headquarters location. Operations at this facility include: divisional headquarters. NASDAQ.

PERPETUAL SAVINGS BANK - F.S.B.
2034 Eisenhower Avenue
Alexandria VA 22314
703/838-6057
Contact Employment Department. A full service financial institution. Offers a wide range of banking services, including NOW accounts, savings accounts (multiple options), retirement plans, convenience services, and loan services. Subsidiary Perpetual Insurance Services offers complete auto, homeowners, life, disability, and commercial insurance; subsidiary PAMCO offers complete line of mortgage banking services. Over 67 branch locations throughout Maryland, Virginia, and District of Columbia. Assets exceed $5.7 billion. Corporate headquarters located in Alexandria, VA. Common positions include: Accountant; Attorney; Bank Officer/Manager; Buyer; Computer Programmer; Credit Manager; Customer Service Representative; Draftsperson; Financial Analyst; Manager; Branch Manager; Department Manager; Management Trainee; Operations/Production Manager; Marketing Specialist; Personnel Specialist; Purchasing Agent; Sales Representative; Systems Analyst. Principal educational backgrounds sought: Accounting; Business Administration; Computer Science; Economics; Finance; Liberal Arts. Company benefits include: medical insurance; dental insurance; pension plan; life insurance; tuition assistance; disability coverage; profit sharing; savings plan; 401 K; mortgage discount.

SOVRAN FINANCIAL CORPORATION
Box 27025
Richmond VA 23261
Contact Employment Department. A major Richmond financial institution.

BOOK & MAGAZINE PUBLISHING

For more information on publishing opportunities in Greater Washington, look for the following professional and trade organizations in Chapter 8, starting on page 265:

American Booksellers Association
Association of American Publishers
Magazine Publishers Association
Writers Guild of America East, Inc.
Writers Guild of America West, Inc.

District of Columbia

ACROPOLIS BOOKS LTD.
2400 17th Street NW
Washington DC 20009
202/387-6805
Contact Personnel Department. A major Washington publishing company.

THE BUREAU OF NATIONAL AFFAIRS INC.
1231 25th Street NW
Room S-100
Washington DC 20037
202/452-4335
Contact Employment Manager. Prepares, publishes, and sells legal and economic periodicals and publications, books, pamphlets, films, and other materials. Also publishes other material, including labor, environmental, and safety services training and communications films. Common positions include: Accountant; Commercial Artist; Computer Programmer; Customer Service Representative; Operations/Production Manager; Marketing Specialist; Personnel & Labor Specialist; Reporter/Editor; Sales Representative; Systems Analyst; Technical Writer/Editor. Principal educational backgrounds sought: Accounting; Art/Design; Business Administration; Computer Science; Finance. Company benefits include: medical insurance; dental insurance; pension plan; life insurance; tuition assistance; disability coverage; profit sharing. Corporate headquarters. Operations at this facility include: research/development; administration. Equal Opportunity Employer.

CHRONICLE OF HIGHER EDUCATION
1255 23rd Street NW
Washington DC 20037
202/466-1000
Contact Lisa Birchard, Office Manager. Publishers of a well-known education journal.

HARCOURT BRACE JOVANOVICH INC.
1666 Connecticut Avenue NW
Suite 300
Washington DC 20009
202/387-3900
Contact Administrative Assistant. Regional office of the well-known publishing company. Also involved in the management of various entertainment enterprises, including Sea World. Corporate headquarters location: Orlando, FL.

THE KIPLINGER WASHINGTON EDITOR INC.
1729 H Street NW
Washington DC 20006
202/887-6400
Contact Nancy Fisher, Director of Personnel. Produces a nationally-distributed newsletter, and Changing Times magazine. Corporate headquarters location.

NATIONAL GEOGRAPHIC SOCIETY
1145 17th Street NW
Washington DC 20036
202/857-7733
Contact Mr. Adrian Loftin, Vice-President/Personnel. One of the foremost research and education organizations in the world, sponsoring field projects in a wide range of areas throughout the world, and publishing articles in the world-respected National Geographic magazine. Corporate headquarters location.

NATION'S BUSINESS
1615 H Street NW
Washington DC 20006-4902
202/463-5650
Contact Paul G. Osborne, Employment Manager. A business magazine published by the U.S. Chamber of Commerce.

THE NEW REPUBLIC
1220 19th Street NW
Suite 600
Washington DC 20036-2405
202/331-7494
Contact Managing Editor. A publisher of a major national magazine with a focus on political stories and current events.

PRENTICE-HALL INFORMATION SERVICES
1819 L Street NW
Suite 400
Washington DC 20036
202/293-0707
Contact Patricia Price, Office Manager. Washington office of a well-known publishing company. Corporate headquarters location: Englewood Cliffs, NJ.

U.S. NEWS & WORLD REPORT
2400 N Street NW
Washington DC 20037
202/955-2000
Contact Carol O'Leary, Personnel Director. A major American news magazine, with more than 20 million readers. Corporate headquarters location.

WASHINGTONIAN MAGAZINE
1828 L Street NW
Washington DC 20036-5014
202/296-3600
Contact Managing Editor. A publisher of a city magazine.

BROADCASTING

For more information on broadcasting opportunities in Greater Washington, look for the following professional and trade organizations in Chapter 8, beginning on page 265:

Broadcast Education Association
Cable Television Association
International Radio and TV Society
National Association of Broadcasters
National Association of Business and Educational Radio
Television Bureau of Advertising
Women in Radio and TV, Inc.

District of Columbia

CBS INC.
2020 M Street NW
Washington DC 20036
202/457-4321
Contact Elaine Scott, Personnel Administrator. A major office for CBS News, one of six divisions in CBS Inc.'s Broadcast Group. Corporate headquarters location: New York, NY. New York Stock Exchange.

NATIONAL PUBLIC RADIO INC.
2025 M Street NW
Washington DC 20036
202/822-2000
Contact Director of Personnel. Headquarters for the public radio broadcasting organization.

UNITED PRESS INTERNATIONAL
1400 Eye Street
Suite 800
Washington DC 20005
202/898-8000
Contact David Wiessler, Bureau Manager. Washington news bureau for the international news, sports, and weather wire service organization. Corporate headquarters location: Brentwood, TN.

Maryland

ARBITRON
4320 Ammendale Road
Beltsville MD 20705
301/982-4600, 982-4742
Contact Gordon Clark, Professional Recruiter. A leading company in the field of broadcast audience measurement. Field staff of more than 3,000 interviews more than two million households, representing a cross-section of Americans in every county, to obtain television and radio listening information. The company produces the Arbitron Television and Radio Reports, which describes television viewing or radio listening patterns in more than 200 marketing areas in the United States. Advertisers and their agencies use the reports when planning, buying, or evaluating their advertising schedules to determine the cost-efficiency of their campaigns. More than 2,000 radio stations, 580 television stations, and 3,500 advertisers and their agencies and buying services use the report. Offices in New York, Chicago, Atlanta, Dallas, Los Angeles, San Francisco, and Washington, DC. Corporate headquarters location: New York, NY.

CHARITABLE / NON-PROFIT / HUMANITARIAN

For more information on charitable/non-profit/humanitarian opportunities in Greater Washington, look for the following professional and trade organizations in Chapter 8, beginning on page 265:

National Association of Social Workers
National Organization for Human Service Education

District of Columbia

B'NAI B'RITH
1640 Rhode Island Avenue NW
Washington DC 20036
202/857-6510
Contact Anne Spiwak, Director of Personnel. Headquarters for the broadly-diversified Jewish social services and political action organization

THE BROOKINGS INSTITUTION
1775 Massachusetts Avenue NW
Washington DC 20036
202/797-6210
Contact Personnel Director. A private nonprofit organization devoted to research, education, and publication in economics, government, foreign policy, and the social sciences generally. Its activities are carried out through three research programs (Economic Studies, Governmental Studies, Foreign Policy Studies), a Center for Public Policy Education, a Social Science Computation Center, and a Publications Program.

FAMILY & CHILD SERVICES OF WASHINGTON DC
929 L Street NW
Washington DC 20001
202/289-1510
Contact Rhoda L. Veney, Executive Director. A private, nonprofit social services organization. Offers a broad range of services, including counseling, adoption, family day care, foster care, summer and winter camping, and services to older Americans. Common positions include: Social Workers; Counselors; Administrative Assistants. Company benefits include: medical and life insurance; pension plan; disability coverage. Corporate headquarters location. Operations at this facility include: service.

MAINSTREAM
1030 15th Street NW
Suite 1010
Washington DC 20005
202/898-1400
Contact Larry Pencak, Executive Director. A leading Washington employment service for persons with physical or mental disabilities. Also provides training and publications for employers.

NATIONAL ALLIANCE OF BUSINESS
1201 New York Avenue NW
Washington DC 20005
202/289-2888
Contact Personnel. A non-profit corporation whose purpose is to increase private-sector training and job opportunities for the economically disadvantaged.

NATIONAL CENTER FOR PUBLIC POLICY RESEARCH
300 Eye Street NE, Suite 3
Washington DC 20002
202/543-1286
Contact Debbie Smith, Personnel. An organization providing material and newsletters for conservative activists.

NATIONAL EDUCATION ASSOCIATION
1201 16th Street NW
Room 221
Washington DC 20036
202/822-7617
Contact Malinda Miles, Employment Manager. A national non-profit membership organization that represents teachers, the teaching profession and educational support personnel. The goals and objectives of the Association are carried out through various activities conducted by the following administrative and program areas: Affiliate Services; Communications; Data Processing; Executive Office; Government Relations; Human and Civil Rights; Instruction and Professional Development; Legal Services; Research and Special Services. Programs and services are specifically designed for teachers of higher education and K-12, and education support personnel. Major programs and functions include research and design, lobbying and other legislative activities, organizing and membership recruitment, communications and public relations, negotiations, and administration. Common positions include: Accountant; Attorney; Commercial Artist; Computer Programmer; Economist; Electrical Engineer; Mechanical Engineer; Information Specialist; Insurance Assistants; Personnel & Labor Relations Specialist; Program Development Specialist; Purchasing Agent; Reporter/Editor; Systems Analyst; Technical Writer/Editor. Principal educational backgrounds sought: Accounting; Art/Design; Business Administration; Communications; Computer Science; Economics; Finance; Liberal Arts; Mathematics. Company benefits include: vacation, sick leave, and personal leave; medical insurance; dental insurance; pension plan; life insurance; tuition assistance; disability coverage; 401K plan. Six regional locations.

NATIONAL WILDLIFE FEDERATION
1412 16th Street NW
Washington DC 20036
Contact Robert Ertter, Director of Personnel. A well-known conservation society dedicated to preserving the nation's wildlife.

PAN AMERICAN HEALTH ORGANIZATION/
PAN AMERICAN SANITARY BUREAU
Regional office of the World Health Organization
525 23rd Street NW
Washington DC 20037
202/861-3200
Contact Mr. Jean Gauthier, Personnel Director. An international agency responsible for assisting Latin and Caribbean governments in instituting national health programs.

THE URBAN INSTITUTE
2100 M Street NW
Washington DC 20037
202/833-7200
Contact Sally Pitofsky, Director of Personnel. A private, nonprofit policy research institution whose staff investigates social and economic problems of the nation's urban communities, and government policies affecting those communities and the people who live in them. Headquarters location.

CHEMICAL & RELATED: PRODUCTION, PROCESSING & DISPOSAL

For more information on chemical opportunities in Greater Washington, look for the following professional and trade organizations in Chapter 8, beginning on page 265:

American Chemical Society
American Institute of Chemical Engineering
American Institute of Chemists
Association of State & Interstate
      Water Pollution Control Administrators
Drug, Chemical and Allied Trades Association
Water Pollution Control Federation

Maryland

AMERICAN CYANAMID COMPANY/ ENGINEERED MATERIALS DEPARTMENT
1300 Revolution Street
Havre de Grace MD 21078
301/939-1910, ext. 235
Contact Peter M. Watts, Personnel Supervisor. American Cyanamid is a research-based biotechnology and chemical company which develops, manufactures and markets medical, agricultural, chemical, and consumer products. Engineered Materials Department produces adhesive, composite and structural materials for the aerospace industry. Common positions include: Accountant; Administrator; Blue-Collar Worker Supervisor; Buyer; Chemist; Computer Programmer; Customer Service Representative; Draftsperson; Chemical Engineer; Mechanical Engineer; Industrial Designer; Department Manager; General Manager; Operations/Production Manager; Personnel & Labor Relations Specialist; Quality Control Supervisor; Sales Representative; Transportation & Traffic Specialist. Principal educational backgrounds sought: Accounting; Business Administration; Chemistry; Computer Science; Engineering; Marketing. Company benefits include: medical, dental, and life insurance; pension plan; tuition assistance; disability coverage; employee discounts; savings plan. Corporate headquarters location: Wayne, NJ. Operations at this facility include: manufacturing; research/development; administration; service; sales. New York Stock Exchange.

THE CELLO CHEMICAL COMPANY
1354 Old Post Road
Havre de Grace MD 21078
301/939-1234
Contact Phyllis Clark, Personnel Director. Produces a wide range of sanitary and cleaning products, including sanitary chemicals, acrylic resins, floor finishes and waxes, deodorants, aerosols, washroom maintenance products, soaps, detergents, liquid and aerosol household cleaners and polishes, floor machines, and insecticides. A subsidiary of Grow Group, Inc. Corporate headquarters location.

FARBOIL COMPANY
8200 Fischer Road
Dundalk MD 21222
301/477-8200
Contact Ron Kester, Personnel Director. Produces a variety of marine, industrial, and architectural paints, specialty coatings, and powder coatings. A subsidiary of Beatrice (Chicago, IL).

FERTILIZER INSTITUTE
501 2nd Street NE
Washington DC 20002
202/675-8250
Contact Pam Lucas, Vice-President of Administration. An association that represents fertilizer manufacturers and supports legislation to aid them.

FMC CORPORATION
P.O. Box 1616
Baltimore MD 21203
301/355-6400
Contact Human Resources. Produces a range of organic chemicals and pesticides. Nationally, the company manufactures and sells a broad range of chemical and machinery products in the following business segments: Industrial Chemicals; Energy Equipment and Services; Military Equipment and Systems; Performance Chemicals; and Diversified Machinery and Equipment. Operates more than 140 production facilities in 33 states and 15 foreign countries. Corporate headquarters location: Chicago, IL. New York Stock Exchange.

GLIDDEN PIGMENTS GROUP/
SCM CORPORATION
3901 Glidden Road
Baltimore MD 21226
301/355-3600
Contact Wayne Staples, Personnel Director. Produces specialized titanium dioxide pigments for industrial and related uses as a division of the well-known manufacturer of paints, coatings, resins and lacquers. A subsidiary of SCM Corporation (New York, NY), a diversified corporation with interests in paper, consumer goods, chemicals, metals, foods and other areas. Corporate headquarters location: Cleveland, OH.

W.R. GRACE & COMPANY/
DAVISON CHEMICAL DIVISION
P.O. Box 2117
Baltimore MD 21203
301/659-9000
Contact James L. Hunt, Personnel Director. Produces a broad range of specialty chemicals, including industrial catalysts, silicas, petroleum and automotive exhaust catalysts, and many others. Second Maryland facility in Beltsville. Nationally, company is a diversified, multinational products and services firm with significant activities in chemicals, natural resources, and consumer products and services. Divisional headquarters location. Corporate headquarters location: Columbia, MD. New York Stock Exchange.

VISTA CHEMICALS COMPANY
3441 Fairfield Road
Baltimore MD 21226
301/355-6200
Contact Mike Doughty, Director of Employee Relations. Produces detergent alkylates, petroleum detergent intermediates, and plasticizers.

Northern Virginia

BASF/FIBERS DIVISION
P.O. Drawer D
Williamsburg VA 23187
804/887-6000
Contact Manager/Personnel Resources. Manufactures and markets industrial chemicals, yarns and man-made fibers. A subsidiary of BASF America Inc. Corporate headquarters location.

COMMUNICATIONS: EQUIPMENT AND SERVICES

For more information on communications opportunities in Greater Washington, look for the following trade and professional organizations in Chapter 8, beginning on page 265:

Communications Workers of America
United States Telephone Association

District of Columbia

CHESAPEAKE & POTOMAC TELEPHONE COMPANY
1710 H Street NW 4th Floor
Washington DC 20006
202/392-1503
Contact Corporate Personnel Office. Furnishes telephone and other communications services throughout the District of Columbia. Also offers other communications services, including data transmission, transmission of radio and television programs, and private line voice and teletypewriter services. Corporate headquarters location. Common positions include: Accountant; Computer Programmer; Marketing Specialist. Principal educational backgrounds sought: Accounting; Computer Science; Marketing. Company benefits include: medical, dental, and life insurance; pension plan; tuition assistance; disability coverage; profit sharing; employee discounts; savings plan.

COMMUNICATION WORKERS OF AMERICA
1925 K Street NW
Washington DC 20006
202/728-2300
Contact Ted Watkins, Executive Assistant to the President. Administrative offices for the nationwide trade union, representing a wide range of professions.

COMSAT CORPORATION
950 L'Enfant Plaza, SW
Washington DC 20024
202/863-6010
Contact Robert Bauman, Personnel Director. A major satellite communications company.

MCI COMMUNICATIONS CORPORATION
1133 19th Street NW
Washington DC 20036
202/872-1600
Contact John Zimmerman, Vice-President/Personnel. Offers long distance intercity telephone service and other telecommunications services to businesses, government, and private customers throughout the United States. Corporate headquarters location. New York Stock Exchange.

Maryland

CASE COMMUNICATIONS INC.
7200 Riverwood Drive
Columbia MD 21046-1194
301/290-7233

Contact Senior Human Resources Consultant. A manufacturer of data communications products including modems, multiplexors, network management systems and message switching systems. Common positions include: Accountant; Administrator; Advertising Worker; Blue-Collar Worker Supervisor; Buyer; Claim Representative; Commercial Artist; Computer Programmer; Credit Manager; Customer Service Representative; Draftsperson; Electrical, Industrial, and Mechanical Engineers; Management Trainee; Operations/Production Manager; Marketing Specialist; Personnel & Labor Relations Specialist; Purchasing Agent; Quality Control Supervisor; Reporter/Editor; Sales Representative; Systems Analyst; Technical Writer/Editor; Transportation & Traffic Specialist. Principal educational backgrounds sought: Accounting; Art/Design; Business Administration; Communications; Computer Science; Engineering; Finance; Marketing; Mathematics. Company benefits include: medical insurance; dental insurance; pension plan; life insurance; tuition assistance; disability coverage; profit sharing; employee discounts; savings plan. Corporate headquarters location. Parent company: Case PLC. Operations include: manufacturing; research/development; administration; service; sales.

HEKIMIAN LABORATORIES INC.
9298 Gaither Road
Gaithersburg MD 20877
301/840-1217
Contact Thomas D. Kruzic, Director of Personnel. Designs and manufactures a wide range of test equipment and computer-based test-systems in support of the major providers and users of telecommunications services. Common positions at this facility include: Accountant; Buyer; Customer Service Representative; Draftsperson; Electrical Engineer; Industrial Engineer; Operations/Production Manager; Sales Representative; Technical Writer/Editor. Principal educational backgrounds sought: Accounting; Business Administration; Communications; Computer Science; Electrical Engineering; Mathematics. Company benefits include: medical insurance; dental insurance; pension plan; life insurance; tuition assistance; disability coverage; profit sharing; savings plan (401K). Corporate headquarters location. Parent company: Axel Johnson, Inc. Operations at this facility include: regional headquarters; divisional headquarters; manufacturing; research/development; administration; service; sales.

PLANTRONICS DATA COMMUNICATIONS GROUP
7630 Hayward Road
P.O. Box 502
Frederick MD 21701-0502
301/662-5901
Contact Vivian Smith-Thompson, Manager, Administration. Designs and markets data communications equipment (circuit switching, packet switching, and radio frequency equipment) on a worldwide basis. Consists of Plantronics Inc, Subsidiaries Plantronics Futurecomms Inc., and Fredericks Electronics Corporation. Common positions include: Accountant; Administrator; Buyer; Computer Programmer; Draftsperson; Electrical Engineer; Mechanical Engineer; Financial Analyst; Department Manager; General Manager; Purchasing Agent; Quality Control Supervisor; Sales Representative; Systems Analyst; Technical Writer/Editor. Principal educational backgrounds sought: Business Administration; Computer Science; Engineering; Marketing. Company benefits include: medical, dental, and life insurance; tuition assistance; disability coverage; profit sharing; savings plan. Corporate headquarters location: Santa Cruz, CA. Operations at this facility include: research/development; administration; sales.

Northern Virginia

CONTEL FEDERAL SYSTEMS
15000 Conference Center Drive
Chantilly VA 22021-3808
703/359-7500
Contact Stephanie Altavilla, Human Resources Assistant. The major Washington-area telephone communications firm. Common positions include: Accountant; Administrator; Buyer; Computer Programmer; Draftsperson; Civil Engineer; Electrical Engineer; Financial Analyst; Department Manager; Marketing Specialist; Personnel & Labor Relations Specialist; Purchasing Agent; Quality Control Supervisor; Systems Analyst; Technical Writer/Editor; Technician. Principal educational backgrounds sought: Accounting; Business Administration; Computer Science; Economics; Engineering; Finance; Marketing; Mathematics; Physics. Company benefits include: medical insurance; dental insurance; pension plan; life insurance; tuition assistance; disability coverage; savings plan. Corporate headquarters located in Atlanta GA. Operations at this facility include: regional headquarters; research/development; administration. New York Stock Exchange.

HOPPMANN CORPORATION
P.O. Box 601
14560 Lee Road
Chantilly VA 22021
703/631-2700
Contact Barbara Ozarkiw, Personnel Director. Produces automated parts handling systems, and audio/video communications systems. Common job positions include: Draftsperson; Electrical Engineer; Mechanical Engineer; Mechanical Designers. Principal educational backgrounds sought: Communications; Engineering; Drafting; Mechanical Design; BA and AA or AS degrees generally preferred. Company benefits include: medical insurance; dental insurance; pension plan; life insurance; tuition assistance; 401K profit sharing plan; 125 flexible benefit plan. Corporate headquarters location. Operations at this facility include: divisional headquarters; manufacturing; research/development; sales.

HUBBELL INC./
PULSECOM DIVISION
2900 Towerview Road
Herndon VA 22071
703/471-2900
Contact Garland Collins, Personnel Department. Produces telecommunications products, and a remote-control supervisory system for industrial processes. Second Virginia facility (Chistianburg) produces outdoor floodlights and industrial lighting. Divisional headquarters location.

TRW
1 Federal Systems Park Drive
Fairfax VA 22033
703/968-1000
Contact Personnel Department. Engaged in communications and systems integration projects. Parent company, TRW, is a diversified technology firm with operations in electronics and space systems, care and truck equipment for both original equipment manufacturers and the replacement market, and a wide variety of industrial and energy components, including aircraft parts, welding systems, and electromechanical assemblies. New York Stock Exhange. Corporate headquarters location: Cleveland, OH.

COMPUTER-RELATED: HARDWARE, SOFTWARE AND SERVICES

For more information on computer opportunities in Greater Washington, look for the following professional and trade organizations in Chapter 8, beginning on page 265:

ADAPSO/The Computer Software and Services Industry Association
Association for Computer Science
Association for Computer Machinery
IEEE Computer Society
Professional Software Programmers Association
Semiconductor Industry Association

District of Columbia

GNOSSOS SOFTWARE
1534 16th Street NW
Washington DC 20036
202/387-0858
Contact Steve Kantor, President. A small, entrepreneurial, PC training, consulting and database applications firm. Expanding to international markets and expert systems. Common positions include: Computer Programmer; Systems Analyst; Management Consultant. Principal educational backgrounds sought: Business Administration; Computer Science; Liberal Arts. Company benefits include: medical insurance; tuition assistance; profit sharing. Corporate headquarters.

SYSCON CORPORATION
1000 Thomas Jefferson Street
Washington DC 20007
202/342-4000
Contact Personnel Department. A major computer programming service.

Maryland

BENDIX FIELD ENGINEERING CORPORATION
BFEC
One Bendix Road
Columbia MD 21045
301/964-7000
Contact Personnel Director. Engaged in computer systems management; engineering and installation services; computer and software services; and maintenance, operating and support services. A wholly-owned subsidiary of Allied Signal Corporation, which serves a broad spectrum of industries through its more than 40 strategic businesses, which are grouped into five sectors: Aerospace; Automotive; Chemical; Industrial and Technology; and Oil and Gas. Allied Signal is one of the nation's largest industrial organizations, and has 115,000 employees in over 30 countries. Corporate headquarters location: Morristown, NJ.

CIRTEK/MARYLAND INC.
P.O. Box 406
New Plant Court
Owings Mills MD 21117
301/363-6900

Contact Ms. Carol Milby, Personnel Director. Engaged in the fabrication of two-sided and ML printed circuit boards. Common positions include: Accountant; Blue-Collar Worker Supervisor; Chemist; Customer Service Representative; Department Manager; Operations/Production Manager; Purchasing Agent; Sales Representative. Company benefits include: medical insurance; life insurance; disability coverage. Operations at this facility include: manufacturing; administration; service; sales. Corporate headquarters location.

COMNET CORPORATION
6404 Ivy Lane
Greenbelt MD 20770-1400
Contact Robert Bowen, President. Provides a broad range of computer services, primarily to agencies or departments of the Federal government, and some commercial customers located throughout the country. Principal services are facilities management (systems tailored for use by a single customer with specific needs), and remote data processing services (variety of customers). Corporate headquarters location.

COMPUTER ENTRY SYSTEMS CORPORATION
2120 Industrial Parkway
Silver Spring MD 20904
301/622-3500
Contact Pat Sellers, Human Resources Manager. Designs, develops, and manufactures microprocessor-based, electro-mechanical optical character-reading equipment. Company markets this equipment for incorporation into computerized document processing systems. Principal purchasers of these systems include major commercial banks, utilities, insurance firms, retail companies, and other businesses handling a high volume of machine-readable documents. CES is a subsidiary of BancTec, Inc. in Dallas TX.

CONTROL DATA CORPORATION
6003 Executive Boulevard
Rockville MD 20852
301/468-8000
Contact Stan Cooper, Personnel Director. A major worldwide computer manufacturer specializing in large computers required for complex scientific, engineering, and similar tasks by such large-volume users as governmental bodies, utilities, institutions, corporations, etc. Also markets interactive time-sharing services in the United States, Canada, Western Europe, Australia, and Japan. Corporate headquarters location: Minneapolis, MN. New York Stock Exchange.

INFORMATION DEVELOPMENT & APPLICATIONS INC. (IDEAS)
10741 Tucker Street
Beltsville MD 20705
301/937-3600, ext. 211
Contact Director of Personnel. A privately-owned, high-technology engineering and manufacturing firm with expertise in the application of state-of-the-art technology to individual product design and custom-engineered systems. A pioneer in microprocessor hardware, firmware, and software design. Common positions include: Accountant; Administrator; Buyer; Computer Programmer; Draftsperson; Electrical Engineer; Department Manager; Operations/Production Manager; Personnel & Labor Relations Specialist; Purchasing Agent; Quality Control Supervisor; Technical Writer/Editor. Principal educational backgrounds sought: Accounting; Computer Science; Engineering; Finance; Liberal Arts. Company benefits include: medical, dental and life insurance; tuition assistance; disability coverage; savings plan. Corporate headquarters location. Operations include: research/development; administration; service.

NCR CORPORATION
2301 Research Boulevard
Rockville MD 20850
301/258-6500
Contact George Tucker, Administrative Manager. Regional sales and research offices; nationally, company develops, manufactures, markets, installs, and services total business information-processing systems for selected worldwide markets. These markets are primarily in the retail, financial, commercial, industrial, healthcare, education, and government sectors. The NCR total-systems-concept encompasses one of the broadest hardware and software product lines in the industry. NCR computers range from small business systems to the most powerful general-purpose processors, and are supported by a complete spectrum of terminals, processors, data communications networks, and an extensive library of software products. Supplemental services and products include field engineering, data centers, systems services, educational centers, and a comprehensive line of media. Corporate headquarters location: Dayton, OH. International facilities. New York Stock Exchange.

TEKTRONIX INC.
700 Professional Drive
Gaithersburg MD 20877
301/948-7151
Contact Personnel Director. Manufactures and markets electronic test and measurement equipment and a highly specialized line of computer graphics terminals and peripherals for the engineering and scientific market. Regional headquarters location. Corporate headquarters location: Beaverton, OR. Operations include: service; sales. Common positions include: Computer Programmer; Electrical Engineer; Sales Representative; Systems Analyst; Sales Engineer; Applications Engineer. Principal educational backgrounds sought: Computer Science; Engineering; Physics. Company benefits include: medical insurance; dental insurance; life insurance; tuition assistance; disability coverage; profit sharing; employee discounts; savings plan.

Northern Virginia

AMERICAN MANAGEMENT SYSTEMS INC.
1777 North Kent Street
Arlington VA 22209
703/841-6000
Contact Patsy Chimini, Personnel Officer. Engaged in the development, installation, and operation of computers and information systems. Corporate headquarters location.

COMPUCARE INC.
12355 Sunrise Valley Drive
Suite 400
Reston VA 22091
703/648-9000
Contact Personnel. A major developer of both hardware and software information systems for hospitals and other health care facilities.

McDONNELL DOUGLAS ELECTRONIC SYSTEMS
COMPANY-WDC
8201 Greensboro Drive
Suite 400
McLean VA 22102
703/442-7960
Contact Employment Representative. A leading northern Virginia software company with contracts in the governmental intelligence community. Common positions include: Computer Programmer;

Software Engineer; Systems Analyst. Principal educational backgrounds sought: Computer Science; Electrical Engineering. Company benefits include: medical insurance; dental insurance; pension plan; life insurance; tuition assistance; disability coverage; profit sharing; savings plan. Corporate headquarters location. Operations at this facility include: administraiton.

SOFTWARE AG OF NORTH AMERICA
11190 Sunrise Valley Drive
Reston VA 22091
Contact Trish Hollar, Manager, Corporate Recruiting. A leading supplier of advanced information system development software. Products include: ADABAS, COM-PLETE, and NATURAL. Operations include: research/development; service; sales. Common positions include: Applications Programmer; Research and Development; Sales Representative; Systems Analyst. Principal educational backgrounds sought: Computer Science. Company benefits include: medical insurance; dental insurance; tuition assistance; life insurance; disability coverage; profit sharing; employee discounts; savings plan; 401 K.

XEROX CORPORATION
1616 North Fort Myer Drive
Arlington VA 22209
703/527-6400
Contact Metro Hiring Center. Area sales and service office for one of the world's largest and best known manufacturers of a broad line of business machines, including copiers, computer systems, word processors, and a wide range of associated and peripheral equipment. Corporate headquarters location: Rochester, NY. New York Stock Exchange.

CONSTRUCTION: SERVICES, MATERIALS & RELATED

For more information on construction opportunities in Greater Washington, look for the following professional and trade associations in Chapter 8, starting on page 265:

Associated Builders and Contractors
Building Officials and Code Administrators International, Inc.
Construction Industry Manufacturers Association
International Conference of Building Officials
National Association of Home Builders

<u>District of Columbia</u>

BLAKE CONSTRUCTION COMPANY
1120 Connecticut Avenue NW
Washington DC 20036
202/828-9000
Contact Kris Olson, Director of Personnel. A major area contractor, engaged primarily in commercial construction activities.

Maryland

THE CECO CORPORATION
9200 Basil Court, Suite 315
Landover MD 20785
301/322-2326
Contact Barbara E. Merritt, Office Supervisor. The Ceco Corporation has been a supplier of construction products and services to the industry for 75 years. the Concrete Construction Division is the Nation's oldest and largest formwork contractor. Through its 35 District Offices, Ceco's Engineers deal with owners, developers, construction managers, and general contractors to produce better, faster, and more economical concrete buildings.

CONGOLEUM CORPORATION
CEDARHURST PLANT
2700 Emory Road
Finksburg MD 21048
301/833-4700
Contact Plant Personnel Manager. Produces flooring felt. Nationally, company is a diversified manufacturer and distributor of one of the nation's largest manufacturers of resilient flooring and other flooring products. Common positions include: Accountant; Blue-Collar Worker Supervisor; Chemist; Department Manager; Operations/Production Manager; Personnel & Labor Relations Specialist; Quality Control Supervisor. Principal educational backgrounds sought: Accounting; Business Administration; Chemistry; Finance; Liberal Arts. Company benefits include: medical insurance; pension plan; life insurance; tuition assistance; disability coverage. Corporate headquarters location: Lawrenceville, NJ. Operations at this facility include: manufacturing; administration.

W.G. CORNELL COMPANY INC.
P.O. Box 216
3520 Bladensburg Road
Brentwood MD 20722
301/779-8200
Contact Frank Salatto, Vice President. A mechanical construction firm primarily engaged in large-scale commercial work.

DEVLIN LUMBER & SUPPLY CORPORATION
1540 Rockville Pike
Rockville MD 20850
301/881-1000
Contact Jonathan England, President. A retailer of building products to both consumers and the commercial construction trade. Products include pressure-treated lumber, wooden building trusses, and many others. Corporate headquarters location.

DIGITAL SYSTEMS CORPORATION
3 North Main Street
P.O. Box 158
Walkersville MD 21793
301/845-4141
Contact Personnel Administrator. Manufactures the proprietary Galaxy Access Control System, special purpose computers for commercial and government markets, and high resolution graphics and video boards for the micro-computer markets. Common positions include: Computer Programmer; Electrical Engineer; Sales Representative. Principal educational backgrounds sought: Engineering; Marketing. Company benefits include: medical insurance; life insurance. Operations at this facility include: regional headquarters; manufacturing; research & development; administration; service; sales.

GAF CORPORATION
P.O. Box 9977
Baltimore MD 21224-0977
301/633-7200

Contact Personnel Manager. Produces roofing products, shingles, builders' board, fiberglass insulation, and protective coatings. Nationally, company offers a diverse product line including building materials, specialty chemicals and plastics, and reprographic products. Second Maryland facility in Hagerstown. Corporate headquarters location: New York, NY. New York Stock Exchange.

GENSTAR STONE PRODUCTS COMPANY
Executive Plaza IV 11350 McCormick Road
Hunt Valley MD 21031
301/527-4216

Contact Steven B. Wheeler, Manager/Personnel Administration. Produces crushed stone, gravel, sand, and similar products as a division of the Redland PLC, a major producer of basic materials and products for the building and construction industries. Facilities are located throughout Maryland, including Baltimore, Rockville, Frederick, and other locations. Common positions include: Accountant; Administrator; Buyer; Chemist; Computer Programmer; Credit Manager; Customer Service Representative; Draftsperson; Mining Engineer; Geologist; Department Manager; General Manager; Management Trainee; Operations/Production Manager; Personnel & Labor Relations Specialist; Purchasing Agent; Quality Control Supervisor; Sales Representative; Systems Analyst; Transportation & Traffic Specialist. Principal educational backgrounds sought: Accounting; Business Adminstration; Chemistry; Communications; Computer Science; Engineering; Finance; Geology; Liberal Arts; Marketing. Company benefits include: medical, dental, and life insurance; pension plan; tuition assistance; disability coverage; employee discounts; savings plan. Corporate headquarters location. Parent company: Redland PLC. Operations at this facility include: divisional headquarters.

GOLD BOND BUILDING PRODUCTS/
NATIONAL GYPSUM COMPANY
2301 South Newkirk Street
Baltimore MD 21224
301/563-5315

Contact Sue Tyber, Personnel Director. Manufactures gypsum wallboard and joint compounds. A division of National Gypsum Company, an integrated, diversified manufacturer of quality products for building, construction, and shelter markets. Common positions at this facility include: Blue-Collar Worker Supervisor; Buyer; Department Manager; General Manager; Operations/Production Manager; Personnel/Labor Relations Specialist; Quality Control Specialist; Quality Control Supervisor; Sales Representative. Educational backgrounds sought: Business Administration. Company benefits include: medical insurance; dental insurance; pension plan; life insurance; tuition assistance; disability coverage; profit sharing; employee discounts; savings plan. Parent company: National Gypsum. Corporate headquarters location: Charlotte, NC. Operations at this facility: manufacturing. New York Stock Exchange.

MARBRO COMPANY INC.
11609 Edmondson Road
P.O. Box 137
Beltsville MD 20705
301/595-5800

Contact Personnel. A contracting firm engaged in sewer and water construction projects.

MILLER & LONG COMPANY INC.
4824 Rugby Avenue
Bethesda MD 20814
301/657-8000

Contact Miles Gladstone, Personnel Director. A major construction firm, specializing in high-rise concrete construction, and other large-scale projects. Corporate headquarters location.

NATIONAL WIRE PRODUCTS CORPORATION
8203 Fischer Road
Baltimore MD 21222-8909
301/477-1700
Contact Richard Holloway, Personnel Administrator. Produces concrete reinforcement products. Operations include: manufacturing; administration; sales. Corporate headquarters location. Common positions include: Accountant; Blue-Collar Worker Supervisor; Computer Programmer; Credit Manager; Draftsperson; Industrial Engineer; Personnel & Labor Relations Specialist; Sales Representative. Principal educational backgrounds sought: Accounting; Business Administration. Company benefits include: medical insurance; pension plan; life insurance; disability coverage.

NS/PAVCO
8700 Ashwood
Capital Heights MD 20743
301/937-0250
Contact Personnel Director. A paving contractor/consultant. Corporate headquarters location. Common positions include: Accountant; Administrator; Blue-Collar Worker Supervisor; Engineer; Purchasing Agent; Sales Representative; Transportation & Traffic Specialist. Principal educational backgrounds sought: Business Administration; Marketing. Company benefits include: medical insurance; life insurance; profit sharing.

SACO SUPPLY COMPANY INC.
21 West Timonium Road
Timonium MD 21093
301/252-3030
Contact Ron Walker, President. Provides a variety of construction and builders products, including lumber, millwork, and brick. Corporate headquarters location.

TRIANGLE PACIFIC BUILDING PRODUCTS
10500 Ewing Road
Beltsville MD 20705
301/937-5000
Contact Ms. Caine, Personnel. Produces lumber, doors, windows, and a wide range of other building products.

Northern Virginia

DAVENPORT INSULATION INC.
8420 Terminal Road
P.O. Box 706
Springfield VA 22150
Contact Carolyn Sprinkle, Personnel. A contracting and retail operation specializing in the installation and servicing on insulation and related products.

DEFENSE RELATED: RESEARCH AND DEVELOPMENT

For more information on defense related opportunities in Greater Washington, look for the following professional organization in Chapter 8, beginning on page 265:

Military Operations Research Society

Maryland

AAI CORPORATION
P.O. Box 126
Hunt Valley MD 21030-0126
301/666-1400
Contact Rick Magill, Senior Personnel Administrator. AAI is an acknowledged leader in the fields of electronic warfare simulation, automatic test systems, combat vehicles, ordnance, remotely piloted vehicles (RPV's) and materials handling equipment. Common positions at this facility include: Accountant; Buyer; Draftsperson; Electrical Engineer; Mechanical Engineer; Systems Analyst; Technical Writer/Editor. Principal educational backgrounds sought: Business Administration; Engineering. Company benefits include: medical insurance; dental insurance; pension plan; life insurance; tuition assistance; disability coverage; employee discounts; savings plan. Corporate headquarters location: New York, NY. Parent company is United Industrial Corporation. Operations at this facility include: manufacturing; research/development; administration. New York Stock Exchange.

ABERDEEN PROVING GROUND
Cdr, USAAPGSA, ATTN: STEAP-CP-RR
Aberdeen Proving Ground MD 21005-5001
301/278-5795
Contact Quinette M. Henderson, College Recruitment Coordinator. APG is a military installation that employs civilians in the research, development, test, and evaluation of military materials that the soldier would use on the battlefield. Corporate headquarters location. Operations include: research/development. Common positions include: Aerospace Engineer; Chemist; Electrical Engineer; Industrial Engineer; Industrial Hygienist; Mechanical Engineer; Physicist; Psychologist. Principal educational backgrounds sought: Engineering. Company benefits include: medical insurance; life insurance; tuition assistance; disability coverage. Corporate headquarters location. Operations at this facility include: research/ development.

GOULD INC.
OCEAN SYSTEMS DIVISION
6711 Baymeadow Drive
Glen Burnie MD 21061
301/760-3100
Contact Mary Frances McDonald, Sr. Human Resources Representative. Produces a number of products and systems for the defense market, including anti-submarine warfare systems, high frequency sonars, other marine and scientific instruments, and process control equipment. Also involved in Research and Development in Artificial Intelligence and Speech Processing. Nationally, company is an integrated manufacturer and developer of electronic, electrical, and industrial products. Common positions include: Accountant; Buyer; Computer Programmer; Draftsperson; Electrical Engineer; Industrial Engineer; Mechanical Engineer; Financial Analyst; Operations/Production Manager; Personnel & Labor Relations Specialist; Systems Analyst. Principal educational backgrounds sought: Accounting; Business Administration; Computer Science; Engineering; Finance. Company benefits

include: medical, dental, and life insurance; pension plan; tuition assistance; disability coverage; profit sharing; employee discounts. Corporate headquarters location: Rolling Meadows, IL. Parent company: Gould, Inc. Operations at this facility include: manufacturing; research/development. New York Stock Exchange.

GRUMMAN AIRCRAFT SYSTEMS
12200 Long Green Pike
Glen Arm MD 21057
301/592-7022
Contact Personnel Administrator. Engaged in the production of machined aerospace components as a division of the Grumman Corporation. Corporate headquarters location: Bethpage, NY. New York Stock Exchange.

HONEYWELL INC.
SIGNAL ANALYSIS CENTER
P.O. Box 391
Annapolis MD 21404
301/266-1700
Contact Susan A. Cianchetta, Personnel Consultant. The Signal Analysis Center, of the Space & Strategic Avionics Division, operates in 4 locations: Annapolis MD; San Antonio TX; Patuxent River MD; and Eatontown NJ. SAC operates through the following 3 divisions: INFOSEC Services, which involve engineering research, test, evaluation, and design of electronics equipment and systems to deny access to sensitive and classified information by unauthorized personnel. TEMPEST (control of electro magnetic emanations), and COMSEC (Communications Security), are subsets of INFOSEC. Electro-Magnetic Interference (EMI), and Electro-Magnetic Compatibility (EMC) services assure that diverse equipment can operate effectively in a common environment. INFOSEC Products, which consists of the modification to commercial grade electronic equipment, usually components of computer systems of computer systems, for use in a secure environment. TEMPEST is the critical technology. Additionally, SAC designs and builds COMSEC Products and modules that enable users to communicate in a secure mode. COMSEC/INFOSEC/SIGINT Systems which combines the services and products to provide customers with complete systems to perform electro-magnetic signal detection and analysis and the transmission/distribution of this information to users. In addition to maintaining the special facilities, engineering personnel and support activities that are required to study, design, and test equipment and systems, SAC contains facilities, professionals, and craftsmen that are required to produce limited numbers of equipment and systems. Common positions include: Electrical Engineer; Mechanical Engineer; Technical Writer/Editor. Principal educational backgrounds sought: Engineering; Mathematics; Physics. Company benefits include: medical, dental, and life insurance; pension plan; tuition assistance; disability coverage; employee discounts; savings plan. Corporate headquarters location: Minneapolis MN. Operations at this facility include: testing; research/development; sales. New York Stock Exchange. American Stock Exchange.

SINGER COMPANY/
LINK DIVISION
11800 Tech Road
Silver Springs MD 20904
301/622-4400
Contact Margaret Bowers, Technical Recruiter. Manufactures controlled-simulation training products, primarily for the defense market. Nationally, company is a highly diversified manufacturer primarily engaged in the design, development, and marketing of aerospace and marine electronic systems for government and industry, the manufacture and sale of consumer products, the worldwide manufacture and sale of sewing products, and the distribution of consumer durables. Corporate headquarters location: Stamford, CT. New York Stock Exchange.

TRACOR APPLIED SCIENCES INC.
1601 Research Boulevard
Rockville MD 20850
301/279-4444,800/638-8512

Contact Jack Hix, Employment Manager. Engaged in the testing and evaluation of U.S. Navy electronics, communications, radar, sonar, and combat systems; and surface ship and submarine maintenance. Common positions include: Biochemist; Buyer; Chemist; Computer Programmer; Draftsperson; Chemical, Communications, Electrical, Industrial, Marine and Mechanical Engineers; Financial Analyst; Branch, Department, and General Manager; Management Trainee; Quality Control Supervisor; Systems Analyst; Technical Writer/Editor; Marine Technicians; Electronic Technicians. Principal educational backgrounds sought: Accounting; Business Administration; Communications; Computer Science; Engineering; Finance. Company benefits include: medical, dental and life insurance; pension plan; tuition assistance; disability coverage; 401K plan. Corporate headquarters location: Austin, TX. Parent company: Tracor, Inc. Operations at this facility include: regional headquarters; research/development; administration; service.

WESTINGHOUSE ELECTRIC CORPORATION/ ELECTRONICS SYSTEMS GROUP
P.O. Box 1693
Mail Stop 4140
Baltimore MD 21203
301/765-2426

Contact Professional Employment. This facility is engaged in research and development, design integration and manufacture of advanced electronic systems for use in radar and electronic countermeasures, command and control systems, communications systems, space systems and other applications for both governmental and commercial customers. Common positions include: Accountant; Administrator; Blue-Collar Worker Supervisor; Buyer; Computer Programmer; Draftsperson; Ceramics Engineer; Electrical Engineer; Industrial Engineer; Mechanical Engineer; Financial Analyst; Department Manager; General Manager; Operations/Production Manager; Marketing Specialist; Personnel & Labor Relations Specialist; Quality Control Supervisor; Systems Analyst; Technical Writer/Editor. Principal educational backgrounds include: Accounting; Business Administration; Computer Science; Engineering; Finance; Mathematics; Physics. Company benefits: medical, dental and life insurance; pension plan; tuition assistance; disability coverage; savings plan. Corporate headquarters located in Pittsburgh PA. Operations at this facility include: divisional headquarters; manufacturing; administration; research/ development; sales. New York Stock Exchange.

Northern Virginia

ANSER (ANALYTIC SERVICES INC.)
Crystal Gateway 3
Suite 800
1215 Jefferson Davis Highway
Arlington VA 22202
703/685-3000

Contact Tom Painter, Sr. Employment Administrator. An independent, not-for-profit scientific research corporation engaged in program analysis, systems analysis, and operations research for the U.S. Air Force and other defense-related agencies. Additional locations in Colorado Springs, CO; and Dayton, OH. Common positions include: Computer Programmer; Economist; Aerospace Engineer; Electrical Engineer; Industrial Engineer; Mechanical Engineer; Operations Research Analyst; Physicist; Statistician; Systems Analyst. Principal educational backgrounds sought: Computer Science; Economics; Engineering; Mathematics; Operations Research; Physics. Company benefits include:

medical insurance; dental insurance; pension plan; life insurance; tuition assistance; disability coverage; employee discounts; savings plan; 20 days paid vacation. Corporate headquarters location.

ATLANTIC RESEARCH CORPORATION
5390 Cherokee Avenue
Alexandria VA 22312
703/642-4000
Contact Employment Manager. Designs, develops and manufactures solid propellant rocket motors for missile systems and other uses, and electromagnetic security systems and professional services. Common positions include: Accountant; Chemist; Computer Programmer; Aerospace Engineers; Chemical, Electrical, Industrial, Mechanical, & Metallurgical Engineers; Department, General, and Operations/Production Managers; Purchasing Agent; Quality Control Supervisor; Systems Analyst; Technial Writer/Editor. Principal educational backgrounds sought: Accounting; Business Administration; Chemistry; Computer Science; Engineering. Company benefits include: medical, dental, and life insurance; pension plan; tuition assistance; disability coverage; savings plan. Corporate and divisional headquarters location. Operations at this facility include: manufacturing; research/development; administration; service; sales.

THE BDM CORPORATION
7915 Jones Branch Drive
McLean VA 22102
703/848-5023
Contact P. Bradford Sterl, Manager, Technical Staffing. Provides professional and technical services for clients in National Defense, Defense Communications (85% of total revenue), Energy and the Environment, Space, Transportation, Manufacturing Industry, Banking and other sectors of public and private endeavors in the United States and abroad. Performs research, analysis, tests, systems design, engineering and integration. Common positions include: Computer Programmer; Electrical Engineer; Mechanical Engineer; Statistician; Systems Analyst; Software Engineer. Principal educational backgrounds sought: Computer Science; Engineering; Mathematics; Physics; Operations Research. Company benefits include: medical, dental, and life insurance; pension plan; tuition assistance; disability coverage; employee discounts; savings plan. Corporate, regional, and divisional headquarters location. Parent company is Ford Aerospace. Operations at this facility include service.

CIVIL ENGINEER CORPS OFFICER/U.S. NAVY
Naval Facilities Engineer Command Code 09MA1
200 Stovall Street
Alexandria VA 22332-2300
202/694-3635
Contact Lieutenant Commander J.E. Surash, Accessions Officer. Responsible for design, construction, maintenance, repair, and operation of the Navy's shore facilities. Corporate headquarters location. Common positions include: Architect; Civil Engineer; Electrical Engineer; and Mechanical Engineer. Worldwide assignment possibilities. Principal educational backgrounds sought: Civil, Mechanical and Electrical Engineering; Architecture. Company benefits include: medical, dental, and life insurance; pension plan; tuition assistance; disability coverage.

DEFENSE CONTRACT AUDIT AGENCY
Cameron Station Room 4B319
Alexandria VA 22304-6178
800/523-2986
Contact Recruitment Officer. DCAA is responsible for auditing the Governments's defense contracts. The company is the largest audit agency in the federal government. Performs all contract audits and provides accounting and financial advisory services to the Department of Defense and 30 other Federal agencies. Common positions include Accountant; Auditor. Principal educational background sought:

Accounting. Company benefits include: medical insurance; pension plan; life insurance; tuition assistance; disability coverage; savings plan.

E-SYSTEMS INC./
MELPAR DIVISION
7700 Arlington Boulevard
Falls Church VA 22046
703/560-5000 ext. 1694
Contact Personnel Representative. A major systems contractor in the areas of remotely controlled reconnaissance, information processing and display, electronic combat operations, digitally controlled communications, and intrusion detection. Divisional headquarters location. Operations at this facility include: manufacturing; research/development. Corporate headquarters location: Dallas, TX. Common positions include: Computer Programmer; Draftsperson; Electrical Engineer; Industrial Engineer; Mechanical Engineer; Physicist; Systems Analyst; Technical Writer/Editor. Principal educational backgrounds sought: Computer Science; Engineering; Mathematics; Physics. Company benefits include: medical, dental, and life insurance; pension plan; tuition assistance; disability coverage; employee discounts; savings plan; employee stock ownership plan; credit union.

ENSCO INC.
5400 Port Royal Road
Springfield VA 22151
703/321-9000
Contact Joanne McDonald, Director of Administration. A research, development, and applied systems engineering firm providing computer and sensor based systems in the areas of defense, physical security, and transportation. Corporate headquarters location. Operations at this facility include: research/development. Common positions include: Computer Programmer; Engineer; Electrical Engineer; Mechanical Engineer; Geophysicist; Department Manager; Physicist; Systems Analyst; Meteorologist. Principal educational backgrounds sought: Computer Science; Engineering; Mathematics; Physics. Company benefits include: medical, dental, and life insurance; pension plan; tuition assistance; disability coverage; employee discounts. Other locations include: Florida, New York, and Maryland. Corporate headquarters location.

ERC INTERNATIONAL
3211 Jermantown Road
P.O. Box 10107
Fairfax VA 22030
703/246-0200
Contact David L. Vernon, Senior Technical Recruiter. A major Washington area research and development corporation specializing in defense contracting. Common job positions include: Accountant; Computer Programmer; Electrical Engineer; Mechanical Engineer; Systems Analyst; Technical Writer/Editor. Principal educational backgrounds sought: Accounting; Business Administration; Computer Science; Engineering; Finance; Mathematics; Physics. Company benefits include: medical, dental, and life insurance; pension plan; tuition assistance; disability coverage; savings plan. Corporate headquarters location. Operations at this facility include: research/development. New York Stock Exchange.

GENERAL RESEARCH CORPORATION
7655 Old Springhouse Road
McLean VA 22102
703/893-5900, ext. 396
Contact Personnel Administrator. A wholly owned subsidiary of Flow General Inc.; provides applied research and analysis in the following areas: radar and infared sensors, high-energy lasers, space technology forecasting, space defense systems, management science, operations research, transportation and logistics, strategic studies, economic and cost analysis, management information

systems, computer software; database systems, energy and the environment. Other offices located in Santa Barbara CA, and Huntsville AL. GRC's technical staff includes more than 500 degreed professionals, over 50% of whom have advanced degrees. Common positions include: Aerospace Engineer; Physicist; Systems Analyst. Principal educational backgrounds sought: Computer Science; Engineering; Mathematics; Physics. Corporate headquarters location: Santa Barbara, CA.

QUESTECH INC.
7600A Leesburg Pike
Fall's Church VA 22043
703/760-1000

Contact David Smith, Employment Representative. QuesTech is a diversified high-technology company that provides scientific, engineering and management services in electronics, computer science, and other advanced technologies to government and industry. These services encompass the entire life cycle of fielded hardware, from research and development through system design and engineering to technical and program management support, test and evaluation and system installation and maintenance. The company's highly trained staff of professionals is dedicated to providing quality services with goals of enhancing national security, fostering a leadership position in research and development and improving industrial productivity. In accomplishing these goals, QuesTech makes use of the latest scientific and engineering approaches, techniques and models, as well as laboratories, computers and systems. The corporation has two operation divisions: QuesTech Research Division (QTRD) and Engineering Resources, Inc. (ERI). Each division is staffed with individuals whose experience and background match these business areas creating a highly effective functional organization. The divisions support each other by providing expertise wherever needed to provide broadly based solutions to complex technical problems. In this way, QuesTech provides its clients with accurate and cost-effective solutions to both narrow, specialized and broad, interdisciplinary problems. Common positions include: Accountant; Buyer; Computer Programmer; Draftsperson; Aerospace Engineer; Ceramics Engineer; Chemical Engineer; Electrical Engineer; Mechanical Engineer; Financial Analyst; Physicist; Statistician; Systems Analyst; Technical Writer/Editor. Principal educational backgounds sought: Accounting; Business Administration; Communications; Computer Science; Economics; Engineering; Finance; Mathematics; Physics. Company benefits include: medical insurance; dental insurance; pension plan; life insurance; tuition assistance; disability coverage; profit sharing; savings plan; vision plan. Corporate, divisional headquarters location. Operations at this facility include: research/development; administration.

U.S. ARMY ENGINEER CENTER
Department of Army, Building 1001
Fort Belvoir VA 22060-5206
703/664-2774

Contact Personnel Department. Approximately 5,000 Federal civilian employees working at Fort Belvoir encompassing seven different Army major commands. Common positions include: Chemist; Chemical Engineer; Civil Engineer; Electrical Engineer; Industrial Engineer; Mechanical Engineer; Metallurgical Engineer; Physicist. Principal educational backgrounds sought: Chemistry; Engineering; Physics. Company benefits include: medical insurance; life insurance. Operations include: research/development/engineering.

ELECTRICAL AND ELECTRONICS

For more information on electronics opportunities in Greater Washington, look for the following professional and trade organizations in Chapter 8, beginning on page 265:

American Electroplaters and Surface Finishers Society
Electrochemical Society
Electronic Industries Association
Electronics Technicians Association
Institute of Electrical and Electronics Engineers
International Brotherhood of Electrical Workers
International Society of Certified Electornics Technicians
National Electrical Manufacturers Association
National Electronics Sales and Services Association

Maryland

CU TRONICS INC.
1925 Greenspring Drive
Timonium MD 21093
301/252-9211
Contact Assistant Director of Personnel. Two facilities in Timonium. A privately-owned electronics firm, manufacturing custom single/double-sided, multilayer printed circuit boards. Other facilities in Nashua, NH, and Norcross, GA. Corporate headquarters location.

DELTA DATA SYSTEMS CORPORATION
7175 Columbia Gateway Drive
Columbia MD 21046
301/290-6400
Contact Joan Kishter, Corporate Personnel Director. A manufacturer of video display terminals.

E.I.L. INSTRUMENTS INC.
10 Loveton Circle
Sparks MD 21152
301/771-4800
Contact Kathryn Marr, Human Resources Manager. Manufactures and distributes a variety of electrical and electronic equipment. Common positions include: Electrical Engineer; Electronic Technician; Branch Manager; Department Manager; Operations/Production Manager; Purchasing Agent; Sales Representative, PMEL Technician. Principal educational backgrounds sought: Accounting; Business Administration; Electronic Technology; Engineering; Marketing. Company benefits include: medical, dental and life insurance; prescriptions; tuition assistance; disability coverage; profit sharing; paid vacation and holidays; prescription drug plan; 401K. Corporate headquarters location. Operations at this facility include: manufacturing; research/development; administration; service; sales.

ENTERPRISE ELECTRIC COMPANY INC.
4204 Shannon Drive
Baltimore MD 21213
301/488-8200
Contact Fred Churchman, Secretary/Treasurer. Engaged in a range of commercial and industrial electrical contracting projects, including pole line and outdoor substation construction. Corporate headquarters location.

HEWLETT PACKARD COMPANY
4 Choke Cherry Road
Rockville MD 20850
301/258-2000

Contact Recruiting Manager. Local facility of a worldwide firm engaged in the design, manufacture, marketing, and servicing of a broad array of precision electronics instruments and systems for measurement, analysis, and computation. Company's line of over 4,000 products are used in industry, business, engineering, science, education, and medicine. Operations are organized into four business segments: electronic data products, electronic test and measurement, medical electronic equipment, and analytical instrumentation. Corporate headquarters location: Palo Alto, CA. New York Stock Exchange.

MECHANICAL PRODUCTS INC.
51 Airport View Drive
St. Mary's Industrial Park
P.O. Box 429
Hollywood MD 20636
301/373-8601
Contact Personnel Director. Manufactures circuit breakers and circuit protection equipment and systems.

MOTOROLA COMMUNICATIONS & ELECTRONICS INC.
7230 Parkway Drive
Hanover MD 21076
301/796-6200
Contact Mark M. Shaklee, Controller. Regional sales offices for one of the world's leading manufacturers of electronic equipment and components, engaged in the design, manufacture, and sale of a diversified line of products such as 2-way radios and other electronic communications systems; semiconductors, including integrated circuits, and discrete components; products for aerospace use; electronic engine controls; digital appliance controls; automobile radios, citizens band radios, and other automotive and industrial electronic equipment; and data communications products such as low, medium, and high-speed modems, multiplexers, and network processors. Common positions include: Accountant; Administrator; Credit Manager; Electrical Engineer; Financial Analyst; Management Trainee; Marketing Specialist; Personnel & Labor Relations Specialist. Principal educational backgrounds sought: Accounting; Business Administration; Computer Science; Engineering; Finance; Marketing. Company benefits include: medical insurance; dental insurance; pension plan; life insurance; tuition assistance; disability coverage; profit sharing; employee discounts; savings plan. Operations at this facility include: regional headquarters; administration; sales. Corporate headquarters location: Schaumburg, IL. New York Stock Exchange.

SOLAREX CORPORATION
1335 Piccard Drive
Rockville MD 20850
301/948-0202
Contact Donna Nunn, Senior Personnel Administrator. Three area locations. Engaged in the research, development, and manufacture of solar electric systems, primarily photovoltaic cells and panels. Corporate headquarters location.

TRANS-TECH INC.
ALPHA INDUSTRIES INC.
5520 Adamstown Road
Adamstown MD 21710
301/695-9400
Contact Judy Eaton, Human Resources Manager. Manufactures a number of electronic-grade ceramic materials used in microwave electronic components, such as telecommunications, and link telephones. A subsidiary of Alpha Industries (Woburn, MA). Divisional headquarters location. Operations include: manufacturing; research/development; administration; sales. Corporate headquarters location:

Woburn, MA. American Stock Exchange. Common positions include: Accountant; Buyer; Chemist; Credit Manager; Ceramics Engineer; Chemical Engineer; Electrical Engineer; Mechanical Engineer; Department Manager; General Manager; Purchasing Agent; Quality Control Supervisor. Principal educational backgrounds sought: Accounting; Chemistry; Engineering; Physics. Company benefits include: medical insurance; dental insurance; AESOP plan; 401K plan; life insurance; tuition assistance; disability coverage.

Northern Virginia

AUTOMATA INC.
1200 Severn Way
Sterling VA 22170
703/450-2600

Contact Patricia C. Bates, Personnel Director. Manufactures printed circuit boards. Common positions include: Accountant; Blue-Collar Worker Supervisor; Buyer; Chemist; Computer Programmer; Customer Service Representative; Industrial Engineer; Mechanical Engineer; Operations/ Production Manager; Personnel & Labor Relations Specialist; Purchasing Agent; Quality Control Supervisor; Sales Representative; Designer - CAD/CAM. Principal educational backgrounds sought: Accounting; Chemistry; Engineering; Marketing. Company benefits include: medical, dental, and life insurance; tuition assistance; disability coverage; profit sharing. Corporate headquarters location. Operation at this facility include: manufacturing; research/development; administration; sales.

COMPUDYNE/VEGA DIVISION
800 Follin Lane
Vienna VA 22180
703/938-6300

Contact Joe Robbins, Personnel Manager. Produces a variety of precision electronics equipment for the defense and communications markets, including portable radar tracking devices, command and control systems, antenna and microwave receiving devices, and related products.

GENICOM CORPORATION
1 Genicom Drive
Waynesboro VA 22980
703/949-1129

Contact Sue Smith, Technical Recruiter. Firm develops, manufactures and markets electronic printers for data processing/word processing applications. Also manufactures and markets high-reliability relays for aerospace and other applications. Common positions include: Accountant; Buyer; Computer Programmer; Electrical Engineer; Industrial Engineer; Mechanical Engineer; Financial Analyst; Marketing Specialist; Software Engineer. Principal educational backgrounds sought: Accounting; Business Administration; Computer Science; Engineering; Finance; Physics. Company benefits include: medical, dental, and life insurance; tuition assistance; disability coverage; savings plan; 401K plan. Corporate headquarters location. Operations at this facility include: manufacturing; research/development; administration.

PEMCO CORPORATION
P.O. Box 1319
Bluefield VA 24605
703/326-2611

Contact Linda Hale, Personnel Records Clerk. Manufacturer of electrical switchgear for surface and underground mining (metal & non-metal), and industrial applications. Corporate headquarters location. Operations include: manufactuing; research/development; administration; service; sales. Common positions include: Accountant; Buyer; Computer Programmer; Credit Manager; Draftsperson; Engineer; Electrical Engineer; Mechanical Engineer; Mining Engineer; Marketing

Specialist; Purchasing Agent; Quality Control Supervisor; Sales Representative. Principal educational backgrounds sought: Accounting; Business Administration; Engineering; Marketing. Company benefits include: medical insurance; life insurance; tuition assistance; disability coverage; profit sharing.

ENGINEERING AND ARCHITECTURE

For more information on engineering and architectural opportunities in Greater Washington, look for the following professional and trade organizations in Chapter 8, beginning on page 265:

American Institute of Architects
American Society for Engineering Education
American Society of Civil Engineers
American Society of Heating, Refrigerating
    and Air Conditioning Engineers
American Society of Landscape Architects
American Society of Naval Engineers
American Society of Plumbing Engineers
American Society of Safety Engineers
Illuminating Engineering Society of North America
Institute of Industrial Engineers
National Academy of Engineering
National Society of Professional Engineers
Society of Fire Protection Engineers
United Engineering Trustees

District of Columbia

AEPA ARCHITECTS ENGINEERS
2421 Pennsylvania Avenue NW
Washington DC 20037
202/822-8320
Contact C. M. Liu, Director of Personnel. A major Washington architecture and engineering firm. Corporate headquarters location.

AMERICAN INSTITUTE OF ARCHITECTS
1735 New York Avenue NW, 4th Floor
Washington DC 20006
202/626-7324
Contact Jeanette J. Jones, Assistant Director of Personnel. A professional association of licensed architects. Acts to promote the aesthetic, scientific, and practical efficiency of architecture; to advance the science and art of planning and building by advancing the standards of architectural education, training, and practice; and to coordinate the building industry and architectural profession to ensure better living standards through improved environment and service. More than 40,000 members nationwide. Common positions include: Accountant; Administrator; Architect; Attorney; Computer Programmer; Customer Service Representative; Civil Engineer; Electrical Engineer; Mechanical Engineer; Marketing Specialist; Public Relations Worker; Purchasing Agent; Technical Writer/Editor. Principal educational backgrounds sought: Accounting; Art/Design; Business Administration; Communications; Computer Science; Economics; Engineering; Finance; Liberal Arts; Marketing. Company benefits include: medical insurance; dental insurance; pension plan; life insurance; disability

coverage; employee discounts; savings plan; credit union; professional development program. Corporate headquarters location. Operations at this facility include: research/development; administration; service.

Maryland

ARINC RESEARCH CORPORATION
2551 Riva Road
Annapolis MD 21401
301/266-4611
Contact Director of Human Resources. An engineering and management consulting firm providing technical studies, analyses, and evaluations of aircraft, ship systems, communications and information systems. Customers include DoD, DoE, DoT and FAA. Other offices in Washington, DC; San Diego, CA; Boston, MA; and Dayton, OH. Corporate headquarters location. Operations include: research/development. Common positions include: Electrical Engineer; Industrial Engineer; Mechanical Engineer; Systems Analyst. Principal educational backgrounds sought: Computer Science; Engineering; Mathematics. Company benefits include: medical insurance; dental insurance; life insurance; pension plan; tuition assistance; disability coverage; profit sharing; savings plan.

GREENHORNE & O'MARA INC.
9001 Edmonston Road
Greenbelt MD 20770
301/982-2800
Contact Human Resources Division. Provides services in the areas of: Engineering; Architecture; Planning; Science; Surveying; Photogrammetry. Corporate headquarters location. Operations include: administration; service; regional and divisional headquarters. Common positions include: Architect; Computer Programmer; Draftsperson; Civil Engineer; Geographer; Landscape Architect; Technical Writer/Editor; Transportation & Traffic Planner. Principal educational backgrounds sought: Computer Science; Civil Engineering; Geology; Landscape Architecture. Company benefits include: medical insurance; life insurance; tuition assistance; disability coverage; employee discounts; travel insurance; profit sharing; savings plan; vacation; sick leave.

KIDDE CONSULTANTS INC.
1020 Cromwell Bridge Road
Baltimore MD 21204
Contact Director of Personnel. Provides planning, engineering, surveying, geotechnical, testing, and construction inspection services. Common positions include: Accountant; Architect; Computer Programmer; Credit Manager; Draftsperson; Civil, Electrical, Industrial and Mechanical Engineers; Technical Writer/Editor; Purchasing Agent; Sales Representative; Transportation & Traffic Specialist. Principal educational backgrounds sought: Accounting; Computer Science; Engineering; Finance. Company benefits include: medical, dental and life insurance; tuition assistance; disability coverage; profit sharing; employee discounts; savings plan; 401(K). Corporate headquarters location: Saddlebrook, NJ. Parent company: Kidde, Inc. New York Stock Exchange (Kidde, Inc.) Operations at this facility include: regional headquarters.

NUS CORPORATION
910 Clopper Road
Gaithersburg MD 20878
301/258-6000
Contact Susan Young, Employment Administrator. An environmental and engineering consulting firm serving utilities, government, and industrial companies. Provides video-based training services through NUS training Corporation. Analytical laboratories provide analytical services to industry, utilities, and government clients, Waste Management Services Group provides engineering and consulting services

to U.S. Government agencies and private companies. Energy Services Group serves utility clients in areas ranging from licensing support and environmental services to all facets of inplant and onsite operations and maintenance needs. Established 1960. Employs approximately 2,000 people in the United States. Common positions include: Biologist; Chemist; Draftsperson; Chemical, Civil, Elecrical, Industrial and Mechanical Engineers; Geologist; Geophysicist; Industrial Designer; Physicist; Systems Analyst; Technical Writer/Editor. Principal educational background: Biology; Chemistry; Engineering; Geology; Mathematics; Physics. Company benefits include: medical insurance; dental insurance; pension plan; life insurance; tuition assistance; disability coverage; profit sharing. Corporate headquarters location. Operations at this facility include: divisional headquarters; research/development; administration.

Northern Virginia

ADVANCED TECHNOLOGY INC.
12005 Sunrise Valley Drive
Reston VA 22091
703/620-8373
Contact Employment Center. Provides engineering and related analytical services in the areas of Information Technology, Computer Science, Logistics, Marine Engineering, Business Application, Commercial Nuclear Engineering, and others. Clients include industry and government. Corporate headquarters location.

CACI, INC. - FEDERAL
8260 Willow Oaks Corp. Drive
Fairfax VA 22031
703/876-2000
Contact Pat Rhubottom, Personnel Manager. CACI is an international high technology and professional services corporation. CACI is a leader in advanced information systems, systems engineering, logistics sciences, proprietary analytical software products, and market analysis consultancy services, information products and systems. Common positions include: Accountant; Computer Programmer; Electrical Engineer; Financial Analyst; Department Manager; Marketing Specialist; Purchasing Agent; Quality Control Supervisor; Systems Analyst; Technical Writer/Editor. Principal educational backgrounds sought: Accounting; Business Administration; Computer Science; Engineering; Finance; Marketing; Mathematics. Company benefits include: medical, dental and life insurance; pension plan; tuition assistance; disability coverage. Corporate headquarters location. Operations at this facility include: administration.

FABRICATED METAL PRODUCTS

For more information on fabricated metal opportunities in Greater Washington, look for the following professional and trade organizations in Chapter 8, beginning on page 265:

American Caste Metals Association
American Powder Metallurgy Institute
Association of Iron and Steel Engineers
National Association of Metal Finishers

District of Columbia

J. B. KENDALL COMPANY
2160 Queens Chapel Road
Washington DC 20018
202/526-2484
Contact Debby Herrity, Personnel. A major steel fabrication corporation.

STROMBERG SHEET METAL WORKS
1235 W Street NE
Washington DC 20018
202/526-8350
Contact Lou Curtain, Production Manager. A major sheet metal manufacturing corporation.

Maryland

BALTIMORE SPECIALTY STEELS CORPORATION
3501 East Biddle Street
Baltimore MD 21213
301/563-5624
Contact Joyce Repko, Personnel Supervisor. BSSC produces stainless steels, alloy steels, billets, bar, rod, wire, special shapes, and nickel-based alloys. New York Stock Exchange. Common positions at this facility include: Accountant; Administrator; Buyer; Computer Programmer; Credit Manager; Electrical Engineer; Mechanical Engineer; Metallurgical Engineer; Financial Analyst; Operations/Production Manager; Purchasing Agent; Quality Control Supervisor; Quality Control Supervisor; Sales Representative; Personnel & Labor Relations Specialist; Product Specialist (Technical Sales Support); Metallurgy or Material Science. Principal educational backgrounds sought: Accounting; Business Administration; Engineering; Finance; Marketing. Company benefits include: medical insurance; life insurance; tuition assistance; disability coverage; profit sharing; savings plan. Corporate headquarters location. Parent company is Armco Inc. Operations at this facility include: manufacturing; administration; service; sales. Nationally, company is a producer of basic and specialty steel mill products, drilling rigs and other equipment for oil and gas industry, and construction products for South American and international markets.

HAMILTON & SPIEGEL INC.
P.O. Box 288
Bladensburg MD 20710-0288
301/322-3150
Contact Bruce Davis, Controller. Sheet metal and roofing constructors; also engaged in stainless steel fabrication. Corporate headquarters location.

MARYLAND SPECIALTY WIRE COMPANY
100 Cockeysville Road
Cockeysville MD 21030
301/785-2500
Contact Allen Fields, Personnel Director. Produces stainless steel and alloy wire used for springs, reinforced hose, wire rope, ball bearings, and other products. Corporate headquarters location.

STEELTIN CAN CORPORATION
1101 Todds Lane
Baltimore MD 21237
301/686-6363
Contact Kendall Strout, Personnel Office. Manufactures a variety of metal and composite cans.

THOMPSON STEEL COMPANY INC.
4515 North Point Road
Baltimore MD 21219
301/477-0400
Contact Art Dietzel, Industrial Relations Manager. Produces cold-rolled strip steel. Corporate headquarters location: Canton, MA. Common positions include: Accountant; Administrator; Blue-Collar Worker Supervisor; Buyer; Claim Representative; Customer Service Representative; Chemical Engineer; Electrical Engineer; Industrial Engineer; Mechanical Engineer; Metallurgical Engineer; Department Manager; Department Manager;General Manager; Operations/Production Manager; Personnel & Labor Relations Specialist; Purchasing Agent; Quality Control Supervisor; Sales Representative. Principal educational backgrounds sought: Accounting; Business Administration; Chemistry; Computer Science; Communications; Engineering; Marketing. Company benefits include: medical insurance; dental insurance; pension plan; life insurance; tuition assistance; disability coverage. Operations at this facility include: manufacturing; administration; service; sales.

Northern Virginia

ATLAS MACHINE & IRON WORKS INC.
13951 Lee Highway
Gainesville VA 22065
703/754-4171
Contact Bill Timmons, Personnel Director. Produces a wide range of fabricated steel plates.

REYNOLDS METALS COMPANY
6601 Broad Street
Richmond VA 23261
804/281-2000
Contact David Thorne, Personnel. Reynolds Metals Company is a producer of metals and other materials through its worldwide operations. Reynolds' core business is as an integrated producer of a wide variety of added-value aluminum products. The company also produces certain plastic products to more fully serve key markets. Reynolds' largest market is containers and packaging, which includes consumer products. Reynolds operates 55 plants in the United States, has plants or interests in 18 other countries and employs 27,600.

FINANCIAL SERVICES/MANAGEMENT CONSULTING

For more information on financial services and management consulting opportunities in Greater Washington, look for the following professional and trade organizations in Chapter 8, beginning on page 265:

American Financial Services Association
American Management Association
American Society of Appraisers
Association of Management Consulting Firms
Federation of Tax Administrators
Financial Analysts Federation
Financial Executives Institute
Institute of Financial Education

Institute of Management Consultants
National Association of Business Economists
National Association of Credit Management
National Association of Real Estate Investment Trusts
National Corporate Cash Management Association
Securities Industry Association

District of Columbia

**AMERICAN EXPRESS TRAVEL
RELATED SERVICES COMPANY**
1150 Connecticut Avenue NW
Washington DC 20036
202/457-1300
Contact Ms. Hang B. Dang, Manager. A large travel services office for the major diversified financial services organization. Nationally, company provides travel and financial services to its customers through more than 700 offices, and more than 800 more representative offices, in addition to thousands of selling outlets throughout the world. Corporate headquarters location: New York NY. New York Stock Exchange.

INTERNATIONAL FINANCE CORPORATION
1850 I Street NW
Room 2001
Washington DC 20433
202/473-7972
Contact Katherine Louthood, Recruitment Officer. An international investment organization whose aim is to foster economic development in developing countries through private enterprise investments. Affiliated with the World Bank. Corporate headquarters location.

JOHNSTON, LEMON & COMPANY INC.
1101 Vermont Avenue NW, 6th Floor
Washington DC 20005
202/842-5500
Contact Gail Lines, Personnel Director. Underwrites, distributes, and deals in corporate and municipal securities, revenue bonds, and mutual funds, and provides related and unrelated business management services. Corporate headquarters location.

MERRILL LYNCH
1111 19th Street
Washington DC 20036
202/659-7333
Contact Greg Franks, Sales Manager. Provides financial services in the following areas: securities, extensive insurance, and real estate and related services. One of the largest securities brokerage firms in the United States, it also brokers commodity futures and options, corporate and municipal securities, and is engaged in investment banking activities. Operations include: sales. Corporate headquarters location: New York, NY. New York Stock Exchange. Common positions include: Customer Service Representative; Branch Manager; Management Trainee; Operations/ Production Manager; Sales Representative. Company benefits include: medical insurance; pension plan; tuition assistance; disability coverage; profit sharing; employee discounts; savings plan.

SYSTEMS CONSULTING ASSOCIATES
1420 16th Street NW
Washington DC 20036
202/234-7333
Contact Personnel Department. A major Washington technical management firm.

USLICO CORP
4601 Fairfax Drive
Washington DC 20006
703/875-3515
Contact Margaret Crandall, Recruiting Manager. USLICO Corporation, with over $2 billion in assets, includes four life insurance companies, a financial planning firm, a broker/dealer and the International Bank Holding Company. United Services Life is the flagship company for the life insurance group which, when combined, ranks in the top 5% of life insurance companies in the United States. Common postitions include: Accountant; Actuary; Claim Representative; Computer Programmer; Customer Service Representative; Financial Analyst; Insurance Agent/Broker; Department Manager; Marketing Specialist; Quality Control Supervisor; Systems Analyst; Underwriter. Principal educational backgrounds sought: Accounting; Business Administration; Computer Science; Finance; Liberal Arts; Marketing; Mathematics; Human Resources. Company benefits include: medical, dental, and life insurance; pension plan; tuition reimbursement; disability coverage; profit sharing; 401 (k) plan; employee discounts; exercise facility; subway; cafeteria. Corporate headquarters location. New York Stock Exchange.

Maryland

APPLIED MANAGEMENT SCIENCES INC.
962 Wayne Avenue, Suite 700
Silver Spring MD 20910
301/585-8181
Contact Jeanmarie Zugel, Personnel Manager. A private, professional services research firm. Established in 1970. Provides a broad range of analytical, technical, and information support services in the energy and environment, defense, health, information and management systems, and human resources fields. These support services reach both the private and public sectors at the national, regional, state, and local levels. Corporate headquarters location. Common positions include: Accountant; Computer Programmer; Economist; Engineer; Chemical Engineer; Civil Engineer; Electrical Engineer; Financial Analyst; Mechanical Engineer; Petroleum Engineer; Geologist; Department Manager; Personnel & Labor Relations Specialist; Statistician; Systems Analyst; Technical Writer/Editor. Principal educational backgrounds sought: Computer Science; Engineering; Mathematics; Economics. Company benefits include: medical insurance; dental insurance; life insurance; tuition assistance; disability coverage; profit sharing; pension plan; two weeks vacation; sick leave. Corporate headquarters location. Operations at this facility include: regional headquarters.

COMMERCIAL CREDIT CO./
PRIMERICA CORP.
300 St. Paul Place
Baltimore MD 21202
301/332-3281
Contact D.A. Wade, Director of Personnel. Primerica is a diversified financial organization consisting of insurance, investment, mortgage banking, and consumer financial services companies. Primerica Corporation and its subsidiaries recruit each year for jobs at various levels of responsibility throughout the United States. Common positions include: Accountant; Administrator; Bank Officer/Manager; Claim Representative; Computer Programmer; Credit Manager; Customer Service Representative; Financial Analyst; Branch Manager; Management Trainee; Personnel & Labor Relations Specialist;

Systems Analyst. Principal educational backgrounds sought: Accounting; Business Administration; Communications; Computer Science; Finance. Company benefits include: medical, dental, and life insurance; pension plan; tuition assistance; disability coverage; savings plan. Corporate headquarters located in New York, NY. Operations at this facility include: divisional headquarters; administration. New York Stock Exchange.

GENERAL BUSINESS SERVICES INC.
20271 Goldenrod Lane
Germantown MD 20874
301/428-1040
Contact Lee Ann Novak, Administrative Assistant. Provides a broad range of small business consulting services, data processing services, record systems, and income tax advisory consulting services. Common positions include: Accountant; Administrator; Department Manager; Operations/Production Manager; Marketing Specialist; Personnel Specialist; Systems Analyst; Technical Writer. Principal educational backgrounds sought: Accounting; Business Administration; Computer Science; Marketing; Secretarial, Data Entry. Company benefits include: medical insurance; pension plan; life insurance; tuition assistance; disability coverage; vacation. Corporate headquarters location. Operations at this facility include: research/development; administration; service; sales.

SECURITY PACIFIC FINANCE
Suite 500
8630 Fenton Street
Silver Springs MD 20910
301/587-7200
Contact Gerald Davis, Regional Director. A money-lending firm, primarily serving individual lenders in a wide range of income levels. Offers home improvement, college expenses, vacations, and other general-purpose loans.

UNION TRUST BANCORP
P.O. Box 1077
Baltimore MD 21203
301/332-5600
Contact Personnel Administrator. A bank holding company ranking in the top five Maryland banks in total deposits. Provides a wide range of banking and trust services through 82 domestic banks in Maryland, and one bank in the Cayman Islands. Subsidiary firms are also engaged in diversified equipment lease financing activities for commercial customers, and consumer loan insurance. Corporate headquarters location.

Northern Virginia

DOMINION BANKSHARES CORPORATION
P.O. Box 13327
Roanoke VA 24040
703/563-7907
Contact David M. Furman, Human Resources Officer. Multi-bank holding company offering financial services. Corporate headquarters location Common position include: Accountant; Bank Officer/Manager; Computer Programmer; Credit Manager; Financial Analyst; Branch Manager; Marketing Specialist; Personnel & Labor Relations Specialist; Systems Analyst; Technical Writer/Editor. Principal educational backgrounds sought: Accounting; Business Administration; Communications; Computer Science; Economics; Finance; Marketing. Company benefits include: medical, dental, and life insurance; pension plan; tuition assistance; disability coverage; employee discounts; savings plan.

FARM CREDIT ADMINISTRATION
1501 Farm Credit Drive
McLean VA 22102-5090
703/883-4135
Contact Personnel. A government agency which regulates and examines the Farm Credit System. Applicants must submit appropriate form (Government Form SF-171) following specific vacancy announcements; unsolicited resumes are disregarded. Ten field locations. Headquarters locations. Common positions include: Credit examiner; Financial Analyst. Limited hiring for the following positions: Accountant; Attorney; Economist; Financial Analyst; Computer Specialist. Principal educational backgrounds sought: Accounting; Business Administration; Economics; Finance. Provides benefits due to federal goverment employees. Operations at this facility include: administration.

FOOD & BEVERAGE RELATED: PROCESSING & DISTRIBUTION

For more information on food & beverage opportunities in Greater Washington, look for the following professional and trade organizations in Chapter 8, beginning on page 265:

American Association of Cereal Chemists
American Society of Agricultural Engineers
American Society of Brewing Chimists
Dairy and Food Industries Supply Association
National Agricultural Chemicals Association
National Dairy Council
United Food and Commercial Workers International Union

Maryland

AMSTAR SUGAR CORPORATION
P.O. Box 838
Baltimore MD 21203
301/752-6150
Contact Ron Frey, Employee Relations Manager. Operates a major cane sugar refinery.

THE BALTIMORE SPICE COMPANY
P.O. Box 5858
Baltimore MD 21208
301/363-1700
Contact Personnel Manager. Produces a wide variety of spices and seasonings. Corporate headquarters location.

EMBASSY DAIRY/
SUBSIDIARY OF MORNINGSTAR FOODS INC
P.O. Box 114
Waldorf MD 20601
301/843-1212
Contact Mr. A.F. Mroz, Personnel Director. Several area facilities, including Washington, DC, and Baltimore. A major area dairy, engaged in the processing of milk and ice cream, and the distribution of those products. Corporate headquarters location.

G. HEILEMAN BREWING COMPANY, INC./
CARLING NATIONAL BREWERY
4501 Hollins Ferry Road
Baltimore MD 21227
301/850-7258
Contact Stanley H. Haas, Division Human Resources Manager. Produces premium beers and other malt beverages. Common positions include: Package Production Supervisor; Brewing Supervisor; Accountant; Customer Service Representative; Electrical and Industrial Engineer; Financial Analyst; Marketing Specialist; Personnel & Labor Relations Specialist; Quality Control Supervisor; Transportation & Traffic Specialist. Principal educational backgrounds sought (but not required): Accounting; Business Administration; Finance; Marketing; Chemistry; Brewing Sciences. Company benefits include: medical insurance; dental insurance; pension plan; life insurance; tuition assistance; disability coverage; savings plan (after one year service). Corporate headquarters location: LaCrosse, WI. Operations at this facility include manufacturing; administration; sales-East. Parent company: Bond Brewing (Australia).

HIGH'S DAIRY STORES
A DIVISION OF THE SOUTHLAND CORP
8920 Whiskey Bottom Road
Laurel MD 20707
301/953-2200
Contact Jean Zyna, Personnel Manager. A manufacturer and retailer of dairy products. Division headquarters location. Corporate headquarters location. Common positions include: Accountant; Administrator; Buyer; Claim Representative; Computer Programmer; Industrial Engineer; Operations/ Production Manager; Management Trainee; Marketing Specialist; Personnel & Labor Relations Specialist; Public Relations Worker; Purchasing Agent; Quality Control Supervisor; Real Estate Developer; Systems Analyst. Principal educational backgrounds sought: Accounting; Biology; Business Administration; Computer Science; Engineering; Marketing. Company benefits include: medical insurance; dental insurance; pension plan; life insurance; tuition assistance; disability coverage; profit sharing; employee discounts. Corporate headquarters are located in Dallas, TX. Parent company is the Southland Corporation. Operations at this facility include: manufacturing; administration. Divisional headquarters location.

MURRY'S STEAKS INC.
8300 Pennsylvania Avenue
P.O. Box 398
Forestville MD 20747-0398
301/420-6400
Contact Barry J. Schlossberg, Director of Personnel. Multiple area locations, including Washington, DC, and Baltimore. Engaged in the production, distribution, and retail and wholesale sale of frozen meats and specialty food items. Corporate headquarters location.

FOOD/TRADE

District of Columbia

GIANT FOOD INC.
P.O. Box 1804
Washington DC 20013
301/341-4267

Contact Employment Manager. A retail food chain. Corporate headquarters location: Landover, MD. American Stock Exchange. Common positions include: Management Trainee. Principal educational background sought: Business Administration. Company benefits include: medical, dental, and life insurance; pension plan; tuition assistance; disability coverage; employee discounts; savings plan.

Maryland

MARS SUPER MARKETS INC.
7183 Holabird Avenue
Baltimore MD 21222
301/282-2100
Contact Randall J. Schults, Director of Human Resources. Operates retail grocery stores. Corporate headquarters location. Common positions include: Accountant; Advertising Worker; Credit Manager; Management Trainee; Personnel & Labor Relations Specialist; Purchasing Agent. Principal educational backgrounds sought: Accounting; Business Administration; Computer Science. Company benefits include: medical insurance; dental insurance; pension plan; life insurance; tuition assistance; disability coverage. Corporate headquarters location.

TESTING ONE TWO THREE COMPANY
3301 Annapolis Road
Baltimore MD 21230
301/355-9400
Contact Mr. Zentgraf, Personnel Manager. Area management offices for the major national supermarket chain. Nationally, company maintains more than 1,000 supermarkets and manufacturing plants throughout the country. Corporate headquarters location: Montvale, NJ.

Northern Virginia

SOUTHLAND CORPORATION/
SEVEN-ELEVEN FOOD STORES
5300 Shawnee Road
Alexandria VA 22312
703/354-2711
Contact Otis Peaks, Divisional Personnel Director. Metropolitan Washington administrative offices for one of the largest operators and franchisors of convenience stores, doing business principally under the name 7-Eleven. Company is also a major processor of dairy products, distributed nationally under 11 regional brand names. Operates more than 6,800 7-Eleven stores worldwide, as well as numerous other food and sandwich stores, auto parts stores, and self-service gasoline outlets, and numerous processing and distribution centers. Corporate headquarters location: Dallas, TX. New York Stock Exchange.

GENERAL MERCHANDISE/TRADE

For more information on merchandise trade opportunities in Greater Washington, look for the following professional organization in Chapter 8, beginning on page 265:

National Retail Merchants Association

District of Columbia

CASUAL CORNER
1017 Connecticut Avenue NW
Washington DC 20036
202/659-8344
Contact Jean Cannon, District Manager. Area management offices for a chain of specialized retail clothing stores.

GARFINCKEL'S
1401 F Street NW
Washington DC 20004
202/628-7730
Contact Director of Personnel. Operates 10 retail specialty stores in Washington, DC metropolitan area and national catalog business. Products include men's, women's and children's clothing, accessories, and home furnishings gift merchandise. Common job positions include: Buyer; Department Manager; Management Trainee; Assistant Buyer. Principal educational backgrounds sought: Business Administration; Liberal Arts; Marketing. Company benefits include: medical insurance; dental insurance; pension plan; life insurance; disability coverage; profit sharing; employee discounts. Corporate headquarters location. Operations at this facility include: divisional headquarters.

WAXIE MAXIE'S
5772 2nd Street NE
Washington DC 20011
202/269-6260
Contact David B. Blaine, Vice President/General Manager. A record, tape, and compact disc retailer. Stores are located throughout Maryland and Virginia, in malls and high traffic strip shopping centers. Corporate headquarters location. Common positions include: Advertising Worker; Blue-Collar Worker Supervisor; Administrative Assistant. Principal educational backgrounds sought: Art/Design; Marketing. Company benefits include: medical insurance; dental insurance; life insurance; disability coverage; paid vacation; employee discounts.

Maryland

W. BELL & COMPANY INC.
12401 Twinbrook Parkway
Rockville MD 20852
301/468-5600
Contact Linda Nahin, Personnel Director. A discount catalog store, offering a wide range of general merchandise to the public. Operates 23 showrooms in the metropolitan areas of Washington D.C., Baltimore MD, Chicago IL, and Houston TX. Common positions include: Accountant; Advertising Worker; Buyer; Comupter Programmer; Branch manager; Department Manager; Management Trainee; Personnel Specialist; Systems Analyst. Principal educational backgrounds sought: Accounting; Business Administration; Computer Science; Finance; Management; Merchandising. Company benefits include: medical, dental and life insurance; tuition assistance; disability coverage; profit sharing; employee discounts. Corporate headquarters location. Operations at this facility include: administration; sales.

CROWN BOOKS
3300 75th Avenue
Landover MD 20785
301/731-1200
Contact Jose Gonzalez, Vice President. One of the largest bookstore chains in the United States, offering a full range of titles at discount prices at all locations. One of the largest bookstore chains in metropolitan Washington, as well as with more than 56 retail locations. Significant retail presence in Southern and Northern California, Seattle, WA; metropolitan Chicago, IL; and Houston, TX. A total of 229 locations in the various areas. A subsidiary of Dart Group. Common positions include: Branch Manager; Management Trainee. Company benefits include: medical insurance; dental insurance; life insurance; disability coverage; savings plan; profit sharing; employee discounts; vacation; sick leave; holidays. Corporate, regional and divisional headquarters location. Operations at this facility include: administration.

DART DRUG STORES INC.
3301 Pennsy Drive
Landover MD 20785
301/772-6000
Contact Ray Green, Personnel Manager. Engaged in the operation of retail discount drug stores in the DC area, including the Maryland and Virginia suburbs, and other locations in Virginia, including Richmond, Charlottesville, and Winchester. Also operates 18 combination drugstore/home centers, Crown Book Stores, Trak Auto Stores, and Total Plus Discount Stores. Corporate headquarters location.

DISTRICT PHOTO INC.
10619 Baltimore Avenue
Beltsville MD 20705
301/937-5300
Contact Timothy Bieber, Personnel Administrator. Engaged in the retail sale of photographic equipment and supplies. Also provides amateur photofinishing services.

GREENBELT COOPERATIVE INC.
8406 Greenwood Place
Savage MD 20763
301/953-2050
Contact Director/Human Resources. Operates furniture stores, and imports a variety of products. Common positions include: Accountant; Advertising Worker; Customer Service Representative; Sales Representative; Systems Analyst. Principal educational backgrounds sought: Art/Design; Business Administration; Marketing. Company benefits include: medical, dental and life insurance; pension plan; tuition assistance; disability coverage; profit sharing; employee discounts; savings plan. Corporate, regional, divisional headquarters location. Operations at this facility include: administration; service.

HAHN STORES
7600 Jefferson Avenue
Landover MD 20785
301/322-4550
Contact Gina Wilkinson, Controller. Area administrative offices for a chain of full-service shoe stores.

LUSKIN'S INC.
7540 Washington Boulevard
Baltimore MD 21227
301/621-1600

Contact Frank Kegel, Personnel Director. Multiple area locations, including Washington, DC, Baltimore, and northern Virginia. Engaged in the retail sale of televisions, appliances, audio equipment, and similar products. Corporate headquarters location.

MERRY GO ROUND ENTERPRISES INC.
3300 Fashion Way
Joppa MD 21085
301/538-1000
Contact Personnel Department. A national retail clothing firm, trading under DJ's, Dejaiz, Attivo, Merry Go Round, and Cignal, with stores coast to coast. Common positions include: all levels of Retail Management; Buyer (occasionally); Management Trainee; Sales Representative; Cashier. Principal educational backgrounds sought: Management; General Academic or College Degree. Company benefits include (for full time only) : medical insurance; pension plan; life insurance; employee discounts; savings plan. Corporate headquarters are located in Harford County MD. Operations at this facility include: regional and divisional headquarters; distribution center; administration.

MONTGOMERY WARD & COMPANY
11160 Veirs Mill Road
Wheaton MD 20902
301/468-5206
Contact Carole Rhinevault, District Personnel Manager. A nationwide retail mass merchandiser offering a broad range of merchandise at each store. Common positions include: Customer Service Representative; Department, General, and Operations/Production Managers; Management Trainee; Personnel & Labor Relations Specialist; Sales Representative; Commission Salesperson; Business Manager. Principal educational backgrounds sought: Accounting; Business Administration; Marketing; Personnel & Labor Relations. Company benefits include: medical, dental and life insurance; employee discounts; savings plan; disability coverage; vacation; personal days. Corporate headquarters location: Chicago, IL. Operations at this facility include: regional headquarters; administration; sales. New York Stock Exchange.

SAKS FIFTH AVENUE
5555 Wisconsin Avenue
Chevy Chase MD 20815
301/657-9000
Contact Ms. Chris McGuiness, Personnel Director. A fashion-forward department store chain with branches in 30 United States cities. Stores emphasize soft-good products, particularly apparel for men, women, and children. Stores emphasize high-quality fashion items, with subsidiary companies operating a catalogue operation and a corporate gift service. Nationally, company is a subsidiary of Gimbel Brothers, Inc., but is operated autonomously with respect to operations, personnel, merchandising, purchasing, and other areas. Corporate headquarters location: New York NY.

SCHWARTZ BROS. INC.
4901 Forbes Boulevard
Lanham MD 20706
301/459-8000
Contact Adele Draiman, Personnel Director. A major East Coast wholesaler of pre-recorded video movies, compact discs, pre-recorded audio products and related accessories. Common positions include: Accountant; Advertising Worker; Buyer; Commercial Artist; Computer Programmer; Credit Manager; Customer Service Representative; Branch Manager; Department Manager; General Manager; Operations/Production Manager; Marketing Specialist; Personnel & Labor Relations Specialist; Editor of Publications; Sales Representative; Warehouse Worker; Graphic Artist; Press Operator. Principal educational backgrounds sought: Accounting; Art/Design; Business Administration; Communications; Computer Science; Finance; Marketing. Company benefits include:

medical, dental, and life insurance; profit sharing; employee discounts; savings plan. Corporate headquarters location. Operations at this facility include: administration; service; sales. NASDAQ.

SEARS, ROEBUCK & COMPANY
10301 Westlake Drive
Bethesda MD 20817
301/469-4000
Contact Personnel Manager. One of the world's largest retailers with subsidiaries engaged in insurance (Allstate Insurance Companies), real estate (Coldwell Banker), and securities brokerage activities (Dean Witter Reynolds). Operates more than 850 retail stores and 2,778 sales offices and other facilities. The company employs approximately 390,000 people worldwide, including part-time employees. Corporate headquarters location: Chicago, IL. New York Stock Exchange.

STIDHAM TIRE COMPANY
3900 Whitetire Road
Landover MD 20785
301/322-3200
Contact Personnel Department. Engaged in retail and wholesale tire sales at 15 area locations. Corporate headquarters location.

ZAYRE CORPORATION
7706 Old Marlboro Pike
Forrestville MD 20747
301/736-6062
Contact Metro Washington Manager. Multiple area locations, including Prince George's and Montgomery counties, MD, and Fairfax, VA. Regional offices for the nationwide general merchandise retailer. Nationally, company maintains and operates more than 250 general merchandise stores under the name "Zayre."

Northern Virginia

KAY JEWELERS INC.
320 King Street
Alexandria VA 22314
703/683-3800
Contact Eric Mayer, Divisional Vice-President/Personnel. Operates the second largest retail jewelry store chain in the United States. Corporate headquarters location. Common positions include: Management Trainee; Career Development program leading to Store Manager Position. Principal educational backgrounds sought: Business Administration; Liberal Arts; Marketing. Company benefits include: medical insurance; dental insurance; pension plan; life insurance; tuition assistance; disability coverage; 401K plan; employee discounts; savings plan. New York Stock Exchange.

LORD & TAYLOR
6211 Leesburg Pike
Falls Church VA 22044
703/536-5000
Contact Denise Warner, Personnel Director. A full-line department store carrying high-quality clothing, accessories, home furnishings, and many other retail items. Stores in many major United States metropolitan areas. A subsidiary of May Department Stores Company (New York, NY). Corporate headquarters location: New York, NY.

T.H. MANDY DIVISION OF U.S. SHOE CORP.

P.O. Box 1685
Merrifield VA 22116
703/698-8909

Contact Human Resources Manager. Washington area based women's specialty retailer with stores in four major metropolitan areas. Common positions include: Accountant; Management Trainee; Assistant Store Manager; Sales Associates. Company benefits include: medical insurance; dental insurance; life insurance; disability coverage; profit sharing; employee discounts. Corporate headquarters location. A subsidiary of U.S. Shoe Corporation. Operations at this facility include: divisional headquarters; administration; sales. New York Stock Exchange.

PEEBLES DEPARTMENT STORES

1 Peebles Street
South Hill VA 23970
804/447-7671

Contact Tim Moyer, Assistant Director of Human Resources. Operates a department store chain, selling moderate to better merchandise. Stores are located in South Carolina, North Carolina, Virginia, Maryland, Delaware, Tennessee, and Kentucky. Corporate headquarters location. Common positions include: Management Trainee (assignments include all seven states). Principal educational backgrounds sought: Business Administration; Liberal Arts; Marketing. Company benefits include: medical and dental insurance; pension plan; life insurance; tuition assistance; disability coverage; employee discounts. Corporate headquarters location. Operations at this facility include: regional headquarters.

GOVERNMENT-RELATED

District of Columbia

FEDERAL BUREAU OF INVESTIGATION

10th Street and Pennsylvania Avenue NW
Washington DC 20535
202/324-3000

Contact David Rarity, Personnel Officer. Central headquarters of the national law enforcement agency.

FEDERAL RESERVE SYSTEM/
BOARD OF GOVERNORS

20th Street and Constitution Avenue NW
Washington DC 20551
202/452-3000

Contact David Shannon, Director of Personnel. Governing office of the Federal Reserve System.

FEDERAL TRADE COMMISSION

6th & Pennsylvania Avenue NW, Room 151
Washington DC 20580
202/326-2020

Contact Larry Tabachnick, Assistant Director for Recruitment. A Federal Government regulatory agency which includes the Bureau of Consumer Protection, Bureau of Competition, and Bureau of Economics. The Federal Trade Commission was created in 1914 to protect the general public (consumers and business) against anticompetitive behavior and deceptive and unfair practices. Headquarters location. Common positions include: Attorney; Economist; and Secretaries. Principal educational background sought: Law. Company benefits include: medical insurance; life insurance; Retirement and Thrift Savings Plan.

INTERNATIONAL MONETARY FUND
Recruitment Division
700 19th Street NW
Washington DC 20431
202/623-7000
Contact Peter Swain, Division Chief. Washington office of the international lending agency, primarily responsible for lending to Third World nations.

METROPOLITAN WASHINGTON
COUNCIL OF GOVERNMENTS
1875 Eye Street NW, Suite 200
Washington DC 20006
202/223-6800
Contact E. Susan Allen, Director of Personnel Services. The only area-wide governmental organization concerned with all aspects of metropolitan development. Works toward solutions of regional problems such as energy, traffic congestion, inadequate housing, air and water pollution, water supply, and land use. Also serves as the regional planning agency, including transportation planning, for metro Washington. Headquarters location.

NATIONAL ACADEMY OF SCIENCES
2101 Constitution Avenue NW
Washington DC 20418
202/334-2000
Contact Personnel Department. The Academy maintains a list of professional vacancies which may be viewed at the employment office. A federally-chartered private corporation of approximately 1,225 members, whose primary aim is to provide an independent source of counsel to the government on matters of science and technology. Academy members are elected. The Academy's research is performed by the National Research Council (NRC). The National Academy operates two fully-autonomous subsidiaries: The National Academy of Engineering, whose 685 members deal with engineering-related studies and national needs; and The Institute of Medicine, whose 300 members examine policy matters pertaining to the public health, with emphasis on providing adequate health services for all sectors of society. Headquarters location.

POSTAL RATE COMMISSION
1333 H Street NW, Suite 300
Washington DC 20268-0001
202/789-6800
Contact Cyril J. Pittack, Personnel Director. Central office of the federal government agency responsible for overseeing U.S. postal rates.

U.S. CHAMBER OF COMMERCE
1615 H Street NW
Washington DC 20062
202/659-6000
Contact Paul G. Osborne, Manager, Employment and Training. Headquarters offices for the nationwide business issues organization, which provides information, opinion, and analysis on legislation, regulation, and programs important to business. Manages department studying more than 50 legislative and regulatory issues of interest to the business community. Chamber of Commerce federation programs and activities encompass more than 30 separate departments, including consulting programs for Chamber members, consumer affairs programs, political action programs, operations programs, informational programs on areas such as regulatory issues or election and campaign laws,

research activities for business, and many others. Also operates a separate communications area, which manages a publishing division producing two Chamber magazines, a broadcasting division, a media relations division, and a special projects division. Common positions include: Accountant; Administrator; Advertising Worker; Attorney; Computer Programmer; Customer Service Representative; Economist; Financial Analyst; Personnel & Labor Relations Specialist; Reporter/Editor; Sales Representative; Systems Analyst. Among educational backgrounds sought are: Accounting; Business Administration; Communications; Computer Science; Finance; Liberal Arts; Marketing. Company benefits include: medical insurance; pension plan; life insurance; tuition assistance; disability coverage; savings plan. Corporate and regional headquarters location. Operations at this facility include: administration.

U.S. GENERAL ACCOUNTING OFFICE
National Recruitment Program
441 G Street NW, Room 4043
Washington DC 20548
202/275-3147
Contact Dinah R. Griggsby, College Relations Office. The independent, nonpolitical federal agency responsible for assisting in congressional oversight of the executive branch of the federal government. Basic mission is to investigate all matters relating to the receipt, disbursement, and application of public funds and make recommendations leading to greater economy and efficiency in public expenditure. Headquarters location. Common positions include: Accountant; Attorney; Computer Scientist; Economist; GAO Evaluator. Principal educational backgrounds sought: Accounting; Business Administration; Computer Science; Economics; Finance; Public Administration. Benefits include: medical insurance; pension plan; life insurance.

U.S. NUCLEAR REGULATORY COMMISSION
Washington DC 20555
301/492-7000
Contact Division of Organization of Personnel. Personnel Resources and Employment Programs Branch. Headquarters location of the national commission responsible for regulation of the nuclear power industry.

U.S. PATENT AND TRADEMARK OFFICE
One Crystal Park One Suite 600
Washington DC 20231
800/327-2909, 703/557-3631
Contact Doris Mouser, Manager/College Relations. Reviews applications for patents and makes legal determinations concerning the granting of patents. Employs more than 1,000 people, primarily scientists and engineers. Corporate headquarters location: Arlington, VA. Common positions include: Architect; Biochemist; Biologist; Chemist; Aerospace Engineer; Biomedical Engineer; Ceramics Engineer; Chemical Engineer; Electrical Engineer; Mechanical Engineer; Metallurgical Engineer; Mining Engineer; Petroleum Engineer; Food Technologist; Industrial Designer; Physist. Principal educational backgroundws sought: Art/Design (Industrial Design, Architecture or Product Design); Biology; Chemistry; Computer Science; Engineering; Physics. Company benefits include: medical, dental, and life insurance; pension plan; tuition assistance; disability coverage; profit sharing. Corporate headquarters location. Parent organization: Department of Commerce of the U.S. Government.

U.S. POSTAL SERVICE
475 L'Enfant Plaza SW
Washington DC 20260-4261
202/268-2000
Contact Headquarters Personnel Division. Resumes should be included. Provides complete range of mail pick-up and delivery services throughout the country and internationally. Also acts as a center for passport acceptance, government program applications, government registration activities, and other

activities. Employs more than 800,000 people nationwide. Corporate headquarters location. Common positions at this facility include: Accountant; Administrator; Advertising Worker; Architect; Attorney; Biologist; Blue-Coller Working Supervisor; Buyer; Chemist; Claim Representative; Commercial Artist; Computer Programmer; Customer Service Representative; Draftsperson; Economist; Civil Engineer; Electrical Engineer; Industrial Engineer; Mechanical Engineer; Metallurgical Engineer; Financial Analyst; Industral Designer; Branch Manager; Department Manager; General Manager; Management Trainee; Operation/Production Manager; Marketing Specialist; Personnel & Labor Relations Specialist; Public Relations Worker; Purchasing Agent; Quality Control Supervisor; Reporter/Editor; Sales Representative; Statistician; Systems Analyst; Technical Writer/Editor; Transportation and Traffic Specialist. Principal educational backgrounds sought: Business Administration; Computer Science; Economics; Engineering. Company benefits: medical insurance; dental insurance; pension plan; life insurance; tuition assistance; disability coverage; savings plan. Corporate headquarters location. Operations at this facility include: administration.

WORLD BANK AND IFC
1818 H Street NW
Washington DC 20433
202/477-1234
Contact William Cosgrove, Vice President of Personnel. A major international agency responsible for assisting with the development policies of Third World countries.

Northern Virginia

DEFENSE INTELLIGENCE AGENCY/
CIVILIAN STAFFING OPERATIONS DIVISION
3100 Clarendon Boulevard
Arlington VA 22201
703/284-1321
Contact Angela C. Yancey, Chief, Recruitment Program. The Defense Intelligence Agency is a major intelligence organization within the Department of Defense. Collects, analyzes, interprets, and disseminates foreign military intelligence. DIA products are used by executive, legislative, and military leaders in the formulation and execution of national security policies. Common positions include: Geographer. Principal educational backgrounds sought: Computer Sciences; Area Studies; International Relations.

HEALTH CARE & PHAMACEUTICALS: PRODUCTS/SERVICES

For more information on health care opportunities in Greater Washington, look for the following professional and trade organizations in Chapter 8, beginning on page 265:

American Academy of Family Physicians
American Academy of Physician Assistants
American Association for Clinical Chemistry
American College of Healthcare Executives
American Dental Association
American Health Care Association
American Medical Association
American Occupational Therapy Association
American Pharmaceutical Association

American Physical Therapy Association
American Society for Biochemistry and Molecular Biology
American Society of Hospital Pharmacists
American Veterinary Medical Association
Cardiovascular Credentialing International
Medical Group Management Association
National Health Council
National Medical Association

District of Columbia

AMERICAN HEALTHCARE ASSOCIATION
1201 L Street, NW
Washington DC 20005
202/842-4444
Contact Sheila McFarland, Personnel Manager. A national association of nursing homes and related long term care facilities. Common positions include: Accountant; Administrator; Advertising Worker; Customer Service Representative; Economist; Department Manager; Marketing Specialist; Personnel & Labor Relations Specialist; Public Relations Worker; Sales Representative; Technical Writer/Editor; Lobbyists. Principal educational backgrounds sought: Business Administration; Finance; Nursing. Company benefits include: medical, dental and life insurance; pension plan; disability coverage. Corporate headquarters location. Operations at this facility include: aministration; service; sales.

GROUP HEALTH ASSOCIATION
4301 Connecticut Avenue
Washington DC 20008
202/364-2000
Contact Personnel Director. A major Washington health maintenance organization.

VISITING NURSE ASSOCIATION OF WASHINGTON DC
5151 Wisconsin Avenue NW
Suite 400
Washington DC 20016
202/686-2862
Contact Donna L. Shea, Employment Manager. Several area locations. A home health care organization providing skilled nursing care to patients in their homes. Serves the District of Columbia, and Montgomery and Prince George's counties in Maryland. Corporate headquarters location. Common positions include: Accountant; Administrator; Claim Representative; Personnel & Labor Relations Specialist; Public Relations Worker; Purchasing Agent; Registered Nurse. Principal educational background sought: Nursing. Company benefits include: medical insurance; dental insurance; pension plan; life insurance; tuition assistance; disability coverage; savings plan.

Maryland

BARRE-NATIONAL INC.
7205 Windsor Boulevard
Baltimore MD 21207
301/298-1000
Contact Personnel Department. One of the nation's largest manufacturers of liquid generic pharmaceuticals, employing more than 500 people. A quality-oriented, non-research generic producer,

specializing in liquids, with a growing product line. Common positions include: Buyer; Chemist; Customer Service Representative; Quality Control Supervisor; Packaging Analyst/ Supervisor.

BAXTER HEALTHCARE CORPORATION
9299 Washington Boulevard
Savage MD 20763
301/725-2800
Contact Jan Jones, Human Resources Manager. Nationally, company develops, manufactures, and markets a wide range of health-care products, systems and services. It offers 120,000 products to health care providers in more thasn 100 countries. Operations include: manufacturing. Corporate headquarters location: Deerfield, IL. New York Stock Exchange. Common positions include: Accountant; Blue-Collar Worker Supervisor; Buyer; Computer Programmer; Draftsperson; Electrical Engineer; Industrial Engineer; Mechanical Engineer; Operations/Production Manager; Personnel Specialist; Quality Control Supervisor; Systems Analyst. Principal educational backgrounds sought: Accounting; Business Administration; Computer Science; Engineering; Finance. Company benefits include: medical insurance; dental insurance; life insurance; tuition assistance; disability coverage; pension plan; savings plan; credit union.

HYNSON, WESTCOTT & DUNNING
250 Schilling Circle
Cockeysville MD 21030
301/771-0100
Contact Human Resources. Manufactures and sells pharmaceutical products and diagnostic test kits as a unit within BBL (Baltimore Biological Laboratory) Division of Becton Dickinson and Company (Paramus, NJ). Operations include: manufacturing; research/development; administration; service; sales. Corporate headquarters location: Paramus, NJ. Common positions include: Biologist; Customer Service Representative; Department Manager; General Manager; Operations/Production Manager; Marketing Specialist; Personnel & Labor Relations Specialist; Purchasing Agent; Quality Control Supervisor; Sales Representative. Principal educational backgrounds sought: Biology; Marketing. Company benefits include: medical insurance; dental insurance; pension plan; life insurance; tuition assistance; disability coverage; employee discounts; savings plan.

MANOR CARE INC.
10750 Columbia Pike
Silver Springs MD 20901
Contact Vice President/Human Resources. Owns, leases, and manages more than 150 health care facilities, with over 19,000 nursing center and hospital beds; and, through Quality Inns subsidiaries, owns, leases, manages and franchises 1,100 inns, containing over 135,000 rooms. Overall, company has more than 20,000 employees in 48 states, Canada, Mexico, Europe and Asia. Common positions include: Accountant; Administrator; Claim Representative; Commercial Artist; Computer Programmer; Dietician; Management Trainee; Personnel & Labor Relations Specialist; Purchasing Agent. Company benefits include: medical, dental, and life insurance; pension plan; tuition assistance; disability coverage; profit sharing; employee discounts; savings plan. Corporate headquarters location. Operations at this facility include: regional headquarters; divisional headquarters; administration; service. New York Stock Exchange.

Northern Virginia

FLOW GENERAL INC.
FLOW LABORATORIES
7655 Old Springhouse Road
McLean VA 22102
703/893-5915

Contact Director of Corporate Affairs. Designs, manufactures and markets biomedical and communications testing products, as well as performing a variety of technological research and analysis services. Operates in two major divisions: Biomedical and Applied Sciences. Biomedical products are used in medical, veterinary and biological research, vaccine production and testing and clinical analysis. Other major subsidiaries are General Research Corporation (research and analysis services), and Moseley Associates (designs manufactures and sells a line of broadcasting and radio communications systems), as well as other minor subsidiaries. Corporate headquarters location. New York Stock Exchange.

HOTEL AND RESTAURANT RELATED

For more information on hotel and restaurant opportunities in Greater Washington, look for the following professional and trade organizations in Chapter 8, beginning on page 265:

The American Hotel and Motel Association
Council on Hotel, Restaurant and Institutional Education
The Education Foundation of the National Restaurant Association

District of Columbia

DUPONT PLAZA HOTEL
1500 New Hampshire Avenue NW
Washington DC 20036
202/483-6000
Contact Mr. Murdoch, General Manager. A major downtown hotel facility, with 314 rooms, banquet facilities, and a restaurant.

INTERNATIONAL HOTEL
Massachusetts & Vermont Avenues NW
Washington DC 20005
202/842-1300
Contact Najiba Hashimi, Personnel Director. Operates a full service hotel facility, with 300 rooms and complete dining facilities.

SHERATON/CARLTON HOTEL
923 16th Street NW
Washington DC 20006
202/638-2626
Contact Vivian Grant, Personnel Director. A major downtown hotel facility, with 250 rooms and complete dining facilities. Second area hotel (Sheraton/Silver Spring, 8727 Colesville Road, Silver Spring MD 20910; 301/589-5200) nearby. Part of the international hotel chain, offering hotel, dining, convention, and meeting facilities at major metropolitan locations throughout the country. Corporate headquarters location: Boston, MA. Common positions include: Accountant; Administrator; Computer Programmer; Credit Manager; Customer Service Representative; Electrical Engineer; Mechanical Engineer; Hotel Manager/Assistant Manager; Department Manager; General Manager; Management Trainee; Personnel & Labor Relations Specialist; Public Relations Worker; Purchasing Agent; Sales Representative; Systems Analyst. Principal educational backgrounds sought: Accounting; Business Administration; Communications; Computer Science; Economics; Engineering; Finance; Liberal Arts;

Marketing; Mathematics. Company benefits include: medical, dental, and life insurance; pension plan; tuition assistance; disability coverage; profit sharing; employee discounts; savings plan.

Maryland

ARA SERVICES INC.
11103 Pepper Road
Hunt Valley MD 21031
215/687-8600
Contact Marge Gulyas, Manager/Human Resources. Regional offices for Business Dining Services operating in the areas of Corporate Dining amd Training Centers. Common positions include: Food Technologist; Hotel Manager/Assistant Manager; General Manager; Management Trainee. Principal educational backgrounds sought: Business Administration; Marketing. Company benefits include: medical, dental and life insurance; pension plan; tuition assistance; disability coverage; profit sharing; savings plan. Corporate headquarters location: Philadelphia, PA. Operations at this facility include: regional headquarters.

Northern Virginia

McDONALD'S CORPORATION
3015 Williams Drive
Fairfax VA 22031
703/698-4000
Contact Cathy Salvano, Personnel Director. Regional offices for the worldwide developer, operator, franchisor, and servicer of a system of restaurants which process, package, and sell a limited menu of fast foods. Overall, company is one of the largest restaurant chains, and the largest food service organization in the world, operating 6,000 McDonald's restaurants in all 50 states and in 26 foreign countries. Corporate headquarters location: Oak Brook, IL. New York Stock Exchange.

INSURANCE

For more information on insurance opportunities in Greater Washington, look for the following professional and trade organizations in Chapter 8, beginning on page 265:

Alliance of American Insurers
American Council of Life Insurance
American Insurance Association
Insurance Information Institute
National Association of Life Underwriters
Society of Actuaries

District of Columbia

AMERICAN COUNCIL OF LIFE INSURANCE
1001 Pennsylvania Avenue NW
Washington DC 20004-2599
202/624-2366

Contact Lorraine Branson, Employment Manager. A major Washington-based trade association. Company benefits include: medical, dental, and life insurance; pension plan; tuition assistance; disability coverage.

GEICO CORPORATION
Geico Plaza
Washington DC 20076
202/986-3000

Contact Patricia Carr, Director, Employment Services. Company's primary business in writing automobile insurance for low-risk customers, such as government employees and military personnel, and homeowners insurance fot the general public. Employs 6,600. Common positions include: Accountant; Actuary; Attorney; Claim Representative; Computer Programmer; Customer Service Representative; Insurance Agent/Broker; Management Trainee; Underwriter. Principal educational backgrounds sought: Accounting; Business Adminstration; Computer Science; Liberal Arts; Marketing; Mathematics. Company benefits include: medical, dental, and life insurance; pension plan; tuition assistance; disability coverage; profit sharing; employee discounts; savings plan; 401K. Corporate headquarters location. New York Stock Exchange.

NATIONAL ASSOCIATION OF LIFE UNDERWRITERS
1922 F Street NW
Washington DC 20006
202/331-6000

Contact Samuel Bohinc, Business Manager. A trade organization representing life underwriters throughout the United States.

Maryland

GEICO CORPORATION
4520 Willard Avenue
Chevy Chase MD 20076
202/986-3904

Contact Kimberly Mulhern, Technical Recruiter. An insurance/financial services firm. Provides property and casualty insurance coverages. Common positions include: Actuary; Claim Representative; Computer Programmer; Management Trainee; Underwriter. Principal educational backgrounds sought: Business Administration; Computer Science; Liberal Arts; Marketing. Company benefits include: medical, dental, and life insurance; pension plan; tuition assistance; profit sharing; employee discounts; 401K plan; employee stock ownership plan. Corporate headquarters location. Operations at this facility include: regional headquarters; administration; service; sales. New York Stock Exchange.

Northern Virginia

ALLSTATE INSURANCE COMPANY
1850 Centennial Park Drive, Suite 400
Reston VA 22091
703/648-1600

Contact John Villard, Human Resource Manager. One of the nation's largest insurance companies; provides life, commercial, and personal property insurance. Reston office serves the company's largest region: Maryland, Virginia and the District of Columbia; with claim and sales offices throughout this territory. Common positions include: Claim Representative; Customer Service Representative; Insurance Agent/Broker; Management Trainee; Personnel Specialist; Statistician; Underwriter. Company benefits include: medical insurance; dental insurance; pension plan; life insurance; tuition assistance; disability coverage; profit sharing; flexible spending. Operations at this facility include: regional headquarters.

USLICO CORPORATION
4601 Fairfax Drive
Arlington VA 22203
703/875-3400
Contact Meg Crandall, Recruiting Manager. A leading life insurance and financial services corporation. Company benefits include: medical insurance; dental insurance; pension plan; life insurance; disability coverage; tuition assistance; employee discounts; savings plan. Corporate headquarters location. Operations at this facility include: administration. New York Stock Exchange. Common positions include: Accountant; Actuary; Administrator; Claim Representative; Computer Programmer; Customer Service Representative; Department Manager; Systems Analyst; Underwriter.

LEGAL SERVICES

For more information on legal service opportunities in Greater Washington, look for the following professional and trade organizations in Chapter 8, beginning on page 265:

American Bar Association
Association of Legal Administrators
Federal Bar Association
National Association for Law Placement
National Association of Legal Assistants
National Association of Legal Administrators
National Federation of Paralegal Associations
National Paralegal Association

District of Columbia

ARENT, FOX, KINTNER, PLOTKIN & KAHN
Washington Square
1050 Connecticut Avenue NW
Washington DC 20036
202/857-6000
Contact Personnel Manager. A major Washington-area law firm, specializing in corporate law. More than 200 attorneys on staff.

ARNOLD & PORTER
1200 New Hampshire Avenue, NW
Washington DC 20036
202/872-6700
Contact Elizabeth Respess, Recruiter. A leading Washington law firm.

COVINGTON & BURLINGTON
P.O. Box 7566
1201 Pennsylvania Avenue NW
Washington DC 20044
202/662-6000

Contact Lorraine Brown, Legal Recruitment Coordinator. A leading Washington law firm.

HOWRY & SIMON
1730 Pennsylvania Avenue NW
Washington DC 20006
202/783-0800
Contact William O'Brien, Hiring Partner. A major Washington law firm.

STEPTOE & JOHNSON
1330 Connecticut Avenue NW
Washington DC 20036
202/429-3000
Contact Rosemary Morgan, Director of Recruiting. A major Washington law firm.

MANUFACTURING: MISCELLANEOUS CONSUMER

For more information on manufacturing opportunities in Greater Washington, look for the following professional and trade organizations in Chapter 8, beginning on page 265:

National Association of Manufacturers
National Machine Tool Builders
National Screw Machine Products Association
National Tooling and Machining Association
The Tooling and Manufacturing Association

Maryland

AW INDUSTRIES
8415 Ardmore Road
Landover MD 20785
301/322-1000, ext. 250
Contact Steve Lieb, Director of Personnel. Engaged in the manufacture of "Serta" mattresses and box springs, sleep sofas, and stationary furniture; and the distribution of carpeting, tile, furniture, and electric appliances. Corporate headquarters location.

BLACK & DECKER
701 East Joppa Road
Towson MD 21204
301/583-3900
Contact Human Resources Department. Engaged in manufacturing, selling, and servicing electric, pneumatic and gasoline-powered tools, including accessories generally used in homes and home workshops, for lawn care and maintenance, in timbering, in the service and maintenance trades, and on farms.

DAVID-EDWARD LTD.
3501 Marmenco Court
Baltimore MD 21230
301/789-0700

Contact Judy Johnson, Vice President. Manufactures custom-made upholstered chairs and sofas. Corporate headquarters location.

GENERAL FURNITURE LEASING COMPANY INC.
8671 Central Avenue
Capitol Heights MD 20743
301/336-7600
Contact Brenda Brantly, Regional Manager. A furniture leasing firm, offering products for both residential and commercial use. Operates 50 offices nationwide; four in the metropolitan DC area. Common positions include: Management Trainee; Sales Representative. Principal educational backgrounds sought: Business Administration; Economics; Marketing. Company benefits: medical and life insurance; pension plan; tuition assistance; disability coverage; profit sharing; employee discounts; savings plan. Corporate headquarters located in Atlanta GA. Operations at this facility include: regional headquarters; sales.

KIRK-STIEFF COMPANY
800 Wyman Park Drive
Baltimore MD 21211
301/338-6030
Contact Personnel Office. Produces sterling silver, pewter, and plated dinnerware and decorative items. Common positions include: Accountant; Administrator; Advertising Working; Blue-Collar Worker Supervisor; Buyer; Commercial Artist; Credit Manager; Computer Programmer; Customer Service Representative; Financial Analyst; Department Manager; Operations/Production Manager; Marketing Specialist; Personnel & Labor Relations Specialist; Purchasing Agent; Quality Control Supervisor; Sales Representative; Systems Analyst; Silversmith/Skilled Precious Metal Worker. Principal educational backgrounds sought: Accounting; Art/Design; Business Administration; Communications; Computer Science; Finance; Liberal Arts; Marketing; Mathematics. Company benefits include: medical, dental, and life insurance; disability coverage; profit sharing; employee discounts; savings plan. Corporate headquarters location. Operations at this facility include: manufacturing; research/development; administration; service; sales.

LEVER BROTHERS COMPANY
5300 Holabird Avenue
Baltimore MD 21224
301/631-5000
Contact Personnel Manager. Produces a variety of soap and detergent products as a division of the major international manufacturer and distributor of soaps and cleaning products, specialty foods, toothpastes, and detergents. Operations include: manufacturing. Corporate headquarters location: New York, NY. New York Stock Exchange. Common positions include: Accountant; Blue-Collar Worker Supervisor; Buyer; Chemist; Computer Programmer; Draftsperson; Chemical Engineer; Electrical Engineer; Industrial Engineer; Mechanical Engineer; Department Manager; Personnel & Labor Relations Specialist; Purchasing Agent. Principal educational backgrounds sought: Accounting; Business Administration; Chemistry; Engineering. Company benefits include: medical insurance; dental insurance; pension plan; life insurance; tuition assistance; disability coverage; profit sharing; savings plan.

SEALY OF MARYLAND & VIRGINIA INC.
Baltimore Beltway at Exit 10
Baltimore MD 21227
301/247-1400
Contact Human Resources. Produces a complete line of nationally-distributed bedding products, including mattresses and box springs. A subsidiary of the Ohio Mattress Company, Cleveland, Ohio.

SHERWIN WILLIAMS COMPANY

2325 Hollins Ferry Road
Baltimore MD 21230
301/625-8220

Contact Personnel Director. Produces a line of paints, varnishes, lacquers, and spray paints as part of the Consumer Division of Sherwin-Williams Company (Cleveland, OH). Common positions include: Chemist; Chemical Engineer. Principal educational backgrounds sought: Chemistry; Engineering. Company benefits include: medical, dental, and life insurance; pension plan; tuition assistance; disability coverage; profit sharing; employee discounts; savings plan. Corporate headquarters location: Cleveland, OH. Parent company: Sherwin-Williams Company. Operations at this facility include: manufacturing. New York Stock Exchange.

TRAK AUTO CORPORATION

3300 75th Avenue
Landover MD 20785
301/731-1200

Contact Personnel Manager. Company sells auto parts at discount in 251 stores in the Washington, Baltimore, Richmond, Chicago and Los Angeles areas. Employs 2,168. Common positions include: Accountant; Computer Programmer; Draftsperson; Management Trainee; Systems Analyst.

THE VALSPAR CORPORATION

1401 Severn Street
Baltimore MD 21230
301/625-7200

Contact Personnel Department. Nationally, company is engaged in the manufacture and distribution of paint and coatings through Consumer Coatings, Industrial Coatings, and Special Products divisions. Consumer Coatings division manufactures and distributes a full line of latex and oil-based paints, stains, and varnishes for consumer and industrial use. Industrial Coatings division manufactures and distributes decorative and protective finishes for OEMs, as well as other specialized industrial coatings. Special Products division produces and markets resins, emulsions, colorants, and paint specialty colors. This facility produces consumer paints, industrial coatings, and synthetic resins. Corporate headquarters location: Minneapolis, MN. American Stock Exchange.

VULCAN-HART CORPORATION

3600 North Point Boulevard
Baltimore MD 21222
301/284-0660

Contact General Manager. A manufacturer of commercial cooking equipment, including gas and electric ovens, ranges, broilers, and fryers. Nationally, other facilities in Louisville, KY; St. Louis, MO; and Compton, CA. Corporate headquarters location: Louisville, KY.

Northern Virginia

BEST PRODUCTS COMPANY

2800 South Randolph Street
Arlington VA 22206
703/578-4600

Contact Personnel Department. A major retailer of jewelry, electronics, sporting goods and other hardline brand name merchandise. Common positions include: Sales; Warehouse; Management. Principal educational backgrounds sought: Business Administration; Marketing. Company benefits include: medical, dental and life insurance; pension plan; tuition assistance; disability coverage; employee discounts; savings plan. Corporate headquarters located in Richmond VA.

STIHL INC.
536 Viking Drive
Virginia Beach VA 23452
804/486-8444
Contact Brenda M. Meadors, Manager/Employment & Compensation. Manufactures world's largest-selling chain saw. Parent company is Andreas Stihl of Waiblingen, West Germany. Manufacturing plant in Virginia Beach is only United States facility. Also manufactures brushcutters, air blowers, "cut-quik" saws, and related power tools. Corporate headquarters location. Operations include: manufacturing. Common positions include: Accountant; Blue-Collar Worker Supervisor; Buyer; Computer Programmer; Draftsperson; Engineer; Industrial Engineer; Mechanical Engineer; Metallurgical Engineer; Financial Analyst; Manager; Department Manager; General Manager; Operations/Production Manager; Marketing Specialist; Personnel & Labor Relations Specialist; Quality Control Supervisor; Sales Representative; Plastics Injection Molding Engineer. Principal educational backgrounds sought: Accounting; Business Administration; Computer Science; Engineering; Finance; Marketing; Tool & Die; Metallurgy; Plastics Injection Molding. Company benefits include: medical insurance; dental insurance; pension plan; life insurance; tuition assistance; disability coverage; profit sharing; employee discounts; 401 K plan; Christmas bonus.

MANUFACTURING: MISCELLANEOUS INDUSTRIAL

District of Columbia

FAIRCHILD INDUSTRIES INC.
Washington-Dulles International Airport
300 West Service Road
P.O. Box 10803
Chantilly VA 22021-9998
703/478-5899
Contact Thomas Haines, Manager, Staffing & Development. Operates nationwide in four business groups: Communications, Electronics and Space, which includes Fairchild Communications & Electronics Company (military avionics and telecommunications equipment), Fairchild Space Company (developer and builder of products and systems for space), Fairchild Control Systems Company (manufacturer of fluid systems hardware and environmental controls for aerospace applications); Commercial Aviation, which includes Fairchild Aircraft Corporation (manufactures executive and commuter aircraft), Commercial/Industrial, which consists of Voi-Shan/Screwcorp and Harco (aerospace fasteners), Greer Hydraulics (fluid energy), Natter Manufacturing (computer cabinetry), Tubing Seal Cap (doorknobs), and Fairchild Industrial Products Company (builder of pneumatic, electropneumatic, and mechanical power controls and systems). Corporate headquarters location. New York Stock Exchange. Common positions include: Accountant; Administrator; Attorney; Financial Analyst; Department Manager; Operations/Production Manager; Personnel & Labor Relations Specialist; Public Relations Worker; Principal educational backgrounds sought: Accounting; Business Administration; Communications; Computer Science; Economics; Engineering; Finance; Liberal Arts. Company benefits include: medical, dental and life insurance; pension plan; tuition assistance; disability coverage; profit sharing; savings plan.

Maryland

AIRFLOW COMPANY
295 Bailes Lane
Frederick MD 21701
301/695-6500
Contact Personnel Manager. Produces a line of specialized air conditioners and dehumidifying equipment and systems.

BALTIMORE AIRCOIL COMPANY
P.O. Box 7322
Baltimore MD 21227
301/799-6204
Contact Shirley Butler, Supv., Personnel Admin. & Employment. A specialist in the design and manufacture of evaporative cooling equipment, producing cooling towers, evaporative condensors, and closed circuit cooling systems at eleven manufacturing plants worldwide. The company's air conditioning products are used in modern heating, ventilating, and air conditioning systems. Refrigeration applications include equipment used in food processing plants, frozen food operations, cold storage warehouses, bottling plants, wineries, breweries, and dairies, and other uses. The company's industrial cooling equipment includes evaporative cooling equipment used by many industries for process and equipment cooling, including steel mills, foundries, chemical processing, power generation, and many others. These products are also used for water conservation. An affiliate, BAC-Pritchard, is a leading manufacturer of field-erected cooling towers (this address). Corporate headquarters location. Common positions include Accountant; Blue-Collar Worker Supervisor; Computer Programmer; Credit Manager; Customer Service Represenative; Draftsperson; Chemical Engineer; Civil Engineer; Industrial Engineer; Mechanical Engineer; Personnel & Labor Relations Specialist; Programmer/Analyst. Principal educational backgrounds sought: Accounting; Business Administration; Computer Science; Engineering. Company benefits include: medical insurance; dental insurance; pension plan; life insurance; tuition assistance; disability coverage. Corporate headquarters location. Parent Company is Amsted Industries, Chicago, IL. Operations at this facility include: manufacturing; corporate headquarters. Company is employee owned.

C.R. DANIELS INC.
3451 Ellicott Center Drive
Ellicott City MD 21043
301/461-2100
Contact John E. Frangos, V. P. of Manufacturing & Engineering. Produces a wide range of aviation accessory products, including seats, nets, and cushions; material handling containers; industrial fabrics and other premium fabric products; canvas and synthetic tarpaulins; and conveyor and elevator belting. Operations include: manufacturing; administration; service; sales. Corporate headquarters location. Common positions include: Accountant; Buyer; Credit Manager; Draftsperson; Industrial Engineer; Mechanical Engineer; Industrial Designer; Department Manager; Quality Control Supervisor. Principal educational backgrounds sought: Business Administration; Engineering.

DAVIS & HEMPHILL INC.
5710 Furnance Avenue
Elkridge MD 21227
301/796-2290
Contact Mr. Francis Duncan, Controller. Manufactures a variety of screw machine products.

ELLICOTT MACHINE CORPORATION
1611 Bush Street
Baltimore MD 21230
301/837-7900

Contact Personnel Director. Produces dredges, dredging machinery, and related equipment. A subsidiary of McConway & Torley Corporation (Pittsburgh, PA), a major steel producer. Corporate headquarters location.

EVAPCO INC.
3120 Frederick Avenue
Baltimore MD 21229
301/945-3400
Contact Bill Gardner, Office Manager. Produces evaporative condensers, closed-circuit coolers, and cooling towers. Corporate headquarters location.

KOPPERS COMPANY/
POWER TRANSMISSION DIVISION
P.O. Box 626
Baltimore MD 21203
301/547-7400
Contact Edward Gerace, Supervisor of Employment. Produces power transmission equipment (couplings), and adjustable-speed transmission drives. Nationally, company is a diversified manufacturer offering specialized engineering and construction capabilities to various industries. Other operations serve the iron and steel industries in the design and construction of basic steel-making facilities. The company also manufactures road paving, roofing, railroad tie, and lumber products; and manufactures machinery for the mining, paper and packaging, and agriculture industries. Two facilities located in Baltimore. Corporate headquarters location: Pittsburgh, PA. New York Stock Exchange.

MEMTEC AMERICA
2033 Greenspring Road
Timonium MD 21093
301/252-0800
Contact Louis Reymann, Corporate Personnel Manager. Produces filters, filtration equipment, strainers, and related items, as well as operating related research facilities. Common positions at this facility include: Chemist; Industrial Engineer; Mechanical Engineer; Metallurgical Engineer; Sales Representative; Principal educational backgrounds sought include: Engineering.

MRC CORPORATION
11212 McCormick Road
Hunt Valley MD 21031
301/771-1300
Contact Mrs. Rose Mary Marovski, Personnel Director. Produces materials handling equipment, control equipment and systems, and automation equipment. A division of Chamberlain Manufacturing Corporation. Corporate headquarters location.

MURRAY CORPORATION
Hunt Valley Industrial Park
260 Schilling Circle
Cockeysville MD 21030
301/771-0380
Contact John Martin, Personnel Department. Produces a variety of automotive and industrial products, including hose, clamps, heating and air conditioning parts, and couplings.

PACIFIC SCIENTIFIC COMPANY
2431 Linden Lane
Silver Springs MD 20910
301/495-7000

Contact Personnel Department. A manufacturer of particle monitoring instrumentation used to size and count particles in air, liquids, and gases. Primary markets (both domestic and international) are pharmaceutical, semiconductor, fluid power and aerospace industries. Common positions include: Accountant; Administrator; Buyer; Chemist; Computer Programmer; Credit Manager; Customer Service Representative; Draftsperson; Electrical Engineer; Industrial Engineer; Department Manager; Operations/Production Manager; Marketing Specialist; Personnel & Labor Relations Specialist; Sales Representative; Technical Writer/Editor; Transportation & Traffic Specialist. Principal educational backgrounds sought: Accounting; Business Administration; Chemistry; Computer Science; Engineering; Finance; Liberal Arts; Marketing; Mathematics; Physics. Company benefits include: medical insurance; dental insurance; pension plan; life insurance; tuition assistance; disability coverage; profit sharing; employee discounts; savings plan. Operations at this facility include: manufacturing; research/development; administration; service; sales. Divisional headquarters location. Corporate headquarters location: Anaheim, CA. Parent company is Pacific Scientific. New York Stock Exchange.

PERMEA/KEMP MANUFACTURING
7280 Baltimore-Annapolis Boulevard
Glen Burnie MD 21061
301/761-5100

Contact Leonard Rauch, Human Resources Specialist. Produces a range of heating equipment, gas generators, and dessicant dryers. Operations include: manufacturing; research/development; administration; service; sales. Corporate headquarters location. Common positions include: Accountant; Administrator; Advertising Worker; Buyer; Computer Programmer; Credit Manager; Customer Service Representative; Draftsperson; Engineer; Chemical Engineer; Electrical Engineer; Industrial Engineer; Mechanical Engineer; Metallurgical Engineer; Marketing Specialist; Personnel & Labor Relations Specialist; Purchasing Agent; Quality Control Supervisor; Reporter/Editor; Sales Representative; Systems Analyst; Transportation & Traffic Specialist. Principal educational backgrounds sought: Accounting; Business Administration; Computer Science; Engineering; Marketing. Company benefits include: medical insurance; dental insurance; pension plan; life insurance; tuition assistance; disability coverage; savings plan.

PULSE INC.
12101 Indian Creek Court
Beltsville MD 20707
301/470-6000

Contact Susan Smith, Personnel Assistant. Engaged in the design, development, and manufacture of machine tools and special machinery; the design, development, and manufacture of aerospace prototypes; and the production of related technical publications.

Northern Virginia

HALIFAX ENGINEERING INC.
P.O. Box 11904
Alexandria VA 22312
703/750-2202

Contact Douglas Randles, Personnel Director. Technical Services Corporation which offers a broad range of professional, technical, and support services which fall into five general areas: Communications/Electronics Installation; Computer Hardware Maintenance; Facilities Operations and Maintenance; Security Services; and Planning, Engineering, and Logistics. Corporate headquarters location. Operations include: service. American Stock Exchange. Common positions include: Electrical Engineer; Mechanical Engineer; Financial Analyst; Manager; Operations/Production Manager; Quality Control Supervisor; Electronic Technician; Computer Technician; Skilled Tradesperson. Principal educational backgrounds sought: Communications; Computer Science; Engineering. Company benefits include: medical insurance; dental insurance; pension plan; life insurance; tuition assistance; disability coverage; profit sharing. Corporate headquarters location. Operations at this facility include: divisional headquarters; administration. American Stock Exchange.

PAKTRON DIVISION/
ILLINOIS TOOL WORKS
P.O. Box 4539
1205 McConville Rd.
Lynchburg VA 24502
804/239-6941
Contact Shirley Maxey, Personnel Manager. Manufactures film capacitors. Divisional headquarters location. Operations include: manufacturing. Corporate headquarters location: Chicago, IL. New York Stock Exchange. Common positions include: Accountant; Buyer; Computer Programmer; Customer Service Representative; Electrical Engineer; Industrial Engineer; Mechanical Engineer; Financial Analyst; General Manager; Operations/Production Manager; Personnel & Labor Relations Specialist; Quality Control Supervisor; Sales Representative; Electronics Engineer. Principal educational backgrounds sought: Accounting; Business Administration; Engineering; Marketing; Physics; Electronics. Company benefits include: medical insurance; dental insurance; pension plan; life insurance; tuition assistance; disability coverage; savings plan.

MISCELLANEOUS SERVICES

District of Columbia

THE AMERICAN ASSOCIATION
FOR THE ADVANCEMENT OF SCIENCE
1333 H Street NW
Office of Human Resources, 8th Floor
Washington DC 20005
202/326-6470
Contact Gregory Stokes, Personnel Associate. Several area locations. One of the largest, most respected scientific societies in the world, with 130,000 members in the United States and in 40 foreign countries, with 285 affiliated scientific and engineering societies. Primary operations include the publication of Science magazine, and related books, films, and publications dealing with 21 different scientific disciplines; planning and support of annual meetings and symposia; improvement of science, math, and engineering education; analysis of federal research and development budget; equal opportunity activities; and issues of scientific freedom and responsibility. Through its programs and policy statements, the AAAS is influential in the formulation of public policy as it affects science and technology, and their impacts on society. Common positions include: Accountant; Administrator; Biochemist; Biologist; Biomedical Engineer; Reporter/Editor; Technical Writer/Editor. Principal educational backgrounds sought: Biology; Communications; Engineering; Liberal Arts; Mathematics. Company benefits include: medical, dental, and life insurance; pension plan; tuition assistance; disability coverage; employee discounts. Headquarters location.

AMERICAN ASSOCIATION OF UNIVERSITY WOMEN
2401 Virginia Avenue NW
Washington DC 20037
202/785-7700
Contact Personnel Director. An organization targeting the needs of women in the college community.

**AMERICAN FEDERATION OF STATE, COUNTY,
AND MUNICIPAL EMPLOYEES (AFSCME)**
1625 L Street NW
Washington DC 20036
202/452-4800
Contact Janet Pullen, Personnel Coordinator. A million-plus member trade union, representing a wide range of professions at the local and state government level. Affiliated with the AFL-CIO. Headquarters location.

AMERICAN HISTORICAL ASSOCIATION
400 A Street SE
Washington DC 20003
202/544-2422
Contact Dr. Samuel R. Gammon, Executive Director. The administrative headquarters of a membership organization for academic and non-academic historians and secondary school teachers.

AMERICAN POSTAL WORKERS UNION
1300 L Street
Washington DC 20005
202/842-4200
Contact Douglas Holbrook, Personnel Director. A major American labor union.

AMERICAN SOCIETY OF INTERNATIONAL LAW
2223 Massachusetts Avenue NW
Washington DC 20008-2864
202/265-4313
Contact Sandra Liebel, Office Administrator. A membership organization and publisher.

ARMS CONTROL ASSOCIATION
11 DuPont Circle NW
Washington DC 20036
202/797-6450
Contact Personnel Department. An organization providing information on arms control issues.

COMPLETE BUILDING SERVICES INC.
2101 Wisconsin Avenue NW
Washington DC 20007
202/333-4977
Contact Joseph Widmayer, President/Mechanical Division. Offers a wide range of commercial and industrial management and maintenance services, including automatic temperature control and pneumatic & electric installation.

DEMOCRATIC NATIONAL COMMITTEE
430 South Capitol Street SE
Washington DC 20003
202/863-8000
Contact Carl Wagner, Transition Director. Administrative offices for the national Democratic Party. Engaged in a wide range of support, fund-raising, publishing, and other activities.

DOGGETT ENTERPRISES INC.
719 10th Street NW
Washington DC 20001
Contact Ernest L. Bryant, II, Director of Operations. Owns, manages, and operates area parking facilities. Common positions include: Cashiers; Management Trainees; Parking Attendants. Company

benefits include: medical and life insurance; disability coverage; uniforms; bonuses. Corporate headquarters location. Operations at this facility include: service.

**GENERAL CONFERENCE OF
SEVENTH-DAY ADVENTISTS**
6840 Eastern Avenue NW
Washington DC 20012
202/722-6000
Contact Jim Harris, Director of Personnel. International headquarters and administrative offices for the Seventh-Day Adventist Church.

INTERNATIONAL BROTHERHOOD OF TEAMSTERS
25 Louisiana Avenue NW
Washington DC 20001
202/624-8773
Contact J. Ann Lloyd, Director of Personnal. International headquarters for one of the nation's largest trade unions. Common positions include: Accountant; Attorney; Computer Programmer; Economist; Financial Analyst; Personnel & Labor Relations Specialist; Purchasing Agent; Reporter/Editor; Systems Analyst; Technical Writer/Editor. Principal educational backgrounds sought: Accounting; Business Administration; Communications; Computer Sciences; Finance. Company benefits include: medical, dental, and life insurance; pension plan; disability coverage. National headquarters location. Operations at this facility include: service.

**INTERNATIONAL UNION OF
ELECTRIC ROAD MACHINERY WORKERS**
1126 16th Street NW
Washington DC 20036
202/296-1200
Contact Dawn Downs, Personnel. National office for a major American labor union.

LABORERS' INTERNATIONAL UNION OF NA
905 16th Street NW
Washington DC 20006
202/737-8320
Contact Angelo Fosco, General President. National headquarters of the trade union organization.

NATIONAL RIFLE ASSOCIATION
1600 Rhode Island Avenue NW
Washington DC 20036
202/828-6000
Contact Susan Snyder, Personnel Manager. A non-profit organization whose primary goal is to further the law-abiding use of firearms in America, through a wide range of programs and services. General areas the NRA is involved in include: Competitions; Education and Training; Law Enforcement Activities; Membership Services; Administrative Services; Data Processing; Publications (The American Rifleman, The American Hunter, The American Marksman); Institute for Legislative Action; Field Services; Hunter Services; Range Development; and NRA Firearms Museum. Common positions include: Attorney; Computer Programmer; Manager; General Manager; Purchasing Agent; Reporter/Editor; Systems Analyst; Technical Writer/Editor; Clerical Support. Principal educational background sought: undergraduate degree in related field. Company benefits include: medical/dental insurance, flexible spending accounts, retirement pension plan, life insurance, longterm disability insurance, on-site cafeteria.

REPUBLICAN NATIONAL COMMITTEE
310 First Street SE
Washington DC 20003
202/863-8500
Contact Beth Hart, Personnel Director. National headquarters for the Republican Party; engaged in a wide range of political and legislative support functions.

SECURITY STORAGE COMPANY OF WASHINGTON
1701 Florida Avenue NW
Washington DC 20009-2621
202/234-5600
Contact Conrad Reid, Sr. V.P. A moving and storage firm, providing the following services: general storage, cold storage, freight forwarding, moving and packing, international trading services, and related insurance services. Corporate headquarters location. Common positions include: Accountant; Administrator; Customer Service Representative; Branch Manager; Department Manager; Marketing Specialist; Quality Control Supervisor. Principal educational backgrounds sought: Accounting; Finance; Marketing. Company benefits include: medical, dental, and life insurance; pension plan; tuition assistance; disability coverage. Corporate headquarters location. Operations at this facility include: service; sales.

Maryland

AMERICAN TOTALISATOR COMPANY INC.
11126 McCormick
Hunt Valley MD 21031
301/771-8700
Contact Human Resources. Provides totalisator service to the pari-mutuel wagering industry. Corporate headquarters location.

COOPERATIVE HOUSING FOUNDATION
1010 Wayne Avenue Suite 240
Silver Springs MD 20910
301/587-4700
Contact Administrative Officer. A major Washington-based foundation serving the needs of the cooperative housing industry both domestically and internationally. Common positions include: Accountant; Architect; Economist; Housing Specialist. Principal educational backgrounds sought: Accounting; Business Administration; Communications; Economics; Engineering; Liberal Arts. Company benefits include: medical insurance; pension plan; life insurance; tuition assistance; disability coverage; credit union. Corporate headquarters location. Regional headquarters location.

KODALUX PROCESSING SERVICES
A DIVISION OF QUALEX, INC.
1 Choke Cherry Road
Rockville MD 20850
301/670-8619
Contact Judith Kontaxis, Human Resources Manager. Offers complete amateur photofinishing and processing services. Common positions include: Entry level production; Entry level secretarial. Principal educational backgrounds sought: High school diploma. Company benefits include: medical insurance; dental insurance; pension plan; life insurance; disability coverage; profit sharing; employee discounts; savings plan. Corporate headquarters location: Durham, NC. Operations at this facility include: manufacturing.

WASHINGTON SUBURBAN SANITARY COMMISSION
1100 West Street
Laurel MD 20707
301/699-4512
Contact Mr. Bill Kay, Senior Personnel Specialist. Operating for more than 60 years; agency is responsible for the design, development, maintenance, and operation of the public water supply and sanitary sewerage systems for a 1,000-square-mile area, embracing most of Montgomery and Prince George's counties. Also has a substantial responsibility for the regulation of plumbing and gasfitting in the suburban Maryland area. Corporate headquarters location. Operations include: service. Common positions include: Accountant; Attorney; Biologist; Blue-Collar Worker Supervisor; Buyer; Chemist; Claim Representative; Computer Programmer; Customer Service Representative; Draftsperson; Engineer; Civil Engineer; Electrical Engineer; Industrial Engineer; Mechanical Engineer; Financial Analyst; Personnel & Labor Relations Specialist; Public Relations Worker; Purchasing Agent; Quality Control Supervisor; Systems Analyst; Corrosion Engineer; Systems Programmer. Principal educational backgrounds sought: Accounting; Biology; Business Administration; Chemistry; Computer Science; Engineering; Mathematics. Company benefits include: medical insurance; dental insurance; pension plan; life insurance; tuition assistance; disability coverage; savings plan; sick/annual leave; paid holidays.

Northern Virginia

AMERICAN PSYCHOLOGICAL ASSOCIATION
1400 North Uhle Street
Arlington VA 22201
703/247-7784
Contact Human Resources. A major Washington-based professional association. Common positions include: Accountant; Administrator; Computer Programmer; Customer Service Representative; Marketing Specialist; Public Relations Worker; Reporter/Editor; Systems Analyst; Technical Writer/Editor. Principal educational backgrounds sought: Accounting; Business Administration; Communications; Computer Science; Liberal Arts. Company benefits include: medical, dental, and life insurance; pension plan; tuition assistance; disabilty coverage; employee discounts; savings plan. Central offices are located at 1200 17th Street, NW, Washington DC 20036. Operations at this facilty include: administration and customer service.

**INTERNATIONAL ASSOCIATION OF
CHIEFS OF POLICE**
1110 N. Glebe Road
Arlington VA 22201
703/243-6500
Contact Personnel Manager. National headquarters for the trade association representing police chiefs and other ranking law enforcement officials. Common positions include: Accountant; Administrator; Computer Programmer; Technical Writer/Editor. Principal educational backgrounds sought: Accounting; Business Administration; Communications; Computer Science. Company benefits include: medical, dental, and life insurance; pension plan; disability coverage; savings plan. Corporate headquarters location.

NEWSPAPER PUBLISHERS

For more information on newspaper publishing opportunities in Greater Washington, look for the following professional and trade organizations in Chapter 8, beginning on page 265:

American Newspaper Publishers Association
American Society of Newspaper Editors
The Dow Jones Newspaper Fund
International Circulation Managers Association
National Newpaper Association
National Press Club
The Newspaper Guild

District of Columbia

AMERICAN NEWSPAPER PUBLISHER ASSOCIATION
P.O. Box 17407 Dulles Airport
Washington DC 20041
703/620-9500
Contact Sandy Wheatley, Personnel Director. A major professional association dedicated to servicing the needs and interest of the newspaper publishing industry.

GANNETT CO. INC.
P.O. Box 7858
Washington DC 20044
703/284-6224
Contact Maria Liggins, Personnel Administrator. Gannett is a nationwide news and information company that publishes 85 daily newspapers, including USA TODAY, 35 non-daily newpapers and USA WEEKEND, a newspaper magazine. It operates 10 television stations, 16 radio stations, Gannett News Services and the largest outdoor advertising company in North America. Gannett also has marketing, television news and program production, research satellite information systems and a national group of commercial printing facilities. Gannett has operations in 41 states, the District of Columbia, Guam, the Virgin Islands, Canada, Great Britain, Hong Kong, Singapore and Switzerland. Common positions include: Accountant; Architect; Attorney; Buyer; Computer Programmer; Financial Analyst; Operations/Production Manager; Personnel & Labor Relations Specialist; Purchasing Agent; Systems Analyst; Secretary; Executive Secretary; Mail Clerk; Stock Clerk. Principal educational backgrounds sought: Accounting; Business Administration; Communications; Computer Science; Finance. Company benefits include: medical, dental, and life insurance; pension plan; tuition assistance; disability coverage. Corporate headquarters location. New York Stock Exchange.

WASHINGTON POST COMPANY
1150 15th Street NW
Washington DC 20071
202/334-6000
Contact Jacqui Thornell, Employment & Affirmative Action Manager. One of the most respected daily newspapers in the United States, with a daily circulation of more than 800,000, and more than 1,000,000 on Sunday. In addition to publishing the Washington Post, the company also publishes the Everett (WA) Herald, Newsweek magazine, books through its publishing division, and television broadcasting through the ownership and operation of four network-affiliated stations in Detroit, Miami, Jacksonville and Hartford. Printing facilities at two other area locations: 7171 Winsatt Road, Springfield VA 21251

and 225 CA Avenue, SE, Washington DC 20003. Corporate headquarters location. American Stock Exchange.

THE WASHINGTON TIMES
3400 New York Avenue NE
Washington DC 20002
202/636-3328
Contact Terri A. Ott, Employment Manager. A major newspaper serving the Washington area. Common positions include: Accountant; Advertising Worker; Buyer; Customer Service Representative; Electrical Engineer; Mechanical Engineer; Personnel & Labor Relations Specialist; Public Relations Worker; Purchasing Agent; Quality Control Supervisor; Reporter/Editor; Sales Representative; Systems Analyst. Principal educational backgrounds sought: Accounting; Art/Design; Business Administration; Communications; Computer Science; Finance; Liberal Arts; Marketing. Company benefits include: medical insurance; dental insurance; pension plan; life insurance; disability coverage; savings plan. Corporate headquarters location. Operations at this facility: manufacturing; research/development; administration; service; sales.

Maryland

THE BALTIMORE SUN
501 North Calvert Street
Baltimore MD 21278
301/332-6268
Contact Employment Specialist. A major publishing company operating various news bureaus around the world. "The Sun" and "The Evening Sun" are two of Baltimore's most widely read newspapers. Principal educational backgrounds sought: Accounting; Business Administration; Communications; Computer Science; Finance; Liberal Arts; Marketing. Company benefits include: medical insurance; dental insurance; pension plan; life insurance; tuition assistance. Corporate headquarters location.

CAPITAL GAZETTE NEWSPAPERS INC.
(ANNAPOLIS EVENING CAPITAL)
P.O. Box 911
Annapolis MD 21404
301/268-5000
Contact Tom Marquardt, Managing Editor. Publishes a daily newspaper. Corporate headquarters location.

LANDMARK COMMUNITY NEWSPAPERS
OF MARYLAND INC.
201 Railroad Avenue
P.O. Box 346
Westminster MD 21157
301/875-5400
Contact Sally Mynes, Business Manager. Provides newspaper publishing, specialty publications, and commercial printing. Operations include: service; sales. Corporate headquarters location: Norfolk, VA. Common positions include: Accountant; Blue-Collar Worker Supervisor; Department Manager; General Manager; Reporter/Editor; Sales Representative; Composing Artist. Principal educational backgrounds sought: Accounting; Art/Design; Business Administration; Communications; Liberal Arts; Marketing. Company benefits include: medical insurance; pension plan; life insurance; tuition assistance; disability coverage; employee discounts; savings plan.

MARYLAND INDEPENDENT NEWSPAPERS/ CHESAPEAKE PUBLISHING CORPORATION

7 Industrial Park Circle
Waldorf MD 20601
301/645-9480

Contact head of department of interest. Publishes five area newspapers: "Enterprise" (circulation: 14,000); "Maryland Independent" (circulation: 12,500); "South County Current" (circulation: 33,000); "Calvert County Recorder" (circulation: 5,500); "Flightline" (circulation: 9,000). Also provides commercial printing services. Divisional headquarters. Operations include: manufacturing; administration; service; sales. Corporate headquarters location (Chesapeake Publishing Corporation): Easton, MD. Common positions include: Accountant; Administrator; Advertising Worker; Credit Manager; Customer Service Representative; Department Manager; General Manager; Operations/Production Manager; Reporter/Editor; Sales Representative. Principal educational backgrounds sought: Accounting; Art/Design; Business Administration; Marketing; Journalism. Company benefits include: medical insurance; pension plan; life insurance; tuition assistance; disability coverage; holidays.

MONTGOMERY COUNTY SENTINEL

7 Palamar Street
Gaithersburg MD 20877
301/990-3140

Contact Rick Levine, General Manager. Publishes a weekly newspaper with a circulation of more than 22,000. Corporate headquarters location.

Northern Virginia

ATLANTIC PUBLICATIONS INC.

P.O. Box 150
Accomac VA 23301
804/787-1111

Contact C. Mark Medders, Vice-President/Administration. Publishers of weekly and twice weekly newspapers, T.M.C., and resort publications in Delaware, Maryland, Virginia, North Carolina, and South Carolina. Corporate headquarters location. Operations at this facility include: administration. Common positions include: Advertising Worker; General Manager; Reporter/Editor; Sales Representative. Company benefits include: medical insurance; profit sharing; employee discounts; bonus plan.

TIMES JOURNAL COMPANIES

6883 Commercial Drive
Springfield VA 22159
703/750-8130

Contact Recruiter. Primarily a newspaper company producing several publications, which include the Times publications covering military and defense issues internationally, and the Journals that serve the local Washington Metropolitan area. Combined circulation: 350,000. Two other major divisions: Commercial Printing and Telemarketing. Common job positions include: Accountant; Advertising Worker; Blue-Collar Worker Supervisor; Commercial Artist; Computer Programmer; Credit Manager; Customer Service Representative; Electrical Engineer; Mechanical Engineer; Management Trainee; Marketing Specialist; Personnel & Labor Relations Specialist; Public Relations Worker; Purchasing Agent; Quality Control Supervisor; Reporter/Editor; Sales Representative; Computer Operators; Administrative Assistants; Secretary; Editorial Assistants; Clerks; Mail Clerks. Principal educational backgrounds sought: Accounting; Art/Design; Computer Science; Marketing; Journalism. Company benefits include: medical insurance; dental insurance; pension plan; life insurance; tuition assistance;

disability coverage; profit sharing; employee discounts; savings plan. Corporate headquarters location. Operations at this facility include: administration; service; sales.

PAPER, PACKAGING & FOREST PRODUCTS/CONTAINERS & GLASS PRODUCTS

For more information on paper/glass industry opportunities in Greater Washington, look for the following professional and trade organizations in Chapter 8, beginning on page 265:

American Paper Institute
Technical Association of the Pulp and Paper Industry

<u>Maryland</u>

CARR-LOWREY GLASS COMPANY
P.O. Box 356
Baltimore MD 21203
301/347-8800
Contact Norm Schmitt, Plant Manager. Produces glass bottles, glass jars, and is engaged in the labeling and decorating of glass products. A division of Anchor-Hocking Corporation (Lancaster, OH), which produces a diversified line of household, hardware, packaging products, and a wide variety of glassware, commercial and institutional chinaware, decorative and convenience hardware, glass containers, and metal and plastic closures. Corporate headquarters location.

CHESAPEAKE FIBER PACKAGING CORPORATION
11000 Gilroy Road
Hunt Valley MD 21031
301/785-2233
Contact Marilyn Weitzenkorn, Office Manager. Produces folding and corrugated boxes. Common positions include Sales Representatives. Principal Educational background sought include: marketing. Company benefits: medical insurance; pension plan; life insurance; disability coverage. Parent company is Chesapeake Paperboard.

CHESAPEAKE PAPERBOARD COMPANY
Fort Avenue and Woodall Street
Baltimore MD 21230
301/752-1842
Contact Nancy Todd, Personnel Director. Produces a variety of paperboard products. Corporate headquarters location.

THE ELSON COMPANY
2116 Sparrows Point Road
Baltimore MD 21219
301/477-3000
Contact Mr. Pete Caltrider, President. Produces wooden boxes, pallets, crates, and corrugated boxes. Corporate headquarters location.

FORT HOWARD CUP CORPORATION
10100 Reisterstown Road
Owings Mills MD 21117
301/363-1111

Contact Employment Manager. Manufactures and distributes paper and plastic cups, containers, bowls, plates, lids, cutlery and drinking straws. Also produces ice-cream cones. Two divisions manufacture packaging and production machinery. Common positions include: Accountant; Computer Programmer; Customer Service Representative; Draftsperson; Electrical Engineer; Mechanical Engineer; Personnel & Labor Relations Specialist; Systems Analyst. Principal educational backgrounds sought: Accounting; Business Administration; Computer Science; Engineering; Liberal Arts; Parent company: Fort Howard Paper Company. Operations at this facility include: manufacturing; research/development; administration.

MARYLAND PAPER BOX COMPANY
4545 Annapolis Road
Baltimore MD 21227
301/789-1700

Contact Clara Snyder, Personnel Director. Manufactures folding cartons, gift boxes, handle shopping bags and gift wrap. Common positions include: Accountant; Credit Manager; Customer Service; General Manager; Operations/ Productions Manager; Marketing Specialist; Purchasing Agent; Sales Representative; Artist. Principal educational backgrounds sought: Accounting; Art/Design; Business Administration; Finance. Company benefits include: medical and life insurance; pension plan; disability coverage; credit union. Corporate headquarters location. Operations at this facility include: regional headquarters; manufacturing; administration; service; sales.

MONARCH SERVICES
4517 Hartford Road
Baltimore MD 21214
301/254-9200

Contact Steve Szekely, Vice President. A commercial printing firm; also manufactures envelopes. Corporate headquarters location.

NATIONAL CAN CORPORATION
2010 Reservoir Road
Sparrows Point MD 21219
301/477-3131

Contact Personnel. Produces metal cans, including sanitary containers, and beverage and other containers. Nationally, company is one of the world's leading manufacturers of packaging products, manufacturing and marketing aluminum and steel cans, glass and plastic blow-molded containers, steel crowns, aluminum closures, and metal and plastic caps for a variety of end-uses. Operates more than 70 manufacturing and support facilities in 10 countries and Puerto Rico. Principal markets include the beer, soft drink, and food processing industries around the world. Corporate headquarters location: Chicago, IL. New York Stock Exchange.

STONE INDUSTRIAL DIVISION/
J.L. CLARK MANUFACTURING
51st Avenue & Cree Lane
College Park MD 20740
301/474-3100

Contact Virginia Hollenbeck, Personnel Office. Manufactures paper tubing products as a division of the national container products firm. Corporate headquarters location: Rockford, IL.

WESTVACO CORPORATION
3400 East Biddle Street
Baltimore MD 21213
301/327-7376
Contact Margaret Sponaugle, Personnel Administrator. Manufactures corrugated fiber cartons. Nationally, company is an international firm specializing in the manufacture of high-quality papers for communications, packaging, and high-technology applications. Products include packaging for both industrial and consumer markets, and envelopes (where company is among the world's largest producers). Other area facilities in Luke, Baltimore, Pasadena, and Laurel, MD. Corporate headquarters location: New York, NY.

Northern Virginia

UNION CAMP CORPORATION
P.O. Box 178
Franklin VA 23851
804/569-4705
Contact Howard N. Soucek, Supervisor, Professional Recruitment. Manufactures paper and building products as well as managing woodlands. Divisional headquarters location. Operations include: manufacturing; service; sales. Corporate headquarters location: Wayne, NJ. New York Stock Exchange. Common positions include: Accountant; Attorney; Blue-Collar Worker Supervisor; Buyer; Chemist; Computer Programmer; Customer Service Representative; Draftsperson; Chemical Engineer; Civil Engineer; Electrical Engineer; Industrial Engineer; Mechanical Engineer; Forester; Department Manager; General Manager; Marketing Specialist; Personnel & Labor Relations Specialist; Programmer; Public Relations Worker; Purchasing Agent; Quality Control Supervisor; Sales Representative; Systems Analyst; Transportation & Traffic Specialist. Principal educational backgrounds sought: Accounting; Business Administration; Chemistry; Computer Science; Engineering. Company benefits include: medical and life insurance; pension plan; tuition assistance; disability coverage; savings plan; stock ownership.

PETROLEUM & ENERGY RELATED/MINING & DRILLING

For more information on petroleum and energy related opportunities in Greater Washington, look for the following professional and trade organizations in Chapter 8, beginning on page 265:

American Association of Petroleum Geologists
American Gas Association
American Geological Institute
American Institute of Mining, Metallurgical and Petroleum
American Nuclear Society
American Petroleum Institute
American Society of Tribologists and Lubrication Engineers
Clean Energy Research Institute
Geological Society of America
Petroleum Equipment Institute
Society of Exploration Geophysicists

District of Columbia

STEUART PETROLEUM COMPANY
4646 40th Street NW
Washington DC 20016
202/537-8900
Contact Ms. Linda D. Browning, Personnel Specialist. An area fuel distributor operating a home heating fuel distributorship and service stations at several area locations. Corporate headquarters location. Common positions include: Accountant; Credit Manager; Customer Service Representative; Financial Analyst; Department Manager; Sales Representative. Company benefits include: medical insurance; dental insurance; life insurance; profit sharing; employee discounts; 410K; sick leave; vacation leave.

Maryland

GRIFFITH-CONSUMERS COMPANY
2510 Schuster Drive
Cheverly MD 20781
301/322-6647
Contact Coniece Washington, Personnel Coordinator. Griffith is a full service, independent retail distributor of petroleum products, principally heating oil and gasoline, operating in Washingon, DC, Maryland, Delaware, Virginia, West Virginia, and portions of New Jersey and Pennsylvania. Griffith also sells diesel fuel, heavy oils, kerosene and products and services related to its energy business. The company has been in the fuel distribution business since 1898. Common posititons include: Accountant; Computer Programmer; Credit Manager; Customer Service Representative; Personnel & Labor Relations Specialist; Sales Representative. Principal educational backgrounds sought: Accounting; Business Administration; Finance; Marketing. Company benefits include: medical, dental, and life insurance; pension plan; tuition assistance; employee discounts. Corporate headquarters location. Operations at this facility include: regional headquarters; divisional headquarters; administration; service; sales.

TELEDYNE ENERGY SYSTEMS
110 West Timonium Road
Timonium MD 21093
301/252-8220
Contact Mrs. Madge Bringle, Personnel Office. A pioneer in space and terrestrial thermoelectric generator development and production. These systems have been used extensively by both NASA and the Department of Defense in earth orbit, deep space, planetary landing and exploration, and remote terrestrial missions. Also produces a product line using this technology for powering remote terrestrial sites for communications, data collection and telemetering, navigation, and cathodic protection. Also actively involved in electrochemical systems development, producing a line of electrolytic hydrogen/oxygen generators for industrial applications and radioactive liquid waste solidification systems, and shipping containers and handling equipment for nuclear power plants. Company is a subsidiary of Teledyne, Inc., a high-technology, multi-product corporation consisting of 130 individual companies employing 50,000 people nationwide. Nationally, company operates in four areas: Aviation and Electronics; Machines and Metals; Engines, Energy, and Power; and Commercial and Consumer. Corporate headquarters location: Beverly Hills, CA. New York Stock Exchange.

PRINTING

For more information on printing opportunities in Greater Washington, look for the following professional and trade organizations in Chapter 8, beginning on page 265:

Binding Industries of America
Printing Industries of America

District of Columbia

McGREGOR PRINTING CORPORATION
2121 K Street NW, Suite 810
Washington DC 20037
202/333-4411
Contact Fred Fearing, Personnel Director. A major Washington printer of business forms.

SAUL'S LITHOGRAPH COMPANY INC.
2424 Evarts Street NE
Washington DC 20018
202/529-9100
Contact Edward Bozzella, President. Offers a complete range of commercial printing services, including offset and lithography services.

Maryland

AMERICAN BANK STATIONERY COMPANY
P.O. Box 17114
Baltimore MD 21203-7114
301/529-7600
Contact Personnel. Engaged in the printing of bank checks, stationery, and other financial and legal documents.

CRAFTSMAN PRESS INC.
3401 52nd Avenue
Bladensburg MD 20710
301/277-9400
Contact Loretta Spring, Executive Secretary. Provides a wide range of commercial printing services.

DIAMOND PRESS
1819 East Preston Street
Baltimore MD 21213
301/327-5600
Contact Mr. Russell Linnell, Personnel Manager. A commercial printer, primarily engaged in the printing of circulars.

DOW JONES & COMPANY
11501 Columbia Pike
Silver Springs MD 20904
301/622-2900

Contact Olive Merson, Business Office Representative. Engaged in printing The Wall Street Journal, as part of the national financial news service and publishing company. Other publications include Barron's, Barron's Educational Book Series, and others. Other services include domestic and international wire services (primarily financial news), and a commercial news retrieval system. Administrative offices are located in South Brunswick, NJ. Corporate headquarters location: New York, NY. New York Stock Exchange.

EDITORS PRESS INC.
6200 Editors Park Drive
Hyattsville MD 20782
301/853-4900
Contact Lois Smith, Personnel Manager. Provides a variety of commercial printing and direct mail services, including the printing of advertising literature, brochures, folders, booklets, pamphlets, maps, catalogs, and periodicals. A subsidiary of Kiplinger Washington Editors (Washington, DC). Corporate headquarters location.

HOLLADAY TYLER PRINTING CORPORATION
7100 Halladay Tyler Road
Glendale MD 20769
301/464-9100
Contact Ms. Geri Whipple, Personnel Director. Provides complete lithography and bookbinding services. Corporate headquarters location.

JOHN D. LUCAS PRINTING COMPANY
1820 Portal Street
Baltimore MD 21224
301/633-4200
Contact Personnel Director. Involved in all aspects of printing and book-making, including books and job printing, composition and binding services, typesetting, and lithography. Common positions include: Customer Service Representative; Sales Representative. Principal educational backgrounds sought: Accounting; Business Administration; Liberal Arts. Company benefits include: medical, dental and life insurance; tuition assistance; disability coverage; profit sharing. Corporate headquarters location. Operations at this facility include: manufacturing; administration; service; sales.

MAXWELL COMMUNICATIONS
7364 Baltimore-Annapolis Boulevard
Glen Burnie MD 21061
301/761-0440
Contact Industrial Relations Manager. Produces newspaper supplements and other printed matter. Company operates offices in most major American cities.

McARDLE PRINTING COMPANY
1140 East-West Highway
Silver Springs MD 20910
301/588-5025
Contact Virgil Wright, Personnel Director. A commercial printing firm.

OPTIC GRAPHICS
101 Dover Road
Glen Burnie MD 21061
301/768-3000
Contact Carolyn Wilder, Personnel Manager. A book manufacturer, utilizing both web and sheet-fed offset equipment. Provides a variety of finishing, including saddle-stitch, perfect binding, wire-o and

plastic binding, loose-leaf binder manufacturing, index tabs printing, and foil stamping. Corporate headquarters location.

Northern Virginia

WILLIAM BYRD PRESS
5408 Port Royal Road
Springfield VA 22151
703/321-8610
Contact Mary Jo Oranburg, Personnel Supervisor. Provides a wide range of typesetting services, including printing periodicals and other commercial printing jobs. Corporate headquarters location.

REAL ESTATE: SERVICES, MANAGEMENT, DEVELOPMENT

For more information on real estate opportunities in Greater Washington, look for the following professional and trade organizations in Chapter 8, beginning on page 265:

Apartment Owners and Managers Association
Building Owners and Managers Association
Institute of Real Estate Management
International Association of Corporate Real Estate Executives
International Real Estate Institute
National Association of Real Estate Investment Trusts
National Association of Realtors

District of Columbia

BRESLER & REINER INC.
401 M Street SW Waterside Mall
Washington DC 20024
202/488-8800
Contact Burton Reiner, Co-owner. Engaged in two primary business segments: Home and Condominium Construction (with completed or planned developments in six Maryland and Virginia communities), and Rental Property Ownership and Management (owns and operates apartment buildings and commercial property for rental). Corporate headquarters location.

OLIVER T. CARR COMPANY
1700 Pennsylvania Avenue NW, Suite 900
Washington DC 20006
202/624-1700
Contact Sandy Mah, Personnel Director. A major area real estate/architectural/construction management firm, with significant operations in the metropolitan District of Columbia area. Operates in four divisions: Acquisitions, which locates, evaluates, and purchases land and buildings that are candidates for improvement; Development, which defines the market, creates the initial design concept, determines economic feasibility, and arranges financing; Construction, which supervises the final design and actualizes the plan from girders to doorknobs; and Operations, which markets and manages the finished product. Company specializes in the construction and/or renovation of mixed-use developments. Corporate headquarters location.

DONOHOE COMPANIES INC.
2101 Wisconsin Avenue NW
Washington DC 20007
202/333-0880
Contact Nora Lauterbach, Personnel Administrator. A leading Washington real estate construction and development company. Common positions include: Accountant; Blue-Collar Worker Supervisor; Computer Programmer; Civil Engineer; Mechanical Engineer; Systems Analyst. Principal educational backgrounds sought: Accounting; Computer Science; Engineering; Marketing. Company benefits include: medical insurance; dental insurance; life insurance; tuition asstance; disability coverage; profit sharing; employee discounts; savings plan. Corporate headquarters location. Operations at this facility include: regional headquarters; divisional headquarters; administration; service; sales.

HOLLADAY CORPORATION
3400 Idaho Avenue NW
Washington DC 20010
202/362-2400
Contact Vice-President. A leading Washington real estate development corporation.

NATIONAL CORPORATION FOR HOUSING PARTNERSHIPS
1225 Eye Street NW
Washington DC 20005
202/347-6247
Contact Stacy S. Lancaster, Manager of Human Resources. Offers a complete range of planning, development, management financing, and technical assistance for projects relating to lower and middle-income family housing. This congressionally-chartered private firm operates through subsidiaries NCHP Real Estate Co. Inc., NCHP Property Management Inc., and NCHP Development Corporation. Corporate headquarters location. Common positions include: Real Estate Property Manager; Real Estate Property Developer. Principal educational backgrounds sought: Business Administration; Computer Science; Economics; Finance. Company benefits include: medical, dental, and life insurance; 401K pension plan; tuition assistance; disability coverage; profit sharing; employee discounts. Operations at this facility include: administration.

Maryland

FEDERAL REALTY INVESTMENT TRUST
4800 Hampden Lane Suite 500
Bethesda MD 20814
301/652-3360
Contact Peggy Fowler, Director of Personnel. An equity real estate investment firm that acquires and improves strip shopping centers along heavily developed highways. Common positions include: Accountant; Attorney; Blue-Collar Worker Supervisor; Computer Programmer. Company benefits include: medical, dental and life insurance; pension plan; FLEX. Corporate headquarters location. Operations at this facility include: administration; service; sales. New York Stock Exchange.

INTERSTATE GENERAL COMPANY L.P.
222 Smallwood Village Center
St. Charles MD 20602
301/843-8600
Contact Nancy M. Davis, Director of Personnel. A real estate investment company that operates through four major divisions: community development; home building, investment property and property management. Common positions include: Accountant; Draftsperson; Civil Engineer; Branch

Manager; Public Relations Worker; Systems Analyst; Tenant Relations; Leasing Consultant; Secretary; Collections; Maintenance; Residential & Commercial Leasing; Property Management Professional. Principal educational backgrounds sought: Accounting; Business Administration; Computer Science; Engineering; Marketing. Company benefits include: medical, dental and life insurance; pension plan; tuition assistance; disability coverage; profit sharing; employee discounts. Corporate headquarters location. Operations at this facility include: regional headquarters; administration. New York Stock Exchange. Pacific Stock Exchange.

W.C. & A.N. MILLER DEVELOPMENT COMPANY
4701 Sangamore Road
Bethesda MD 20816
301/229-4000
Contact James Ward, Personnel Office. Engaged in real estate planning, development, and construction.

Northern Virginia

SMITHY BRAEDON COMPANY
3040 Williams Drive
Fairfax VA 22031
703/641-8000
Contact Barbara M. Early, Corporate Secretary/Dir. of Personnel. Four area locations, including the District of Columbia, Alexandria, VA, Baltimore, MD, and Bethesda, MD. A full service commercial real estate firm covering Maryland, Virginia, and the District of Columbia. Common positions include: Accountant; Administrator; Claim Representative; Financial Analyst; Insurance Agent/Broker; Branch Manager; Management Trainee; Marketing Specialist; Public Relations Worker; Sales and Leasing Representative; Systems Analyst. Principal edcational backgrounds sought: Accounting; Business Administration; Communications; Computer Science; Economics; Finance and Investments; Marketing. Company benefits include: medical insurance; life insurance; disability coverage; savings plan; 401K; accidental death/dismemberment. Corporate, regional headquarters location. Operations at this facility include: administration; sales; leasing; property management; corporate communications; finance and investments; insurance.

RESEARCH & DEVELOPMENT

Maryland

BECTON DICKINSON DIAGNOSTIC
INSTRUMENT SYSTEMS
383 Hillen Road
Towson MD 21204
301/337-8700, ext. 324
Contact Rita Bajkowski, Supervisor/Human Resources. A biological research and development firm producing bacterial detection systems, culture media, nuclear radiation monitoring equipment, and other electronic laboratory products. A division of Becton Dickinson and Company (Paramus, NJ). Divisional headquarters location. Operations include: manufacturing; research/development. Corporate headquarters location: Franklin Lakes, NJ. New York Stock Exchange. Common positions include: Accountant; Biochemist; Buyer; Chemist; Credit Manager; Customer Service Representative; Computer Programmer; Draftsperson; Biomedical Engineer; Chemical Engineer: Industrial Engineer:

Electrical Engineer; Mechanical Engineer; Department Manager; Financial Analyst; Industrial Designer; General Manager; Operations/Production Manager; Personnel & Labor Relations Specialist; Purchasing Agent; Quality Control Supervisor; Systems Analyst; Technical Writer/Editor. Sales Representative. Principal educational backgrounds sought: Biology; Business Administration; Computer Science; Chemistry; Liberal Arts . Company benefits include: medical insurance; dental insurance; pension plan; life insurance; tuition assistance; disability coverage; employee discounts; savings plan; profit sharing.

JOHNS HOPKINS UNIVERSITY/
APPLIED PHYSICS LABORATORY
Professional Recruitment Office
Johns Hopkins Road
Laurel MD 20707
301/953-5270

Contact Daniel T. King, Staffing Supervisor. A division of The Johns Hopkins University; conducts advanced technical research programs for the Navy, NASA, the Department of Defense, the National Institute of Health, and other agencies. APL has made contributions ranging from major defense systems to biomedical devices. Corporate headquarters location. Operations include: research/development. Common positions include: Computer Engineer; Computer Programmer; Aerospace Engineer; Electrical Engineer; Mechanical Engineer; Physicist; Systems Analyst. Principal educational backgrounds sought: Computer Science; Engineering; Mathematics; Physics. Company benefits include: medical insurance; dental insurance; pension plan; life insurance; tuition assistance; disability coverage. Operations at this facility include: research/development. Corporate headquarters location.

MICROBIOLOGICAL ASSOCIATES INC.
9900 Blackwell Road
Rockville MD 20850
301/738-1000

Contact Connie Kepner, Director of Personnel. Main business operations are biotechnology, molecular virology, toxicology, and gentic toxicology. Common positions include: Biologist; Technical Writer/Editor; Technicians; Animal Handlers; Janitors; Secretaries. Principal educational backgrounds sought: Biology; Molecular Biology; Microbiology, Immunology/Virology. Company benefits include: medical, dental and life insurance; tuition assistance; disability coverage; savings plan; 401k; Credit Union. Corporate headquarters location. Toxicology facility located in Bethesda, MD. Operations include: administration; research/development; biological testing.

Northern Virginia

ALLIED/
RESEARCH & DEVELOPMENT
P.O. Box 31
Petersburg VA 23804
804/520-3000

Contact Personnel Department. An area technical and research center employing approximately 600 people. Parent company, Allied Signal Corporation, serves a broad spectrum of industries through its more than 40 strategic businesses, which are grouped into five sectors: Aerospace; Automotive; Chemical; Industrial and Technology; and Oil and Gas. Allied Signal is one of the nation's largest industrial organizations and has 115,000 employees in over 30 countries. Corporate headquarters location: Morristown, NJ.

CERBERONICS INC.
5600 Columbia Pike
Baileys Crossroads VA 22041
703/379-4500
Contact Lucy Erikson, Personnel. A major research and development company with a focus on federal government contract work.

HAZLETON LABORATORIES AMERICA, INC.
9200 Leesburg Turnpike
Vienna VA 22182
703/893-5400
Contact Lyn Murphy, Personnel Administrator. A major life sciences firm, providing biological and chemical research services; also a major supplier of laboratory animals and biological products. Clients include research institutes, industrial companies, government agencies, and manufacturers of pharmaceuticals, chemicals, food, and cosmetics. Common positions include: Biochemist; Biologist; Chemist. Principal educational backgrounds sought in Biology and Chemistry. Company benefits include: medical insurance; dental insurance; pension plan; life insurance; tuition assistance; disability coverage; profit sharing; employee discounts; 401K plan. Operations include research/development and administration. Parent company is Corning Glass Works, located in Herdon, VA.

RUBBER & PLASTICS

For more information on rubber and plastics opportunities in Greater Washington, look for the following professional and trade organizations in Chapter 8, beginning on page 265:

Society of Plastics Industry
Society of Plastic Engineers

<u>Maryland</u>

AMETEK/
SPECIAL FILAMENTS DIVISION
8335 Telegraph Road
P.O. Box 339
Odenton MD 21113
301/569-4500
Contact Billie Clark, Personnel Administrator. Produces a wide variety of synthetic filaments, including saran, polypropylene, polyethylene, polyester, and nylon. Nationally, company designs, develops, manufactures, and markets in the following business segments: Electromechanical; Process Equipment; Precision Instruments; and Industrial Materials (includes this facility). Corporate headquarters location: New York, NY. New York Stock Exchange.

J.L. CLARK MANUFACTURING COMPANY INC./
STONE INDUSTRIAL
51st Avenue and Cree Lane
College Park MD 20740
301/474-3100
Contact Virginia Hollenbeck, Personnel. Produces paper tubing and tubes, high-temperature plastic tubing, and heat-shrinkable plastic tubing. Nationally, company operates in three industry segments:

packaging items (metal and plastic containers, metal tubes, composite containers, and various specialty chemicals); filters (oil, air, fuel, coolant, hydraulic fluid, and chemical solution filters used in a variety of products and industries); and paper and plastic tubes. Second facility in Havre de Grace produces decorated metal ends, battery sleeves, and metal signs, and is engaged in flat sheet decorating. Corporate headquarters location: Rockford, IL.

FAWN PLASTICS COMPANY INC.
International Circle, Suite 140
Hunt Valley MD 21030
301/584-1300
Contact Dean Robbins, Sales Manager. Produces a range of molded plastic products, including electronic assembly products. Corporate headquarters location.

MALCO PLASTICS INC.
9800 Reisterstown Road
Garrison MD 21055
301/363-1600
Contact Carol Barnes, Personnel Director. A plastics products manufacturer, producing such diverse items as credit cards and advertising specialties, as well as providing screen process printing, lithography, and embossing services.

SEWELL PLASTICS INC.
P.O. Box 498
350 Old Bay Lane
Havre de Grace MD 21078
301/939-1500
Contact Ms. Pat McPartland, Personnel Officer. Produces a variety of plastic containers, including plastic beverage bottles. Corporate headquarters location: Atlanta, GA.

TRANSPORTATION: EQUIPMENT & SERVICES

For more information on transportation opportunities in Greater Washington, look for the following professional and trade organizations in Chapter 8, beginning on page 265:

Air Line Employees Association
Air Transport Association of America
American Institute of Aeronautics and Astronautics
American Society of Travel Agents
American Trucking Association
Association of American Railroads
Automotive Service Association
Automotive Service Industry Association
Aviation Maintenance Foundation
Future Aviation Professionals of America
Institute of Transportation Engineers
Marine Technology Society
Motor Vehicle Manufacturers Association
National Aeronautic Association of USA
National Automotive Dealers Association
National Institute For Automotive Service Excellence

National Marine Manufacturers Association
Professional Aviation Maintenance Association
Shipbuilders Council of America

District of Columbia

AEROSPACE INDUSTRIES ASSN. OF AMERICA
1250 I Street NW
Washington DC 20005
202/371-8400
Contact Jane Weeden, Personnel Director. An organization representing companies involved in aerospace research, development and manufacturing.

AMERICAN BUS ASSOCIATION
1015 15th Street NW, Suite 250
Washington DC 20006
202/842-1645
Contact Personnel Department. An organization representing the inter-city bus industry. Common positions include: Advertising Worker; Public Relations Worker; Clerical Worker. Principal educational backgrounds sought: Business Administration; Communications; Liberal Arts. Company benefits include: medical insurance; dental insurance; pension plan; life insurance; tuition assistance. Corporate headquarters location. Operations at this facility include: administration.

Northern Virginia

ALLIED SIGNAL/
AEROSPACE HEADQUARTERS
1000 Wilson Boulevard
Arlington VA 22209
703/276-2000
Contact Personnel Department. Headquarters for the Aerospace sector of Allied Signal Corporation. Parent company serves a broad spectrum of industries through its more than 40 strategic businesses, which grouped into five sectors: Aerospace; Automotive; Chemical; Industrial and Technology; and Oil and Gas. Allied Signal is one of the nation's largest industrial organizations and has 115,000 employees in over 30 countries. Corporate headquarters location: Morristown, NJ.

AVIS RENT-A-CAR SYSTEM INC.
501 East Monroe Avenue
Alexandria VA 22301
703/684-2266
Contact Mike Bowling, Car Sales Manager. Multiple area locations. Area management offices for the major international vehicle renting and leasing firm. Operates through three divisions: car rental, truck rental, and car leasing. Corporate headquarters location: New York, NY.

NEWPORT NEWS SHIPBUILDING
4101 Washington Avenue
Newport News VA 23607
804/380-4878
Contact J.O. Dunn, Supervisor of Recruiting. Engaged in the design, construction, repair, overhaul, and refueling of conventional and nuclear-powered merchant and naval surface ships and submarines. Parent company is Tenneco, Inc. Common positions include: Design Engineer; Test Engineer. Principal educational backgrounds sought: Mechanical and Electrical Engineering. Company benefits

include: medical insurance; dental insurance; pension plan; life insurance; tuition assistance; disability coverage; savings plan. Corporate headquarters location. Operations include: manufacturing; research/development; administration. New York Stock Exchange.

TRW SYSTEMS
1 Federal System Park Drive
Fairfax VA 22033
703/734-6000
Contact Personnel Director. Nationally, company operates in three business segments: Car and Truck Components, which produces chassis, engines, and other components for cars, trucks, buses, farm machinery, and off-highway vehicles, and a variety of products for the replacement parts markets; Electronic and Space Systems, which manufactures electronic components for use in the telecommunications, computer, automotive, and home entertainment industries; and Industrial and Energy segment, which manufactures tools, fasteners, and bearings for industrial users, pumps and valves used by the petroleum industry, and aircraft components for commercial and military aircraft. Corporate headquarters location: Cleveland, OH. New York Stock Exchange.

U.S. AIR INC.
2345 Crystal Park Four
Arlington VA 22227
703/892-7000
Contact Manager of Employment Services. A major American airline serving a variety of regions.

UTILITIES

For more information on utility opportunities in Greater Washington, look for the following professional organization in Chapter 8, beginning on page 265:

American Water Works Association

District of Columbia

EDISON ELECTRIC INSTITUTE
1111 19th Street NW 9th Floor
Washington DC 20036
202/778-6492
Contact Personnel Assistant. A major Washington-based association whose membership includes all investor-owned electric utility companies in the United States. Common positions include: Accountant; Administrator; Advertising Worker; Attorney; Computer Programmer; Economist; Electrical Engineer; Mechanical Engineer; Financial Analyst; Department Manager; Marketing Specialist; Public Relations Worker; Purchasing Agent; Statistician; Systems Analyst; Technical Writer/Editor; Lobbyist; Policy Analyst; Librarian. Principal educational backgrounds sought: Accounting; Business Administration; Communications; Computer Science; Economics; Engineering; Finance; Liberal Arts; Marketing. Company benefits: medical insurance; dental insurance; pension plan; life insurance; tuition assistance; disability coverage; savings plan. Corporate headquarters location. Operations at this facility include: service.

NATIONAL RURAL ELECTRIC
COOPERATIVE ASSOCIATION
1800 Massachusetts Avenue NW
Washington DC 20036
202/857-9610

Contact George Simpson, Manager of Employment. A national service organization of nearly 1,000 rural electric systems (more than 950 cooperatively owned), which provide power to more than 25 million people in 46 states. Operates through five departments: Government Relations, Energy and Environmental Policy, Public and Association Affairs, Management Services, and Retirement/Safety/Insurance, with 20 divisions within these departments handling such matters as legislation, technical information and training, an overseas assistance program, insurance and employee benefits, publications, and public relations. Common positions include: Accountant; Actuary; Claim Representative; Computer Programmer; Customer Service Representative; Insurance Agent/Broker; Public Relations Worker; Reporter/Editor; Underwriter; Claims Processor. Company benefits include: medical, dental, and life insurance; pension plan; tuition assistance; disability coverage; 410K savings plan; vision care plan. Corporate headquarters location.

POTOMAC ELECTRIC POWER COMPANY
1900 Pennsylvania Avenue NW
Washington DC 20068
202/872-2449

Contact Blanche Moose, Personnel Representative. A major Washington-area electric service.

WASHINGTON GAS LIGHT COMPANY
1100 H Street NW
Washington DC 20080
750-5943

Contact Yvonne B. Willis, Manager of Employment. Engaged in the purchase, sale, and distribution of natural gas in metropolitan Washington DC, including portions of Maryland and Virginia, through seven operating subsidiaries. Total population of service area exceeds three million. Corporate headquarters location. New York Stock Exchange. Common positions include: Accountant; Civil Engineer; Computer Programmer; Mechanical Engineer; Financial Analyst. Principal educational backgrounds sought: Accounting; Computer Science; Economics; Engineering; Finance. Company benefits include: medical, dental, and life insurance; pension plan; tuition assistance; employee discounts; savings plan.

Northern Virginia

DOMINION RESOURCES
Box 26532
Richmond VA 23261
804/775-5700

Contact Anne Grier, Manager of Personnel. Dominion Resources, Inc. is a holding company principally involved in the electric power business. It is also active in natural gas, real estate, and investment management businesses.

GOVERNMENT JOBS

WORKING FOR THE FEDERAL GOVERNMENT

Most of the jobs you know about, and many you may never have heard of, exist in the Federal civil service.

The Federal Government needs all kinds of skills to serve a nation of over 200 million people, 24 hours a day, every day of the year. Government employees work in offices, shipyards, laboratories, national parks, hospitals, military bases, and many other settings across the country and around the world. (About 12 percent of the jobs are in Washington, D.C.) This section should answer many of your questions about working for the Federal Government. If you need more information, contact a Federal Job Information Center, a State Employment Service Office, or a Federal agency where you want to work.

The Competitive Service

Most Federal civilian jobs are in the competitive service, which means that people applying for them compete with other applicants and must be evaluated by the Office of Personnel Management or agencies under delegated authority. The information in this section applies only to competitive service jobs.

The Excepted Service

Some agencies (for example, the U.S. Postal Service, the Foreign Service of the Department of State, and the Tennessee Valley Authority) are excepted from competitive service procedures. **If you are interested in an excepted service job, you should not apply through the Office of Personnel Management, but should contact agencies directly.** A list of excepted agencies is included in a separate section of this book.

About Applying

The Office of Personnel Management (OPM) accepts applications for Federal employment based on the current and projected hiring needs of Government agencies.

After you apply, OPM examines your application to see whether you are qualified for the kind of work you want. If you are qualified, your name goes on a list with the names of other people who are qualified for the same kinds of jobs.

When Government hiring officials have vacancies, they

may ask OPM for the names of people qualified to fill the jobs. The best qualified applicants' names are referred from OPM lists for hiring consideration by the agency.

Your chances of being hired depend on your qualifications, how fast vacancies are occurring in the area where you want to work, the number of qualified applicants who want the same kind of job, and the salary level you say you will accept.

Many factors affect whether Government agencies will be hiring and the number of jobs of various types they will fill. Among them are such factors as current policy and program priorities, budget and workload levels, labor market conditions, and rates of turnover.

When there are enough qualified applicants on its lists, OPM stops accepting applications. Also, because Government hiring needs vary by location, you might be able to apply for the same type of job one place, but not in another. However, if you are a veteran, you may be able to take advantage of the following exceptions: 1) If applications were accepted during the time they were on active duty, returning veterans may apply within 120 days after discharge or release from a hospital, even if applications are not being accepted from non-veterans. 2) People entitled to 10-point veteran preference (see **Veteran Preference** later in this section) may apply at any time for a position for which the OPM maintains a list or is about to establish a list, or for which a non-temporary appointment was made in the preceding three years. (See **Kinds of Appointments** below.)

Federal Job Information Centers

The Office of Personnel Management maintains Federal Job Information Centers in several major metropolitan areas across the country. They are listed under "U.S. Government" in the white pages of local phone books; a directory of these facilities is included in a separate section of this book. Federal job opportunities are also posted in State Job Service (State Employment Security) Offices.

HOW JOBS ARE FILLED

First, see the Office of Personnel Management. For most Federal jobs, you must be on an OPM list and be referred to the agency as being among the most highly qualified applicants for the job. In order to get on the list, contact a Federal Job Information Center (or State Job Service Office) to see whether applications are being accepted in your area for the kind of work you want. If you're not sure what kind of work you want, job information specialists may be able to suggest a type of work for which your education and experience might qualify you. The qualifications information and application forms you'll need can be obtained in person or by mail from a Federal Job Information Center.

Qualifications Required

Read the Qualifications Information Statement -- QIS (sometimes called an "announcement") carefully. It tells what education and/or experience you need and whether a written test is required for the job. If it states that persons must have one year of experience in a certain field, and you lack that experience, don't apply. If applications are being accepted for jobs in a certain location only and you don't want to work there, don't file. Many disappointed applicants waste valuable time and effort applying for jobs which they either do not want or are not qualified to do, simply because they don't read job information carefully.

Competitive service jobs are classified by grade levels based on the level of responsibility required for the job. Salaries correspond to the grades; the higher the grade, the higher the salary. (An outline of the pay grade system appears later in this section.)

To qualify for most Federal jobs, you must have the amount of education and/or experience specified for the grade level you want. However, for some jobs there is no rigid requirement as to the number of years of education or experience. For these, you must show that you have the knowledge, skills, and abilities needed to do the work by providing information to supplement your application. The qualifications material for the job you want will tell you the particular requirements needed.

Filling Out The Forms

Be sure to fill out the forms carefully and completely, following the directions on each. Describe your background in full, since credit cannot be given for qualifications you fail to tell about.

Answer every question on the application, being sure to sign it. If you don't, the Office of Personnel Management will have to write to you to get the missing information, which will delay processing your application.

If a deadline is given for filing your application, be sure to send it to the address specified in the instructions on or before the deadline date.

Volunteer Experience

Unpaid experience or volunteer work in community, cultural, social service or professional associations will count the same as paid experience if it is of the type and level acceptable as paid expericence for the job you want. When you are filling out your application forms, be sure to describe the work fully, showing the actual number of hours a week spent on the activity, in order to receive credit for it.

Written Tests

Written tests are not required for many government jobs. For some jobs, however -- including certain law-enforcement and clerical positions -- a written exam is required. If the qualifications information says that a written test is required for the kind of job you want, you will receive a notice in the mail telling you when and where to go for the test, or an information sheet will list the dates and times when the test is given.

The test will be practical. It will test your ability to do the job you applied for or it will measure your ability to learn how to do it. It is not necessary to prepare for the test by taking a "Civil Service" course. No school can guarantee that you will be found qualified or that you will be offered a job.

Tests for Handicapped Persons

Special examinations can be arranged for handicapped persons to assure that their abilities are fairly assessed. Blind persons are provided with readers or, if they prefer, may use certain tests which have been placed on cassette tape or printed in braille. Certain verbal test requirements have been waived, and sign language interpreters may be used to ensure that deaf applicants clearly understand the instructions for those tests that are not waived. Applicants having difficulty in writing may be given extra time on their tests, and examiners may mark their answer sheets at the applicants' instruction.

In some cases, handicapped applicants can be hired

without competing with other applicants. Ask about selective placement assistance at Federal Job Information Centers, at OPM Regional Offices (listed at the end of this section) or the selective placement coordinator in an agency where you want to work.

How You Are Rated

If you take a written test, you will receive a notice of your score and your name will be placed on a civil service list according to the score. Applicants are referred to agencies for job consideration in order of their standing on the list and in accordance with veteran preference laws. (See **Veteran Preference** below.)

If you apply for a job that doesn't require a written test, your rating will be based on the experience, education, and training you describe on your application, along with supplemental information you may be asked to provide. Your qualifications may also be verified with former employers and supervisors.

If you are qualified for salaries higher than you applied for, you may also be rated at the higher salary levels. You will not be rated for jobs with salaries lower than you say you will accept.

You will be told of the status of your application by the office to which you applied. The notice will usually tell you what your score is for each grade for which you qualified and how long your name will remain on the list for referral to agencies.

If you did not qualify and feel you should have, or if you have questions about your rating, you should contact the office it came from. If you do write the OPM office, be sure to give your full name, the job and grade level for which you applied, the rating you received, your date of birth, your Social Security number, and any identification number that appears on your Notice of Rating.

If there is any important change in your status (such as a change of address or name or the area where you want to work), be sure to keep the office informed.

Referral for Jobs

Federal hiring officials fill jobs in several ways. They can promote an employee who was hired at a lower level and has progressed to the point of assuming greater responsibility; they can hire an employee who wants to transfer from another agency or a former career employee who wants to be reinstated; or they can request the names of qualified applicants from an OPM list.

When the OPM receives a request, it sends to the agency the names of people highest on the list. If the job to be filled has specialized requirements, OPM sends the names of the top persons who meet the special requirements. Applicants who have indicated that they do not want to work in the place where the job is located are not considered.

The "Rule of Three"

The hiring official in the agency makes a choice from among the top three available applicants on the list of names sent by the Office of Personnel Management. By law, the agency official does not have to choose the top person, but has a choice of any of the top three -- so long as he or she doesn't pass over a veteran to hire a non-veteran. This explains why a person whose name is at the top of the list sometimes doesn't get a job, when people lower on the list may. The names of applicants who aren't selected go back to the OPM list and will stay on the list until they are hired, their eligibility expires, or the list is terminated.

Appeals

If you believe you have been discriminated against by a Federal agency on the basis of race, color, religion, sex, physical or mental handicap or national origin, you may file a written complaint with the agency within 30 days of the date of the incident.

If you believe a hiring practice administered or required by OPM was not fair or was not based on the ability to do the job, you may appeal to OPM no later than 15 days from the date the practice was applied or the results made known.

Veteran Preference

If you are a veteran, you may be eligible for special consideration and assistance in getting a Government job and also in keeping it after you are hired. For example, if you are found basically qualified for the kind of work you want, veteran preference will add 5 or 10 points to your score.

The following people receive 10 points: (1) a veteran who received a Purple Heart or has a service-connected disability; (2) the spouse of a veteran who is unable to qualify for Federal employment because of a service-connected disability; (3) the unremarried widow or widower of a veteran who served in the armed forces during a war, in a campaign or expedition for which a campaign badge was authorized, or during the period beginning April 28, 1952, and ending July 1, 1955; (4) certain mothers of veterans who died or were permanently disabled while on active duty.

Most other honorably discharged veterans get 5 points provided their service began before October 5, 1976.

Under certain circumstances, Vietnam Era veterans may be hired without competing with other applicants. Any veteran with a compensable disability of 30% or more may also be hired non-competitively. As of October 1, 1980, non-disabled veterans who held the rank of major (or its equivalent) or above will not be entitled to veteran preference when applying for a Government job.

Federal Job Information Centers and veterans placement coordinators in Federal Government agencies can give you more detailed information about who is entitled to veteran preference and what its benefits are.

Kinds of Appointments

If you are offered a job, the letter or telegram you receive will tell you what kind of appointment you are being offered. Most appointments are either temporary, term, career-conditional, or career. Their conditions are as follows:

A **temporary appointment** is an appointment for one year or less. Temporary workers can't be promoted and can't transfer to another Government job. They are not under the retirement system and are not entitled to health or life insurance benefits.

A **term appointment** is made for work on a specific project that will last more than one year but less than four years. Term employees can be promoted or reassigned to other positions within the project for which they were hired. They are not under the retirement system, but they are eligible for health and life insurance benefits. If you accept a temporary or term appointment, your name will stay on the list from which you were hired. This means that you will not hurt your chances to be considered for career-conditional or career appointments by accepting temporary or term appointments.

A **career-conditional appointment** leads after three years of continuous service to a career appointment, which gives an employee career tenure and rights and privileges not available to other employees. During this time, employees must demonstrate that they can do satisfactory work and may be dismissed for failure to do so. After the probationary period, career-conditional employees cannot be dismissed without evidence of misconduct, delinquency, or inefficiency on the job. Career-conditional employees have transfer and promotion privileges. After achieving career status, an employee is in the last group to be affected during a layoff period. Employees who leave the Federal service after achieving career status may reenter at any time without taking a written test or being reevaluated by the Office of Personnel Management. (This is "reinstatement".)

A **career appointment** is rarely offered to new employees unless they are transferring from another merit system under which they have already served three years.

Part-Time Work

Most Government agencies hire employees who work less than full time. Some work part-time on a permanent basis, for a few hours each day or on a temporary basis, for a limited number of weeks or months.

You apply for part-time work, showing on your application form the number of hours you want to work. Permanent part-time workers are eligible for most of the same fringe benefits, including retirement, health and life insurance, as full-time workers. Temporary employees, both full and part-time, generally receive only Social Security coverage and leave benefits.

GETTING A JOB THROUGH OPM

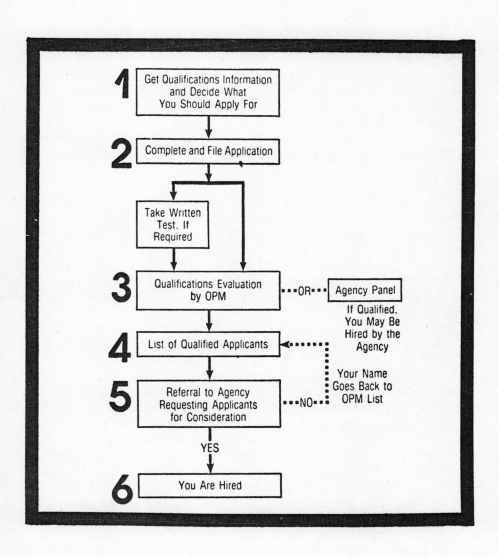

EMPLOYMENT REQUIREMENTS

When you are being considered for a job, and at the time you are hired, there are requirements which must be taken into account in addition to your being able to do the work.

Probationary Periods

As mentioned earlier, competitive service employees may be let go during their probationary periods if they do not perform satisfactorily on the job. (They may be removed after that time, too; but the procedures are more complex.)

Another trial period exists for employees who move into supervisory or management jobs; before their appointments become final, they must show that they can perform well as managers or supervisors. If they do not, they may be removed to positions at the same grade without supervisory or managerial responsibilities.

Suitability

Federal employees are expected to have reputations as honest, reliable , trustworthy, and loyal persons. It is not surprising, then, that there is a requirement that everyone entering the Government be investigated. The Office of Personnel Management and the agency which employs you have joint responsibility for determining your fitness. When and how you are investigated will depend upon the type of position you are considered for or appointed to. If the position is sensitive from the standpoint of national security, you will probably be investigated before you are appointed. This investigation will consist of personal interviews with employers, teachers, friends, acquaintances, etc., as well as a check of various records. If the position you are appointed to is not sensitive, an investigation of lower intensity will be conducted immediately after you are employed. This investigation consists of a check of various records and written inquiries to employers and references. In either case, your fingerprints will be checked against the records of the Federal Bureau of Investigation.

The application form asks you to disclose discharges from employment and certain criminal convictions. However, having been fired or convicted will not automatically disqualify you.

Travel

If you have to move in order to report for duty, you ordinarily pay your own way. The Government pays initial moving or travel expenses for only a few hard-to-fill positions.

Political Activity

The law protects Federal employees from improper political pressures by placing restrictions on their political activity. As a Federal worker, you may, of course, vote as you please and express your opinions as a private citizen. Fed Facts 2, a leaflet on political activities of Federal employees, gives details.

Holding Outside Employment

As a Federal employee, you are permitted to engage in any spare-time work which does not interfere with your Government work. If you intend to take on an outside job, you should discuss your plan with your supervisor or agency personnel officer to determine whether it will be compatible with your regular job.

Jobs in Foreign Countries

In most instances where U.S. installations are established in foreign countries, vacancies are filled by hiring U.S. citizens residing in the area, or residents of the foreign country.

OTHER REQUIREMENTS

Age

Some jobs have special minimum and maximum age limits. (For example, many law enforcement officers must not have passed their 35th birthday before starting work.) Check the qualifications information for the job you want before you apply. The usual minimum age at which you can be hired is 18, although you can apply for most jobs at age 16 if you are a high school graduate. If you are 16 or 17 and are out of school but haven't graduated, you may be hired in a permanent position only if (1) you have successfully completed a formal training program preparing you for work, sponsored by public or private organizations concerned with providing work training for youths; or (2) if you have been out of school for at least 3 months, not counting summer vacation, and school authorities write a letter on their official stationery agreeing with your preference for work instead of additional schooling.

Student Employment

Job opportunities are best if you graduate. If you can, you should complete your education before you apply for full-time work. In order to encourage students to complete their education, there are special Government employment opportunities for disadvantaged youth and for students enrolled in vocational education programs. Students who meet certain requirements can be hired to work during school vacations as summer aides and part-time as student aides during the school year if they are 16 and (1) the part-time work schedule is set up through agreement with the school; (2) the school certifies that the student can maintain good standing in school while working; and (3) the student stays in school. To find out whether you qualify for the Stay-In-School or Summer Aid Programs, contact a Federal Job Information Center or local offices of your State Employment Service. Information on the Cooperative Education Program may be obtained from your school guidance counselor.

Other students who want to apply for summer jobs must be 18 (or at least 16 and a high school graduate) at the time they are hired. If you are interested, you should ask about summer employment opportunities early in the school year for a job the following summer. Information is available at Federal Job Information Centers or at the agency where you wish to work.

Some Federal agencies may have programs in which students may work on a volunteer (unpaid) basis in jobs which add to their experience in their chosen career field. Interested students should check with an agency nearby.

Citizenship

Generally, only American citizens may apply for and be appointed to jobs in the competitive civil service. This restriction does not apply to positions overseas or in the excepted service (see **The Excepted Service** above). The laws on citizenship are very complex, and are described in OPM pamphlet BRE-27, Federal Employment of Noncitizens. This pamphlet may be obtained at Federal Job Information Centers.

The best source of information on whether an agency can hire noncitizens is the particular agency where an applicant wants to work.

Physical Requirements

You must be physically able to perform the duties of positions you apply for, and must be emotionally and mentally stable. A physical or mental handicap or a prior emotional problem will not disqualify you if you can do your work efficiently without being a hazard to yourself or to others.

For a few positions (among them air traffic controllers, Federal mine inspectors, and many law enforcement jobs) applicants must pass rigid physical examinations before beginning work. When the duties of positions require strict physical standards, the requirements are described in detail in the application information.

Selective placement assistance is available for applicants with physical or mental disabilities (including mentally restored persons). This assistance may include job information; special testing for applicants with visual, hearing, or motor impairments; and referral to agency coordinators for selective placement. If you wish assistance, you should contact your nearest Federal Job Information Center.

ON THE JOB

After being selected on the basis of merit, Government employees are paid and promoted on the same basis. Federal salaries are based on the principle of equal pay for work of equal value. When jobs in higher grades are open, they are often filled by promoting employees in lower grades who have become qualifed to perform more difficult duties.

Pay

The pay grades of Government jobs are established after position classifiers study the duties involved. They find out how difficult the duties are, how much responsibility is involved, and what knowledge, skill, or experience goes into performing the duties. Then they classify the jobs in appropriate grades under standards set by the Office of Personnel Management.

A Government employee's pay is determined by the level of the job he or she fills, not necessarily by the employee's qualifications. (For example, if you are qualified for a GS-9, but accept a job at the GS-5 level, you would be paid the GS-5 salary, not the GS-9 salary.)

Government policy is that the salaries of Federal employees should be comparable with those paid by private employers for work of the same difficulty and responsibility. Salaries are reviewed periodically and adjusted so that, over the years, people choosing Government careers can expect pay which is realistically geared to the economy. The current salaries are published by OPM and are available at Federal Job Information Centers. There are several schedules of pay grades, the most common being the General Schedule and the Wage Grade Schedule.

The General Schedule

The General Schedule (GS) pay system applies to most white-collar jobs and to protective occupations, such as guards -- a total of about 45 percent of Federal employees. Under the General Schedule, positions are graded by number according to how difficult the work is, starting with GS-1 and going up to GS-18. Clerical workers generally start at GS-1, 2, or 3; guards at GS-4, and white-collar workers with experience or education equal to a college degree at GS-5. The salaries of each grade are set by the President and approved by Congress.

Wage Grades

Most blue-collar positions are covered under Wage Grade pay rates which vary according to the location where the employee is working. Wage Grade salaries are adjusted from time to time to bring them into line with prevailing wages paid for the same work by private industry in the same locality.

Other Pay Systems

A few Federal agencies and a few classes of employees have other pay plans. The Tennessee Valley Authority, the Foreign Service of the Department of State, and physicians, dentists, and nurses in the Department of Medicine and Surgery of the Veterans Administration are among them.

Within-Grade Steps

Each Grade has a set salary range of within-grade "steps". New employees almost always are hired at the first step of a grade. If they do their work well, they receive within-grade raises at intervals until the top rate of the grade is reached. Employees may be awarded additional within-grade increases for exceptionally outstanding work.

Merit Pay

Managers and supervisors in grades GS-13, 14, and 15 do not receive standard within-grade increases based on length of service. Instead, they are eligible for increases based on a formal appraisal of their performance and the performance of the organizations they direct.

The Senior Executive Service includes top-level managers (GS-16 or above) who are paid according to their performance.

Hours of Work

The usual Government work week is 40 hours, 5 days a week, Monday through Friday. However, in some cases (for example, nurses and building guards) the nature of the work may require different hours.

As in any other business, employees sometimes have to work overtime. Employees who do so are either paid for the overtime or given time off to make up for the extra time worked. For jobs which require work after 6 pm, a higher rate of pay (night differential) may be paid.

Several government agencies have instituted flexible work schedules, which allow employees to vary their hours of work, while continuing to work a 40-hour week.

Advancement and Training

Many of the people in top jobs in Government began their careers at the bottom of the ladder. They did their jobs well, took advantage of training opportunities, and learned more and more about the work of their agencies. As they became more qualified, they were promoted to increasingly important positions. Whenever possible, most agencies fill vacancies by promoting their own employees. Promotion programs in every agency are designed to make sure that promotions go to the employees who are among the best qualified to fill higher positions. How fast employees are promoted depends upon openings in the higher grades and upon their own ability and effort.

Federal employees receive on-the-job training. They may also receive additional job-related training in their own agencies, in other agencies and at facilities outside Government.

It is not always necessary to move to a new job in order to advance in grade. Sometimes, because of changes in work assignments, responsibilities of an employee's job may increase to the extent that it should be placed in a higher grade, resulting in a promotion for the employee.

Transfers

One advantage of working for the Federal Government is the possibility of moving to a better job by transferring from one agency to another without going through the examining process over again. However, in order to transfer, an employee would have to locate his or her own job by checking for vacancies and interviewing with officials in other agencies. If a position is vacant, and the hiring official is impressed with an individual's qualifications, arrangements may be made for the transfer.

Performance on the Job

At regular intervals, employee job performance is evaluated. These evaluations are taken into account when an employee is considered for a promotion or transfer to another agency and when an agency has to lay people off. Employees whose performance is unsatisfactory may be dismissed or assigned to other jobs with duties which they can be expected to learn to do satisfactorily.

Incentive Awards

Government agencies encourage their employees to suggest better, simpler, and more economical ways of doing their jobs. They may give a cash award to an employee for a suggestion or invention that results in saving money or giving improved service. They may also reward outstanding job performance or other acts which are especially deserving of recognition.

Vacation and Sick Leave

For vacations and other purposes, most Federal employees earn annual leave according to the number of years (civilian plus creditable military service) they have been in the

Federal service: 13 days a year for the first three years, 20 days a year for the next 12 years. After 15 years, they earn 26 days of annual leave each year.

Sick leave is intended for use for illnesses serious enough to keep you away from work, and for appointments with doctors, dentists, or opticians. Sick leave that is not used accumulates for future use. It is one of the best forms of insurance an employee can have in case of extended periods of sickness.

Occupational Health Program

The Federal Government maintains an occupational health program for the health and fitness of its employees. This includes emergency medical treatment, health maintenance examinations, immunizations, and programs for assistance with alcoholism and drug abuse problems.

Retirement

Seven percent of employees' salaries is withheld from all paychecks as employee shares in a retirement fund. The Government also contributes seven percent to the fund, which provides employees and their families or survivors with an income after completing their working careers.

If you work for the Government for 30 years, you can retire at age 55 and get a lifetime annual income equal to 56 1/4% of the highest average salary you earned during any three consecutive years of your working career. An employee who becomes disabled after at least five years of Government service may retire on an annuity at any age.

If you leave the Government before you complete five years of service, you will not be entitled to an annuity and the money you put into the retirement fund can be returned to you. If you leave after completing five or more years of service, you have a choice of having your money returned or leaving it in the fund. If you leave it in the fund, you will get an annuity starting when you are 62.

Layoffs

Government layoffs are called reductions in force, and may be caused by such factors as a cut in appropriations, closing of a facility, or a decrease in workload. During a reduction in force (RIF) the four things that determine the order in which an employee may be displaced are: the type of appointment held, whether the employee has veteran preference for this purpose (most 20-year retired veterans do not), how long an employee has worked for the Government, and the quality of the employee's job performance.

If you are separated from your job because your agency had to undertake a reduction in force, the Federal Government has a commitment and an obligation to assist you, to the maximum extent possible, in obtaining other employment. OPM supplements the placement efforts of agencies actually running reductions in force by operating placement assistance programs which ensure that you receive first consideration for other available Government positions for which you qualify before outside candidates can be considered.

Unemployment Compensation

If unemployed, Federal workers are entitled to unemployment compensation similar to that provided for employees in private industry. They are covered by the unemployment insurance system under conditions set by the State in which they worked.

Severance Pay

A Federal employee who is involuntarily separated through RIF, or for other reasons which are no fault of his or her own (in other words, an employee whose termination is free from problems such as misconduct, delinquency, or inefficiency), and who is not entitled to an immediate retirement annuity, may be eligible for severance pay. This pay is based on years of service and age over 40, and may not exceed a year's basic salary.

Employee Organizations

There are a number of unions and other employee organizations in the Federal Government. Some of them are for special groups, such as postal employees, while others have a general membership throughout Government agencies. As a Federal employee, you are free to join or refrain from joining such organizations.

OPM Regional Offices

The Office of Personnel Management has regional offices in Atlanta, GA; Boston, MA; Chicago, IL; Dallas, TX; Denver, CO; New York, NY; Philadelphia, PA; St. Louis, MO; San Francisco, CA; and Seattle, WA. The central office is located in Washington, DC, 20415. A complete directory of the OPM offices which provide Federal job information and testing services follows.

OPM FACILITIES AND TEST CENTERS NATIONWIDE

The Office of Personnel Management operates area offices and Federal job test centers in the cities listed below. These offices provide general information on Federal employment, explain how to apply for specific jobs, supply application materials, and conduct written examinations, when required.

You can get information by mail, by telephone, or by visiting these offices. Usually, the easiest method, if you want information or application material for a specific job or occupation and can identify it clearly, is to write. The number of hours each office is open to the public varies from one office to another. Because of the large number of people who seek information by telephone, the lines are frequently busy or callers must hold for a time before someone can speak to them. Fortunately, many offices provide recorded messages which give hours of service, general information, and in some cases, even supply the best opportunities for Federal employment.

OPM also provides Federal employment information to State Job Service (State Employment Security) offices, and for college-entry jobs, to college placement offices. In addition, many Federal agencies recruit directly for their own vacancies and provide a variety of information services.

ALABAMA
Huntsville:

> Southerland Building
> 806 Governors Drive, Southwest
> Huntsville AL 35801
> 205/453-5070

ALASKA
Anchorage:

> Federal Building
> 701 C Street, Box 22
> Anchorage AK 99513
> 907/271-5821

ARIZONA
Phoenix:

U.S. Postal Service Building
522 North Central Avenue
Phoenix AZ 85004
602/261-4736

ARKANSAS
Little Rock:

Federal Building, Third Floor
700 West Capitol Avenue
Little Rock AR 72201
501/378-5842

CALIFORNIA
Los Angeles:

Linder Building
845 South Figueroa
Los Angeles CA 90017
213/688-3360

Sacramento:

1029 J Street
Room 202
Sacramento CA 95814
916/440-3441

San Diego:

880 Front Street
San Diego CA 92188
714/293-6165

San Francisco:

211 Main Street, Second Floor
San Francisco CA 94105
415/974-9725

COLORADO
Denver:

1845 Sherman Street
Denver CO 80203
303/837-3509

CONNECTICUT
Hartford:

> Federal Building, Room 613
> 450 Main Street
> Hartford CT 06103
> 203/722-3096

DISTRICT OF COLUMBIA
Metro Area:

> 1900 E Street NW
> Washington DC 20415
> 202/737-9616

FLORIDA
Orlando:

> Federal Building and U.S. Courthouse
> 80 North Hughey Avenue
> Orlando FL 32801
> 305/420-6148 or 305/420-6149

GEORGIA
Atlanta:

> Richard B. Russell Federal Building, 9th Floor
> 75 Spring Street Southwest
> Atlanta GA 30303
> 404/221-4315

GUAM
Agana:

> Pacific News Building
> 238 O'Hara Street, Room 308
> Agana GU 96910
> 344-5242

HAWAII
Honolulu (and Island of Oahu)

> Federal Building, Room 1310
> 300 Ala Moana Boulevard
> Honolulu HI 96850
> 808/546-8600

ILLINOIS
Chicago:

> 55 East Jackson, Room 1401
> Chicago IL 60604
> 312/353-5136

INDIANA
Indianapolis:

46 East Ohio Street, Room 124
Indianapolis IN 46204
317/269-7161

IOWA
Des Moines:

210 Walnut Street, Room 191
Des Moines IA 50309
515/284-4545
(In Scott and Pottawattamie Counties, dial
402/221-3815)

KANSAS
Wichita:

One-Twenty Building, Room 101
120 South Market Street
Wichita KS 67202
316/269-6106
(In Johnson, Leavenworth, and Wyandotte
Counties, dial 816/374-5702.)

LOUISIANA
New Orleans:

F. Edward Hebert Building
610 South Street, Room 849
New Orleans LA 70130
504/589-2764

MARYLAND
Baltimore:

Garmatz Federal Building
101 West Lombard Street
Baltimore MD 21201
301/962-3822

DC Metro Area:

1900 E Street NW
Washington DC 20415
202/737-9616

MASSACHUSETTS
Boston:

3 Center Plaza
Boston MA 02108
617/223-2571

MICHIGAN
Detroit:

> 477 Michigan Avenue, Room 565
> Detroit MI 48226
> 313/226-6950

MINNESOTA
Twin Cities:

> Federal Building
> Fort Snelling
> Twin Cities MN 55111
> 612/725-4430

MISSISSIPPI
Jackson:

> 100 West Capitol Street, Suite 335
> Jackson MS 39620
> 601/960-4585

MISSOURI
Kansas City:

> Federal Building, Room 134
> 601 East 12th Street
> Kansas City MO 64106
> 816/374-5702

St. Louis:

> Old Post Office, Room 400
> 815 Olive Street
> St. Louis MO 63101
> 314/425-4285

NEBRASKA
Omaha:

> U.S. Courthouse and Post Office Building, Room 1010
> 215 North 17th Sttreet
> Omaha NE 68102
> 402/221-3815

NEW HAMPSHIRE
Portsmouth:

> Thomas J. McIntyre Federal Building, Room 104
> 8 Daniel Street
> Portsmouth NH 03801
> 603/436-7220, ext. 762

NEW JERSEY
Newark:

> Peter W. Rodino, Jr., Federal Building
> 970 Broad Street
> Newark NJ 07102
> 201/645-3673
> (In Camden, dial 215/597-7440)

NEW MEXICO
Albuquerque:

> Federal Building
> 421 Gold Avenue Southwest
> Albuquerque NM 87102
> 505/766-5583

NEW YORK
New York City:

> Jacob K. Javits Federal Building
> 26 Federal Plaza
> New York NY 10278
> 212/264-0422

Syracuse:

> James N. Hanley Federal Building
> 100 South Clinton Street
> Syracuse NY 13260
> 315/423-5660

NORTH CAROLINA
Raleigh:

> Federal Building
> 310 New Bern Avenue, P.O. Box 25069
> Raleigh NC 27611
> 919/755-4361

OHIO
Dayton:

> Federal Building
> 200 West Second Street
> Dayton OH 45402
> 513/225-2720

OKLAHOMA
Oklahoma City:

> 200 Northwest Fifth Street, Room 205
> Oklahoma City OK 73102
> 405/231-4948

OREGON
Portland:

Federal Building
1220 Southwest Third Street
Portland OR 97204
503/221-3141

PENNSYLVANIA
Harrisburg:

Federal Building, Room 168
Harrisburg PA 17108
717/782-4494

Philadelphia:

William J. Green, Jr., Federal Building
600 Arch Street
Philadelphia PA 19106
215/597-7440

Pittsburgh:

Federal Building
1000 Liberty Avenue
Pittsburgh PA 15222
412/644-2755

PUERTO RICO
San Juan:

Federico Degetau Federal Building
Carlos E. Chardon Street
Hato Rey, PR 00918
809/753-4209

RHODE ISLAND
Providence:

John O. Pastori Federal Building, Room 310
Kennedy Plaza
Providence RI 02903
401/528-5251

SOUTH CAROLINA
Charleston:

Federal Building
334 Meeting Street
Charleston SC 29403
803/724-4328

TENNESSEE
Memphis:

100 North Main Street, Suite 1312
Memphis TN 38103
901/521-3956

TEXAS
Dallas:

1100 Commerce Street, Room 6B4
Dallas TX 75242
214/767-8035

Houston:

701 San Jacinto Road, 4th Floor
Houston TX 77002
713/226-2375

San Antonio:

643 East Durango Boulevard
San Antonio TX 78206
512/229-6611

VIRGINIA
Norfolk:

Federal Building, Room 220
200 Granby Mall
Norfolk VA 23510
804/441-3355

D.C. Metro Area:

1900 E Street, NW
Washington DC 20415
202/737-9616

WASHINGTON
Seattle:

Federal Building
915 Second Avenue
Seattle WA 98175
206/442-4365

WEST VIRGINIA
Charleston:

Federal Building
500 Quarrier Street
Charleston WV 25301
304/343-6181, ext. 226

GOVERNMENT AND INTERNATIONAL ORGANIZATIONS HIRING INDEPENDENTLY

Certain Federal organizations are excepted from the competitive civil service and fill their jobs through their own hiring systems. To get one of these jobs, you do not have to pass an Office of Personnel Management examination.

If you are interested in a job with one of these organizations, you should contact that organization directly at the address given below.

An asterisk (*) indicates that under certain conditions, employees of the agency in question may transfer to positions in the competitive civil service without first having to qualify by passing an OPM examination.

U.S. Government Organizations

Defense Intelligence Agency
Civilian Personnel Operations Division
Pentagon
Washington DC 20301

Federal Bureau of Investigation
10th Street and Pennsylvania Avenue NW
Washington DC 20535

Federal Reserve System, Board of Governors
20th Street and Constitution Avenue NW
Washington DC 20551

General Accounting Office
Room 4650
441 G Street NW
Washington DC 20548

International Development Cooperation Agency*
320 21st Street NW
Washington DC 20523

International Monetary Fund
Recruitment and Training Division
700 19th Street NW
Washington DC 20431

Pan American Health Organization
Pan American Sanitary Bureau
Regional Office of the World Health Organization
525 23rd Street NW
Washington DC 20037

United Nations Children's Fund (UNICEF)
Recruitment and Placement Section
Division of Personnel
866 United Nations Plaza
New York NY 10017

United Nations Development Programme
Division of Personnel
1 United Nations Plaza
New York NY 10017

United Nations Fund For Population Activites
220 East 42nd Street
New York NY 10017

United Nations Institute for Training and Research
801 United Nations Plaza
New York NY 10017

United Nations Secretariat
Office of Personnel Services
Recruitment Programmes Section
New York NY 10017

World Bank and IFC
Director, Personnel Management Department
Recruitment Division
1818 H Street NW
Washington DC 20433

EMPLOYMENT SERVICES

Employment services fall into three basic categories: executive search firms; employment agencies and counseling services. There are also important distinctions among the types of organizations listed within each basic category.

Executive search firms, often called "head hunters" can be divided into two types -- those that operate on retainer for their client companies, and those that operate on a contingency basis. Executive search firms handle only experienced executives, focus on positions in the higher salary ranges, and generally do not specialize in any particular industry.

Executive search firms are always hired by and compensated by the employer. They are as likely to contact and recruit a candidate who is not even considering switching jobs as one who is currently in the job market. They will only be interested in executives with an established record of success in a position that is directly applicable to the specific needs of current or future recruiting assignments. Executive search firms will often keep on file the names of tens of thousands of possible candidates for placement.

After receiving an assignment, the search firm will go through its records, as well as other sources, and quickly limit its search to a few dozen or a few hundred names, depending on the importance of the position being filled. Then, after intensive study of these candidates, and after discussions with sources in the industry, the executive search firm might interview a few dozen candidates. Finally, the firm will present the strongest few candidates to its client firm for final selection. If you are an experienced executive, you may want to send in your resume to one or more of the executive search firms listed below, but don't bother to follow up with a phone call -- and don't expect an interview unless your background happens to match their current needs.

Employment agencies must first be divided into private agencies, and those agencies operated by state governments. State employment agencies place a broad range of individuals, including hard to place workers, such as the unemployed and low-skilled people. In some states, private employment agencies are allowed to charge the employee a fee. But the vast majority of private employment agencies are "fee-paid" (by the employer). The employment agencies will charge the employer a fee, usually based on a percentage of the first year's salary after employment commences. The fee ranges from 10 to 25 percent or more of the first year's salary.

Employment agencies do not have the reputation for being the most reputable of industries. Firms specializing in lower end placement and office help are notorious for running ads for positions they do not have and for pitching candidates to employers that do not exist. With placement fees often running over $2000 even for a secretarial placement, many agencies will not hesitate to push a job-seeker to take a position they know the person will not really like. Some agencies will have the job seeker stop by their office both before and after job interviews to try to monopolize the candidate's time and thereby prevent the person from using another agency. On the other hand, many empolyment agencies, especially those operating in only one industry (where word-of-mouth travels fast) place great importance upon their reputation, and operate with a high sense of integrity.

Employment agencies that place professionals usually specialize in a particular industry or profession. Employment agencies are particularly active in the higher demand professions such as computer programming and engineering. Other professions with specialized employment agencies include: accounting, banking, finance, advertising, data processing, medicine, insurance, publishing, retailing, sales, and a variety of technical fields. Like executive search firms, employment agencies that place professionals are not interested in individuals without experience, or people hoping to switch careers. But these employment agencies fill fewer senior positions than executive search firms, and hence can sometimes place professionals with only five to ten years of relevant work experience. If you are well qualified in a certain area, a specialized employment agency may also be quite interested in meeting you and trying to place you.

Employment agencies are licensed by the state in which they operate. Some states will furnish you with the number of business complaints that have been lodged against a particular employment agency.

Counseling services are even more diverse. Many non-profit organizations offer counseling services for very low fees or even for free. These organizations include colleges and universities, as well as private associations. For-profit counseling services charges a broad range of fees. Services offered include individual career counseling, internship programs, specialized workshops in areas such as resume and interview preparation, and aptitude and interest testing.

EMPLOYMENT AGENCIES AND TEMPORARY SERVICES OF THE DISTRICT OF COLUMBIA

ATLAS PERSONNEL AGENCY
1660 L Street N.W.
Suite 309
Washington DC 20036
Contact Dolores K. Ebert, President. 202/293-7210. Employment agency. Appointment requested. Founded 1940. Branch office located in Rockville, MD. Nonspecialized. Positions commonly filled include: Accountant; Administrative Assistant; Bank Officer/Manager; Bookkeeper; Clerk; Contracts Administrator; Contracts Manager; Credit Manager; Customer Service Representative; Data Entry Clerk; Financial Analyst; Legal Secretary; Medical Secretary; Receptionist; Secretary; Stenographer; Typist; Word Processing Specialist. Company pays fee. Number of placements per year: 201-500.

CREATIVE OPTIONS CORPORATION/TEMPORARY OPTIONS, INC.
1629 K Street NW
Suite 800
Washington DC 20006
Contact Alison Walisko or Fran Rea, Personnel Coordinators. 202/785-9377. Temporary help service. Founded 1980. Specializes in the areas of: Creative Personnel; Graphics; Technical. Positions commonly filled include: Production Artist; Proofreader; Reporter/Editor; Technical Writer/Editor; Typesetter; Copywriter; Designers; Computer Graphics Specialist. Company pays fee. Number of placements per year: 501-1000.

DURHAM PERSONNEL INC.
1725 K Street N.W.
Suite 608
Washington DC 20006
Contact Mike Jameson, Branch Manager. 202/861-0355. Temporary help service. No appointment required. Founded 1967. Member, National Association of Temporary Services. Branch offices in: Atlanta, Dallas, San Antonio, and western New York. Nonspecialized. Positions commonly filled include: Accountant; Administrative Assistant; Bookkeeper; Clerk; Computer Operator; Computer Programmer; Construction Worker; Customer Service Representative; Data Entry Clerk; Demonstrator; Dietician; Driver; Factory Worker; General Laborer; General Manager; Legal Secretary; Light Industrial Worker; Medical Secretary; Model; Office Worker; Receptionist; Secretary; Stenographer; Typist; Word Processing Specialist. Company pays fee. Number of placements per year: 1000+.

EXCLUSIVE TEMPORARIES OF WASHINGTON
1156 15th Street N.W.
Suite 530
Washington DC 20005
Contact Denise Madison, Operations Manager. 202/659-0944. Temporary help agency. Appointment required. Founded 1979. Specializes in the areas of: Secretarial and Clerical. Positions commonly filled

include: Accountant; Administrative Assistant; Architect; Bookkeeper; Civil Engineer; Claims Representative; Computer Programmer; Customer Service Rep; Data Entry Clerk; Draftsperson; Driver; EDP Specialist; Executive Secretary; Factory Worker; General Laborer; Legal Secretary; Light Industrial Worker; Marketing Specialist; Mechanical Engineer; Medical Secretary; Model; Nurse; Receptionist; Secretary; Stenographer; Systems Analyst; Typist; Word Processor. Number of placements per year: 501-1000.

THE PERSONNEL INSTITUTE
1000 Connecticut Avenue N.W.
Suite 702
Washington DC 20036
Contact Dr. William E. Stuart, President. 202/223-4911. Employment consultants. No appointment required. Founded 1963. Equipped to perform psychological testing and staffing studies. The Personnel Institute has an ongoing Outplacement Division as well as an Executive Search Department. Specializes in the areas of: Computer Hardware and Software; Engineering; Manufacturing; MIS/EDP; Minorities; Technical and Scientific; Veterans; Women. Positions commonly filled include: Aerospace Engineer; Bank Officer/Manager; Biologist; Biomedical Engineer; Computer Programmer; EDP Specialist; Economist; Electrical Engineer; Financial Analyst; Government Relations Specialist; Industrial Designer; Industrial Engineer; MIS Specialist; Marketing Specialist; Mechanical Engineer; Operations/Production Specialist; Physicist; Quality Control Supervisor; Systems Analyst; Washington Representative. Company pays fee. Number of placements per year: 201-500.

SPANISH CATHOLIC CENTER
3055 Mount Pleasant Street N.W.
Washington DC 20009
202/483-1520
Contact Sandra Aguilar, Director of Employment. Employment agency. No appointment required. Founded 1967. Provides employment assistance to newly arrived immigrants from Spanish speaking countries, Portuguese speaking countries, Ethiopia, Haiti, and others. Specializes in the areas of: Bilingual; Construction; Minorities; Nonprofit. Positions commonly filled include: Busperson; Construction Worker; Driver; Factory Worker; General Laborer; Housekeeper; Legal Secretary; Receptionist; Secretary; Waiter; Waitress. Number of placements per year: 501-1000.

STAFF BUILDERS INC. OF WASHINGTON, D.C.
1001 Connecticut Avenue N.W.
Suite 238
Washington DC 20036
703/734-8230
Temporary help service. Appointment requested. Founded 1961. Branch offices located in: Arizona; California; Connecticut; District of Columbia; Florida; Georgia; Illinois; Indiana; Kansas; Louisiana; Maryland; Massachusetts; Michigan; Minnesota; Missouri; Nevada; New Jersey; New Mexico; New York; Ohio; Oklahoma; Oregon; Pennsylvania; Rhode Island; Tennessee; Texas; Virginia; Washington. Nonspecialized. Positions commonly filled include: Accountant; Administrative Assistant; Bookkeeper; Clerk; Companion; Computer Operator; Computer Programmer; Customer Service Representative; Data Entry Clerk; Demonstrator; Driver; EDP Specialist; Factory Worker; General Laborer; Health Aide; Legal Secretary; Light Industrial Worker; Medical Secretary; Nurse; Office Worker; Public Relations Worker; Receptionist; Sales Representative; Secretary; Stenographer; Technician; Typist; Word Processing Specialist. Company pays fee. Number of placements per year: 1001+.

TAC/TEMPS INC. OF DISTRICT OF COLUMBIA
1717 K Street N.W.
Suite 402
Washington DC 20006
202/466-2495
Temporary help service. No appointment required. Branch offices located in: California; Connecticut; District of Columbia; Maryland; Massachusetts; New Hampshire; New York; Pennsylvania; Rhode Island; Virginia. Specializes in the areas of: Accounting and Finance; Advertising; Banking; Clerical; Education; Health and Medical; Insurance; Legal; Manufacturing; Nonprofit; Personnel and Human Resources; Printing and Publishing; Sales and Marketing; Transportation. Positions commonly filled include: Bookkeeper; Clerk; Data Entry Clerk; Demonstrator; Driver; Factory Worker; General Laborer; Legal Secretary; Light Industrial Worker; Medical Secretary; Office Worker; Receptionist;

Secretary; Typist; Word Processing Specialist. Company pays fee. Number of placements per year: 1001+.

WSS TEMPORARY SERVICE
2020 K Street N.W.
Suite 310
Washington DC 20006
202/457-1848
Contact Robbie Sison, Director of Operations and Development. Employment agency; temporary help service. No appointment required. The Washington School for Secretaries has been in business for over 60 years. Specializes in the areas of: Clerical; Legal; Word Processing. Positions commonly filled include: Administrative Assistant; Advertising Worker; Bookkeeper; Clerk; Computer Operator; Computer Programmer; Customer Service Representative; Data Entry Clerk; Demonstrator; Factory Worker; General Laborer; Legal Secretary; Light Industrial Worker; Medical Secretary; Office Worker; Public Relations Worker; Receptionist; Secretary; Stenographer; Systems Analyst; Typist; Word Processing Specialist. Company pays fee. Number of placements per year: 1001+.

EXECUTIVE SEARCH FIRMS OF THE DISTRICT OF COLUMBIA

MANAGEMENT RECRUITERS OF WASHINGTON, D.C.
1707 H Street N.W.
Suite 400
Washington DC 20006-1806
202/785-3000; FAX 202/785-5195
Contact Frank Black, Manager. Executive search firm. Appointment required; no phone calls; unsolicited resumes accepted. Founded 1965. World's largest contingency search firm. Five hundred offices nationwide, doing business under the names "Management Recruiters", "Sales Consultants", "CompuSearch" and "OfficeMates5". Specializes in mid-management/professional positions, $25,000-75,000 per annum. Specializes in the areas of: Accounting; Administration, MIS/EDP; Advertising; Affirmative Action; Architecture; Banking and Finance; Chemicals and Pharmaceuticals; Communications; Computer Hardware and Software; Construction; Electrical; Engineering; Food Industry; General Management; Health and Medical; Human Resources; Industrial and Interior Design; Insurance; Legal; Manufacturing; Operations Management; Printing and Publishing; Procurement; Real Estate; Retailing; Sales and Marketing; Technical and Scientific; Textiles; Transportation. Contingency.

MRI
1660 L Street NW
Suite 606
Washington DC 20036
202/785-3000
Contact Clay Clark, Manager. Executive search firm. Appointment required; no phone calls; unsolicited resumes accepted. Founded 1965. World's largest contingency search firm. Five hundred offices nationwide, doing business under the names "Management Recruiters", "Sales Consultants", "CompuSearch" and "OfficeMates5". Specializes in mid-management/professional positions, $25,000-75,000 per annum. Specializes in the areas of: Accounting; Administration, MIS/EDP; Advertising; Affirmative Action; Architecture; Banking and Finance; Chemicals and Pharmaceuticals; Communications; Computer Hardware and Software; Construction; Electrical; Engineering; Food Industry; General Management; Health and Medical; Human Resources; Industrial and Interior Design; Insurance; Legal; Manufacturing; Operations Management; Printing and Publishing; Procurement; Real Estate; Retailing; Sales and Marketing; Technical and Scientific; Textiles; Transportation. Contingency.

THE N.P.S. GROUP
2020 Pennsylvania Avenue #217
Washington DC 20006
(301) 292-8214
Contact Lewis C. Norman. A member of Abraham & London Ltd/Affluence International, "a cooperative executive placement network". The practice was founded in 1977 by the current director, Richard London. It offers a cooperative placement system to its clients. The national headquarters are in Los Angeles, California. The practice has a nationwide network of offices and 400+ independent consultants to serve its national client list, and an international network of 100+ independent consultants serving other countries for its multinational clients. Abraham & London's practice concentrates on middle management to senior management placements. Affluence International's practice concentrates on executive level appointments. Both divisions work a wide spectrum of industries and commerce including Accounting, Banking, Data Processing, Engineering, Financial Services, Insurance, and many more. It prides itself on building a personal relationship with its clients and enjoys a high percentage of repeat business. Its attitudes in doing business are wisdom, integrity, and distinction. In 1986 the practice completed hundreds of executive placement assignments. This firm specializes in the areas of: Data Processing; Financial; Management; Medical.

THE PERSONNEL INSTITUTE
1000 Connecticut Avenue N.W.
Washington DC 20036
202/223-4911
Contact Dr. William E. Stuart, President. Employment consultants. No appointment required. Founded 1963. Equipped to perform psychological testing and staffing studies. The Personnel Insitute has an ongoing Outplacement Division as well as an Executive Search Department. Specializes in the areas of: Computer Hardware and Software; Engineering; MIS/EDP; Manufacturing; Minorities; Technical and Scientific; Veterans; Women. Positions commonly filled include: Aerospace Engineer; Bank Officer/Manager; Biologist; Biomedical Engineer; Computer Programmer; EDP Specialist; Economist; Electrical Engineer; Financial Analyst; Goverment Relations Specialist; Industrial Designer; Industrial Engineer; MIS Specialist; Marketing Specialist; Mechanical Engineer; Operations/Production Specialist; Physicist; Quality Control Supervisor; Systems Analyst; Washington Representative. Company pays fee. Number of placements per year: 201-500.

SALES CONSULTANTS OF WASHINGTON, D.C.
1660 L Street NW
Suite 250
Washington DC 20036
202/452-9100
Contact Brian Hoffman, Manager. Executive search firm. Appointment required; no phone calls; unsolicited resumes accepted. Founded 1965. World's largest contingency search firm. Five hundred offices nationwide, doing business under the names "Management Recruiters", "Sales Consultants", "CompuSearch" and "OfficeMates5". Specializes in mid-management/professional positions, $25,000-75,000 per annum. Specializes in the areas of: Accounting; Administration, MIS/EDP; Advertising; Affirmative Action; Architecture; Banking and Finance; Chemicals and Pharmaceuticals; Communications; Computer Hardware and Software; Construction; Electrical; Engineering; Food Industry; General Management; Health and Medical; Human Resources; Industrial and Interior Design; Insurance; Legal; Manufacturing; Operations Management; Printing and Publishing; Procurement; Real Estate; Retailing; Sales and Marketing; Technical and Scientific; Textiles; Transportation. Contingency.

MARYLAND EMPLOYMENT AGENCIES AND TEMPORARY SERVICES

ADIA PERSONNEL SERVICES
1104 Kenilworth Drive
Suite 104
Towson MD 21204
301/494-1055

Contact Kitty Davis, Branch Manager. Full service personnel company including temporary and permanent placement. Specializes in Clerical and Light Industrial placement including: Accounting; Communications; Data Processing; Factory/Warehouse Work; Secretarial; Word Processing. Company pays fee.

BUTLER SERVICE GROUP, INC.
4977 Mercantile Road
Baltimore MD 21236
301/529-2250
Contact Jan Stauffer, Branch Administrator. Temporary help service. Appointment requested. Founded 1974. Specializes in the areas of: Engineering; Manufacturing; Technical and Scientific. Positions commonly filled include: Aerospace Engineer; Architect; Buyer; Computer Operator; Computer Programmer; Data Entry Clerk; Draftsperson; Electrical Engineer; General Laborer; Industrial Engineer; Mechanical Engineer; Operations/Production Specialist; Purchasing Agent; Technical Writer/Editor; Technician. Number of placements per year: 101-200.

CAREERS III INC.
7658 Standish Place
Suite 115
Rockville MD 20855
301/251-1255
Contact Pat Busbice, President. Employment agency. Appointment requested. Founded 1981. Branch offices located in: Rockville, MD; Washington, DC. Specializes in the area of: Clerical. Positions commonly filled include: Administrative Assistant; Bookkeeper; Clerk; Customer Service Representative; Data Entry Clerk; Legal Secretary; Medical Secretary; Office Worker; Receptionist; Secretary; Stenographer; Technical Writer/Editor; Typist; Word Processing Specialist. Company pays fee. Number of placements per year: 201-500.

CONTINENTAL ASSISTANCE & SEARCH AGENCY INC./CASA
914 Silver Spring Avenue
Suite 205
Silver Spring MD 20910
301/587-0135
Contact Mr. Marc Jeanty, Executive Director, or Renee Pierce, Assistant Director. Employment agency; temporary help agency. No appointment required. Founded 1970. Specializes in the areas of: Bilingual; Fashion; Finance; Health and Medical; Legal; Real Estate. Positions commonly filled include: Accountant; Aerospace Engineer; Agricultural Engineer; Architect; Attorney; Biomedical Engineer; Ceramics Engineer; Chemical Engineer; Civil Engineer; Clerk; Companion; Computer Operator; Computer Programmer; Construction Worker; Electrical Engineer; Factory Worker; General Maintenance Worker; Houseworker; Industrial Engineer; Legal Secretary; Mechanical Engineer; Medical Secretary; Metallurgical Engineer; Mining Engineer; Nurse; Office Worker; Petroleum Engineer; Receptionist; Restaurant and Hotel Employee; Secretary; Typist. Company pays fee; individual pays fee. Number of placements per year: 51-100.

DUNHILL OF ROCKVILLE, INC.
414 Hungerford Drive
Suite 220
Rockville MD 20850
301/654-2115
Contact Gordon Powers, President. Employment agency; temporary help service. Founded 1974. Specializes in the areas of: Accounting and Finance; Banking; Clerical. Positions commonly filled include: Accountant; Bank Officer/Manager; Bookkeeper; Financial Analyst; Legal Secretary; Medical Secretary; Office Worker; Purchasing Agent; Receptionist; Secretary; Statistician; Stenographer; Typist. Company pays fee. Number of placements per year: 50.

EDUCATIONAL SALES - TA TECHED
5020 Sunnyside Avenue
Suite 220
Beltsville MD 20705
301/474-6266

Contact Frank R. Petts, President. Employment agency. Appointment preferred. Founded 1973. Specializes in the areas of: Computer Hardware and Software; Engineering; Sales and Marketing; Technical and Scientific. Positions commonly filled include: Computer Programmer; EDP Specialist; Electrical Engineer; MIS Specialist; Physicist; Sales Representative; Statistician; Systems Analyst; Technical Writer/Editor. Company pays fee.

GARLISS AND ASSOCIATES INC.
Suite 100
RCM and D Building
555 Fairmont Avenue
Towson MD 21204
301/823-6061

Contact Linda Gross, Executive Recruiter. Employment agency. Appointment requested. Founded 1983. Specializes in the areas of: Accounting and Finance; Banking; Health and Medical; Insurance; Legal; Manufacturing; MIS/EDP; Personnel and Human Resources; Real Estate; Sales and Marketing. Positions commonly filled include: Accountant; Actuary; Architect; Attorney; Bank Officer/Manager; Bookkeeper; Claim Representative; Clerk; Computer Operator; Credit Manager; Customer Service Representative; Data Entry Clerk; EDP Specialist; Financial Analyst; General Manager; Hotel Manager/Assistant Manager; Insurance Agent/Broker; Legal Secretary; Medical Secretary; Office Worker; Personnel and Labor Relations Specialist; Purchasing Agent; Quality Control Supervisor; Secretary; Statistician; Stenographer; Systems Analyst; Technical Writer/Editor; Typist; Word Processing Specialist. Number of placements per year: 101-200.

J. R. ASSOCIATES
152 Rollins Avenue
Suite 200
Rockville MD 20852
301/984-8885

Contact Daniel Keller, President. Employment agency. Appointment requested. Founded 1981. Specializes in the areas of: Computer Hardware and Software; Engineering; MIS/EDP; Sales and Marketing; Technical and Scientific. Positions commonly filled include: Classified High-Tech Specialist; Computer Analyst; Computer Programmer; Data/Telecommunications Specialist; EDP Specialist; Financial Analyst; MIS Specialist; Marketing Representative; Sales Engineer; Sales Representative. Company pays fee. Number of placements per year: 51-100.

MITCHELL, McDERMOTT, SPIWACK & FINKS
8601 Georgia Avenue
Suite 704
Silver Spring MD 20910
301/565-3900

Contact Mr. Robert L. McDermott, President. Employment agency; temporary help service. Appointment requested. Founded 1974. Specializes in the areas of: Accounting and Finance; Banking; Clerical; Computer Hardware and Software; MIS/EDP; Mortgage Industry; Sales and Marketing; Women. Positions commonly filled include: Accountant; Administrative Assistant; Bank Officer/Manager; Bookkeeper; Clerk; Computer Operator; Computer Programmer; Credit Manager; Customer Service Representative; Data Entry Clerk; EDP Specialist; Legal Secretary; Medical Secretary; Office Worker; Receptionist; Sales Clerk; Sales Representative; Secretary; Stenographer; Typist; Word Processing Specialist. Company pays fee. Number of placements per year: 501-1000.

MICRO/TEMPS AND EDP/TEMPS
A TECHNICAL AID COMPANY
7500 Greenway Center Drive
Suite 420
Greenbelt MD 20770
301/474-9063

Temporary help service. No appointment required. Founded 1976. Branch offices located in: California; Connecticut; Illinois; Maryland; Massachusetts; Michigan; New York; Ohio; Pennsylvania; Virginia. Specializes in the areas of: Computer Software; Engineering; MIS/EDP; Technical and Scientific. Positions commonly filled include: Applications Programmer; Communications Engineer; Computer Operator; EDP Specialist; MIS Specialist; Software Engineer; Systems Analyst;

Systems and Design Engineer; Systems Programmer; Technical Writer/Editor. Company pays fee. Number of placements per year: 1001+.

SNELLING & SNELLING
91 Aquahart Road
Suite 117
Glen Burnie MD 21061
301/761-8600
Contact Seymour Shapiro, Manager. Employment agency. Appointment required. Founded 1977. A franchise of nationwide Snelling & Snelling, Inc., in business since 1951. Nonspecialized. Positions commonly filled include: Accountant; Actuary; Administrative Assistant; Aerospace Engineer; Architect; Attorney; Bank Officer/Manager; Biomedical Engineer; Bookkeeper; Buyer; Ceramics Engineer; Chemical Engineer; Claim Representative; Clerk; Credit Manager; Customer Service Rep; Data Entry Clerk; Draftsperson; Electrical Engineer; Electronic Technician; Executive Secretary; Financial Analyst; General Manager; Industrial Designer; Industrial Engineer; Insurance Agent/Broker; Legal Secretary; Marketing Specialist; Mechanical Engineer; Medical Secretary; Metallurgical Engineer; Office Worker; Operations/Production Specialist; Personnel and Labor Relations Specialist; Personnel Director; Physicist; Purchasing Agent; Quality Control Supervisor; Receptionist; Sales Manager; Sales Representative; Secretary; Stenographer; Technical Writer/Editor; Technician; Typist; Underwriter; Word Processor. Company pays fee (80%); individual pays fee (20%). Number of placements per year: 101-200.

STAFF BUILDERS INC. OF MARYLAND
Baltimore: 301/837-4555;
Columbia: 301/992-1940;
Landover: 301/577-5700;
Rockville: 301/424-0313;
Severna Park: 301/544-3122;
Timonium: 301/561-0700.
Temporary help service. Appointment requested. Founded 1961. Branch offices located in Arizona; California; Connecticut; District of Columbia; Florida; Georgia; Illinois; Indiana; Kansas; Louisiana; Maryland; Massachusetts; Michigan; Minnesota; Missouri; Nevada; New Jersey; New Mexico; New York; Ohio; Oklahoma; Oregon; Pennsylvania; Rhode Island; Tennessee; Texas; Virginia; Washington. Nonspecialized. Positions commonly filled include: Accountant; Administrative Assistant; Bookkeeper; Clerk; Companion; Computer Operator; Computer Programmer; Customer Service Representative; Data Entry Clerk; Demonstrator; Draftsperson; Driver; EDP Specialist; Factory Worker; General Laborer; Health Aide; Legal Secretary; Light Industrial Worker; Medical Secretary; Nurse; Office Worker; Public Relations Worker; Receptionist; Sales Representative; Secretary; Stenographer; Technician; Typist; Word Processing Specialist. Company pays fee. Number of placements per year: 1001+.

TAC/TEMPS INC. OF MARYLAND
8923 Shady Grove Court
Gaithersburg MD 20877
301/963-9590
Temporary help service. No appointment required. Branch offices located in: California; Connecticut; District of Columbia; Maryland; Massachusetts; New Hampshire; New York; Pennsylvania; Rhode Island; Virginia. Specializes in the areas of: Accounting and Finance; Advertising; Banking; Clerical; Education; Health and Medical; Insurance; Legal; Manufacturing; Nonprofit; Personnel and Human Resources; Printing and Publishing; Sales and Marketing; Transportation. Positions commonly filled include: Bookkeeper; Clerk; Data Entry Clerk; Demonstrator; Driver; Factory Worker; General Laborer; Legal Secretary; Light Industrial Worker; Medical Secretary; Office Worker; Receptionist; Secretary; Typist; Word Processing Specialist. Company pays fee. Number of placements per year: 1001+.

TECH/AID OF MARYLAND
7008 Security Boulevard
Suite 118
Baltimore MD 21207
301/597-9550

Temporary help service. No appointment required. Founded 1969. Tech/Aid is a division of Technical Aid Corporation which has branch offices located in: Arizona; California; Connecticut; Illinois; Maryland; Massachusetts; New Hampshire; Pennsylvania; Rhode Island; Texas; Virginia. Specializes in the areas of: Architecture; Cable Television; Computer Hardware and Software; Construction; Engineering; Manufacturing; Technical and Scientific. Positions commonly filled include: Aerospace Engineer; Architect; Ceramics Engineer; Chemical Engineer; Civil Engineer; Buyer; Draftsperson; Electrical Engineer; Estimator; Factory Engineer; Industrial Designer; Industrial Engineer; Mechanical Engineer; Metallurgical Engineer; Mining Engineer; Operations and Production Specialist; Petroleum Engineer; Purchasing Agent; Quality Control Supervisor; Technical Writer and Editor; Technician. Company pays fee. Number of placements per year: 1001+.

TELESEC TEMPORARY PERSONNEL, INC.
6526 Bellcrest Road
Suite 610
Hyattsville MD 20782
301/699-5054
Temporary help service. No appointment required. Founded 1948. Branch offices located in: Washington, DC; Hyattsville, MD; Falls Church, VA. Specializes in the areas of: Construction; Engineering; Handicapped; Health and Medical; Manufacturing; Teaching. Positions commonly filled include: Administrative Assistant; Bookkeeper; Claim Representative; Clerk; Customer Service Representative; Demonstrator; General Laborer; Legal Secretary; Librarian; Library Technician; Light Industrial Worker; Medical Secretary; Office Worker; Receptionist; Secretary; Stenographer; Typist; Word Processing Specialist.

TELESEC TEMPORARY PERSONNEL, INC.
10408 Montgomery Avenue
Kensington MD 20895
301/949-3110
Contact Mary Beth Marsden, Recruiting Coordinator. Temporary help service. No appointment required. Founded 1948. Branch offices located in: Washington, DC; Hyattsville, MD; Falls Church, VA. Specializes in the areas of: Construction; Engineering; Handicapped; Health and Medical; Manufacturing; Teaching. Positions commonly filled include: Administrative Assistant; Bookkeeper; Claim Representative; Clerk; Customer Service Representative; Demonstrator; General Laborer; Legal Secretary; Librarian; Library Technician; Light Industrial Worker; Medical Secretary; Office Worker; Receptionist; Secretary; Stenographer; Typist; Word Processing Specialist.

TEMP FORCE OF TOWSON
One Investment Place
Suite G-7
Towson MD 21204
301/828-0778
Contact Ruth Abrams, Manager. Temporary help service. No appointment required. Founded 1965. Branch offices located in: Alabama; Arkansas; California; Colorado; Connecticut; Florida; Illinois; Indiana; Kansas; Maryland; Massachusetts; Michigan; Mississippi; Nevada; New Jersey; New Mexico; New York; Ohio; Oklahoma; Pennsylvania; Tennessee; Utah; Vermont; Virginia. Nonspecialized. Positions commonly filled include: Accountant; Bookkeeper; Clerk; Computer Operator; Computer Programmer; Customer Service Representative; Data Entry Clerk; Demonstrator; Driver; Factory Worker; General Laborer; Legal Secretary; Light Industrial Worker; Medical Secretary; Office Worker; Purchasing Agent; Receptionist; Secretary; Statistician; Stenographer; Typist; Word Processing Specialist.

T.G.I.F. INC. OF MARYLAND
Post Office Box 3158
Baltimore MD 21228
Contact Nelly Schwab, Manager. Search firm for In-Home employees. No appointment required. Founded 1982. Also search for hourly and weekly paid employees to help in homes. Branch offices located in: Colorado; Connecticut; Kentucky; Ohio; Oregon; Tennessee; Texas; Utah; Virginia; Washington. Specializes in the areas of: Elderly; Personnel and Human Resources; Private Family Needs; Women. Positions commonly filled include: Companion; Cook; Driver; Housekeeper; Nanny; Nurse. Company pays fee. Number of placements per year: 501-1000.

TIME IS MONEY PERSONNEL SERVICES
Eight Sudbrook Lane
Pikesville MD 21208
301/486-1088
Contact Beverly Fishman, President. Employment agency. Appointment required. Founded 1981. Specializing in the placement of Actuaries. Positions commonly filled include: Actuary; Insurance Worker; Secretary. Secretary; Insurance. Company pays fee. Number of placements per year: 0-50.

VICTOR TEMPORARY SERVICES OF BALTIMORE
40 West Chesapeake Avenue
Suite 207
Towson MD 21204
301/828-8071
Temporary help service. Appointment requested. Founded 1954. Victor Temporary Services has over 100 offices throughout the United States. Nonspecialized. Positions commonly filled include: Bookkeeper; Clerk; Computer Operator; Customer Service Representative; Data Entry Clerk; Demonstrator; Draftsperson; Electronic Assembler; Factory Worker; General Laborer; Legal Secretary; Light Industrial Worker; Medical Secretary; Office Worker; Receptionist; Secretary; Stenographer; Technician; Typist; Word Processing Specialist. Company pays fee. Number of placements per year: 1001+.

EXECUTIVE SEARCH FIRMS OF MARYLAND

COMPUSEARCH OF BALTIMORE
Suite 801,
9515 Deereco Road
Timonium MD 21093
301/252-6616; FAX 301/252-7076
Contact Ken Davis, General Manager, John LaMartina, Manager, Rich Sezov, Sales Manager, or Dick Forder, Manager of Advanced Training. Executive search firm. Appointment required; no phone calls; unsolicited resumes accepted. Founded 1965. World's largest contingency search firm. Five hundred offices nationwide, doing business under the names "Management Recruiters", "Sales Consultants", "CompuSearch" and "OfficeMates5". Specializes in mid-management/professional positions, $25,000-75,000 per annum. Specializes in the areas of: Accounting; Administration, MIS/EDP; Advertising; Affirmative Action; Architecture; Banking and Finance; Chemicals and Pharmaceuticals; Communications; Computer Hardware and Software; Construction; Electrical; Engineering; Food Industry; General Management; Health and Medical; Human Resources; Industrial and Interior Design; Insurance; Legal; Manufacturing; Operations Management; Printing and Publishing; Procurement; Real Estate; Retailing; Sales and Marketing; Technical and Scientific; Textiles; Transportation. Contingency.

MANAGEMENT RECRUITERS OF ANNAPOLIS
Sovran Bank Building
Suite 5A
2083 West Street
Annapolis MD 21401-3030
301/261-8411 (Baltimore)
301/841-6600 (Washington)
Contact John Czajkowski, Manager. Executive search firm. Appointment required; no phone calls; unsolicited resumes accepted. Founded 1965. World's largest contingency search firm. Five hundred offices nationwide, doing business under the names "Management Recruiters", "Sales Consultants", "CompuSearch" and "OfficeMates5". Specializes in mid-management/professional positions, $25,000-75,000 per annum. Specializes in the areas of: Accounting; Administration, MIS/EDP; Advertising; Affirmative Action; Architecture; Banking and Finance; Chemicals and Pharmaceuticals; Communications; Computer Hardware and Software; Construction; Electrical; Engineering; Food Industry; General Management; Health and Medical; Human Resources; Industrial and Interior Design; Insurance; Legal; Manufacturing; Operations Management; Printing and Publishing;

Procurement; Real Estate; Retailing; Sales and Marketing; Technical and Scientific; Textiles; Transportation. Contingency.

MANAGEMENT RECRUITERS OF BALTIMORE
Suite 801
9515 Deereco Road
Timonium MD 21093
301/252-6616;
FAX 301/252-7076
Contact Ken Davis, General Manager, John LaMartina, Manager, Rich Sezov, Sales Manager, or Dick Forder, Manager of Advanced Training. Executive search firm. Appointment required; no phone calls; unsolicited resumes accepted. Founded 1965. World's largest contingency search firm. Five hundred offices nationwide, doing business under the names "Management Recruiters", "Sales Consultants", "CompuSearch" and "OfficeMates5". Specializes in mid-management/professional positions, $25,000-75,000 per annum. Specializes in the areas of: Accounting; Administration, MIS/EDP; Advertising; Affirmative Action; Architecture; Banking and Finance; Chemicals and Pharmaceuticals; Communications; Computer Hardware and Software; Construction; Electrical; Engineering; Food Industry; General Management; Health and Medical; Human Resources; Industrial and Interior Design; Insurance; Legal; Manufacturing; Operations Management; Printing and Publishing; Procurement; Real Estate; Retailing; Sales and Marketing; Technical and Scientific; Textiles; Transportation. Contingency.

MANAGEMENT RECRUITERS OF COLUMBIA
Three Lakefront North
Suite 210
5570 Sterrett Place
Columbia, MD 21044
301/995-1040;
FAX 301/730-9044
Contact Brian Brenton, General Manager. Executive search firm. Appointment required; no phone calls; unsolicited resumes accepted. Founded 1965. World's largest contingency search firm. Five hundred offices nationwide, doing business under the names "Management Recruiters", "Sales Consultants", "CompuSearch" and "OfficeMates5". Specializes in mid-management/professional positions, $25,000-75,000 per annum. Specializes in the areas of: Accounting; Administration, MIS/EDP; Advertising; Affirmative Action; Architecture; Banking and Finance; Chemicals and Pharmaceuticals; Communications; Computer Hardware and Software; Construction; Electrical; Engineering; Food Industry; General Management; Health and Medical; Human Resources; Industrial and Interior Design; Insurance; Legal; Manufacturing; Operations Management; Printing and Publishing; Procurement; Real Estate; Retailing; Sales and Marketing; Technical and Scientific; Textiles; Transportation. Contingency.

MANAGEMENT RECRUITERS OF GAITHERSBURG
One Bank Street
Suite 220
Gaithersburg MD 20878-1504
301/840-0440
FAX 301/926-4128
Contact John L. Butts, Jr. or Ginnabeth Butts, Co-Managers. Executive search firm. Appointment required; no phone calls; unsolicited resumes accepted. Founded 1965. World's largest contingency search firm. Five hundred offices nationwide, doing business under the names "Management Recruiters", "Sales Consultants", "CompuSearch" and "OfficeMates5". Specializes in mid-management/professional positions, $25,000-75,000 per annum. Specializes in the areas of: Accounting; Administration, MIS/EDP; Advertising; Affirmative Action; Architecture; Banking and Finance; Chemicals and Pharmaceuticals; Communications; Computer Hardware and Software; Construction; Electrical; Engineering; Food Industry; General Management; Health and Medical; Human Resources; Industrial and Interior Designer; Insurance; Legal; Manufacturing; Operations Management; Printing and Publishing; Procurement; Real Estate; Retailing; Sales and Marketing; Technical and Scientific; Textiles; Transportation. Contingency.

MANAGEMENT RECRUITERS OF MONTGOMERY COUNTY
232 North Washington Street
Rockville MD 20850
301/251-8505
Contact Tom Hubin, Manager. Executive search firm. Appointment required; no phone calls; unsolicited resumes accepted. Founded 1965. World's largest contingency search firm. Five hundred offices nationwide, doing business under the names "Management Recruiters", "Sales Consultants", "CompuSearch" and "OfficeMates5". Specializes in mid-management/professional positions, $25,000-75,000 per annum. Specializes in the areas of: Accounting; Administration, MIS/EDP; Advertising; Affirmative Action; Architecture; Banking and Finance; Chemicals and Pharmaceuticals; Communications; Computer Hardware and Software; Construction; Electrical; Engineering; Food Industry; General Management; Health and Medical; Human Resources; Industrial and Interior Design; Insurance; Legal; Manufacturing; Operations Management; Printing and Publishing; Procurement; Real Estate; Retailing; Sales and Marketing; Technical and Scientific; Textiles; Transportation. Contingency.

MARK ALLEN ASSOCIATES, INC.
10451 Twin Rivers Road
Suite 245
Columbia MD 21044
301/997-3493
Contact Alan Levin, C.P.C., President. Executive search firm. Appointment requested; no unsolicited resumes accepted. Founded 1983. Nonspecialized. Contingency. Number of searches conducted per year: 25.

OFFICEMATES5 OF BALTIMORE (DOWNTOWN)
300 E. Lombard Street
Suite 935
Baltimore MD 21202
301/547-6600
Contact Ken Davis, Owner, or Julie Wood, Manager. Executive search firm. Appointment required; no phone calls; unsolicited resumes accepted. Founded 1965. World's largest contingency search firm. Five hundred offices nationwide, doing business under the names "Management Recruiters", "Sales Consultants", "CompuSearch" and "OfficeMates5". Specializes in mid-management/professional positions, $25,000-75,000 per annum. Specializes in the areas of: Accounting; Administration, MIS/EDP; Advertising; Affirmative Action; Architecture; Banking and Finance; Chemicals and Pharmaceuticals; Communications; Computer Hardware and Software; Construction; Electrical; Engineering; Food Industry; General Management; Health and Medical; Human Resources; Industrial and Interior Design; Insurance; Legal; Manufacturing; Operations Management; Printing and Publishing; Procurement; Real Estate; Retailing; Sales and Marketing; Technical and Scientific; Textiles; Transportation. Contingency.

OFFICEMATES5 OF FREDERICK
Suite 202
201 Thomas Johnson Drive
Frederick MD 21701
301/663-0600
FAX 301/663-0454
Contact Pat Webb, Co-Owner/Manager, or Dick Bates, Co-Owner. Executive search firm. Appointment required; no phone calls; unsolicited resumes accepted. Founded 1965. World's largest contingency search firm. Five hundred offices nationwide, doing business under the names "Management Recruiters", "Sales Consultants", "CompuSearch" and "OfficeMates5". Specializes in mid-management/professional positions, $25,000-75,000 per annum. Specializes in the areas of: Accounting; Administration, MIS/EDP; Advertising; Affirmative Action; Architecture; Banking and Finance; Chemicals and Pharmaceuticals; Communications; Computer Hardware and Software; Construction; Electrical; Engineering; Food Industry; General Management; Health and Medical; Human Resources; Industrial and Interior Design; Insurance; Legal; Manufacturing; Operations Management; Printing and Publishing; Procurement; Real Estate; Retailing; Sales and Marketing; Technical and Scientific; Textiles; Transportation. Contingency.

OFFICEMATES5 OF MONTGOMERY COUNTY
232 North Washington Street
Rockville MD 20850
301/251-8505

Contact Theresa Hubin, Manager. Executive search firm. Appointment required; no phone calls; unsolicited resumes accepted. Founded 1965. World's largest contingency search firm. Five hundred offices nationwide, doing business under the names "Management Recruiters", "Sales Consultants", "CompuSearch" and "OfficeMates5". Specializes in mid-management/professional positions, $25,000-75,000 per annum. Specializes in the areas of: Accounting; Administration, MIS/EDP; Advertising; Affirmative Action; Architecture; Banking and Finance; Chemicals and Pharmaceuticals; Communications; Computer Hardware and Software; Construction; Electrical; Engineering; Food Industry; General Management; Health and Medical; Human Resources; Industrial and Interior Design; Insurance; Legal; Manufacturing; Operations Management; Printing and Publishing; Procurement; Real Estate; Retailing; Sales and Marketing; Technical and Scientific; Textiles; Transportation. Contingency.

SALES CONSULTANTS OF BALTIMORE
Suite 801
9515 Deereco Road
Timonium MD 21093
301/252-6616;
FAX 301/252-7076

Contact Ken Davis, General Manager, John LaMartina, Manager, Rich Sezov, Sales Manager, or Dick Forder, Manager of Advanced Training. Executive search firm. Appointment required; no phone calls; unsolicited resumes accepted. Founded 1965. World's largest contingency search firm. Five hundred offices nationwide, doing business under the names "Management Recruiters", "Sales Consultants", "CompuSearch" and "OfficeMates5". Specializes in mid-management/professional positions, $25,000-75,000 per annum. Specializes in the areas of: Accounting; Administration, MIS/EDP; Advertising; Affirmative Action; Architecture; Banking and Finance; Chemicals and Pharmaceuticals; Communications; Computer Hardware and Software; Construction; Electrical; Engineering; Food Industry; General Management; Health and Medical; Human Resources; Industrial and Interior Design; Insurance; Legal; Manufacturing; Operations Management; Printing and Publishing; Procurement; Real Estate; Retailing; Sales and Marketing; Technical and Scientific; Textiles; Transportation. Contingency.

SALES CONSULTANTS OF BALTIMORE (DOWNTOWN)
300 Russell Street
Baltimore MD 21230
301/727-5750

Contact Steve Braun, Manager. Executive search firm. Appointment required; no phone calls; unsolicited resumes accepted. Founded 1965. World's largest contingency search firm. Five hundred offices nationwide, doing business under the names "Management Recruiters", "Sales Consultants", "CompuSearch" and "OfficeMates5". Specializes in mid-management/professional positions, $25,000-75,000 per annum. Specializes in the areas of: Accounting; Administration, MIS/EDP; Advertising; Affirmative Action; Architecture; Banking and Finance; Chemicals and Pharmaceuticals; Communications; Computer Hardware and Software; Construction; Electrical; Engineering; Food Industry; General Management; Health and Medical; Human Resources; Industrial and Interior Design; Insurance; Legal; Manufacturing; Operations Management; Printing and Publishing; Procurement; Real Estate; Retailing; Sales and Marketing; Technical and Scientific; Textiles; Transportation. Contingency.

SALES CONSULTANTS OF PRINCE GEORGES COUNTY
7515 Annapolis Road,
Suite 404
Hyattsville MD 20784
301/731-4200

Contact Tom Hummel, Manager. Executive search firm. Appointment required; no phone calls; unsolicited resumes accepted. Founded 1965. World's largest contingency search firm. Five hundred offices nationwide, doing business under the names "Management Recruiters", "Sales Consultants", "CompuSearch" and "OfficeMates5". Specializes in mid-management/professional positions, $25,000-75 000 per annum. Specializes in the areas of: Accounting; Administration, MIS/EDP; Advertising;

Affirmative Action; Architecture; Banking and Finance; Chemicals and Pharmaceuticals; Communications; Computer Hardware and Software; Construction; Electrical; Engineering; Food Industry; General Management; Health and Medical; Human Resources; Industrial and Interior Design; Insurance; Legal; Manufacturing; Operations Management; Printing and Publishing; Procurement; Real Estate; Retailing; Sales and Marketing; Technical and Scientific; Textiles; Transportation. Contingency.

SALESWORLD INC.
901 Dulaney Valley Road
Suite 508
Towson MD 21204
301/296-5600
Contact Nelson White, Regional Branch Manager. Executive recruiting firm. Appointment required. Specializes in the areas of: Engineering; Sales and Marketing. Positions commonly filled include: Advertising Executive; Aerospace Engineer; Agricultural Engineer; Bank Officer/Manager; Biomedical Engineer; Civil Engineer; Electrical Engineer; General Manager; Hotel Manager; Industrial Engineer; Insurance Agent/Broker; Marketing Specialist; Mechanical Engineer; Metallurgical Engineer; Mining Engineer; Personnel Director; Petroleum Engineer; Sales Representative; Underwriter. Number of placements per year: 201-500.

WHITE RIDGELY & ASSOC. INC.
2201 Old Court Road
3rd Floor
Balitmore MD 21208
301/296-1900
Contact Charles White, President. Executive search firm. Appointment required; unsolicited resumes accepted. Founded 1982. Started in Financial area; spread to other disciplines. Geographical area - south of NYC and north of Atlanta. Work with a few strong clients. Multiple searches. References available. Specializes in the areas of: Accounting; Administration, MIS/EDP; Banking and Finance; Construction; Health and Medical; Human Resources; Insurance; Printing and Publishing; Sales and Marketing; Women. Contingency. Number of searches conducted per year: 51-100.

PERSONNEL SERVICES AND TEMPORARY AGENCIES OF NORTHERN VIRGINIA

ADIA TEMPORARY SERVICES
45 West Boscawen Street
Winchester VA 22601
703/667-1916
Contact C. Lynn Weakley, Jr., Owner/Manager. Temporary help service. No appointment required. Founded 1971. Nonspecialized. Positions commonly filled include: Administrative Assistant; Advertising Worker; Bookkeeper; Clerk; Computer Operator; Computer Programmer; Construction Worker; Customer Service Representative; Data Entry Clerk; Demonstrator; Draftsperson; EDP Specialist; Factory Worker; General Laborer; Lab Technician; Legal Secretary; Light Industrial Worker; Medical Secretary; Nurse; Office Worker; Personnel and Labor Relations Specialist; Quality Control Worker; Receptionist; Secretary; Technician; Typist; Word Processing Specialist. Company pays fee. Number of placements per year: 201-500.

BAFINEX ASSOCIATES
4660 Kenmore Avenue
Suite 316
Alexandria VA 22304
703/751-7106
Contact Michael D. McIver, President, or Ronald Miller, Executive Vice President. Employment agency. Appointment requested. Founded 1975. Specializes in the areas of: Banking; Real Estate. Positions commonly filled include: Bank Officer/Manager; Credit Manager; Financial Analyst. Company pays fee. Number of placements per year: 51-100.

CECORP OF VIRGINIA
7127 Little River Turnpike
Suite 206
Annandale VA 22003
703/941-1200

Contact James Hill, President. Employment agency. No appointment required. Founded 1983. Specializes in the areas of: Insurance Claims; Sales and Marketing. Positions commonly filled include: Claim Representative; Retail Manager; Sales Manager; Sales Representative; Technician. Company pays fee. Number of placements per year: 51-100.

COMPUTER ENGINEERING CONSORTIUM (CEC)
7353 McWhorter Place
Suite 202
Annandale VA 22003
703/922-8770

Contact George Lytle, Owner. Employment agency. Appointment requested. Specializes in the areas of: Computer Hardware and Software; Defense and Military; Engineering; MIS/EDP; Technical and Scientific. Positions commonly filled include: Aerospace Engineer; Computer Operator; Computer Programmer; Computer Scientist; Customer Service Representative; Data Base Designer; Electrical Engineer; MIS Specialist; Operations/Production Specialist; Software Engineer; Systems Analyst; Systems Programmer; Technical Writer/Editor. Company pays fee. Number of placements per year: 201-500.

DELANEY ASSOCIATES, INC.
6462 Little River Turnpike
Suite E
Alexandria VA 22312
703/914-0055

Contact Janice E. Delaney, President. Employment agency; temporary help service. Appointment requested. Founded 1979. Specializes in the areas of: Accounting and Finance; Advertising; Associations; Banking; Clerical; Consulting Firms; Engineering; Legal; Minorities; Nonprofit; Women. Positions commonly filled include: Accountant; Administrative Assistant; Bookkeeper; Clerk; Computer Operator; Data Entry Clerk; Legal Secretary; Office Worker; Receptionist; Secretary; Stenographer; Technical Writer/Editor; Typist; Word Processing Specialist. Company pays fee. Number of placements per year: 201-500.

BFI BELL SEARCH INC.
6491 Little River Turnpike
Post Office Box 11497
Alexandria VA 22312
703/354-7227

Contact Jean Mona, President. Employment agency. Founded 1981. Member of Dunhill Personnel System, which has 300 franchise offices throughout the United States. Specializes in the areas of: Engineering; Health and Medical; Technical and Scientific. Positions commonly filled include: Analyst; Office Support; Professional and Middle Level Management; Programmer; Programmer/Analyst; Systems Analyst; Systems Programmer;

DUNHILL OF TYSONS
8229 Boone Boulevard
Suite 310
Vienna VA 22182
703/790-5393

Contact Harvey Silver, President. Employment agency; temporary help service. Appointment requested. Founded 1973. Member of Dunhill Personnel System, which has 300 franchise offices throughout the United States. Specializes in the areas of: Computer Hardware and Software. Positions commonly filled include: Administrative Assistant; Clerk; Computer Programmer; Customer Service Representative; EDP Specialist; Legal Secretary; Medical Secretary; Receptionist; Sales Representative (computer-related); Secretary; Stenographer; Systems Analyst; Typist; Word Processing Specialist. Company pays fee.

HALBRECHT & COMPANY, INC.
10195 Main Street
Suite L
Fairfax VA 22031
703/359-2880
Contact Thomas Maltby, Vice President/Manager. Employment agency. Appointment required. Founded 1957. Company recruits for leading corporations and management consulting firms. Does not mass mail resumes. Specializes in the areas of: Computer Hardware and Software; MIS/EDP; Technical and Scientific. Positions commonly filled include: Actuary; Computer Programmer; EDP Specialist; Electrical Engineer; Financial Analyst; Management Consultant; Petroleum Engineer; Statistician; Systems Analyst. Company pays fee.

KEY ACCOUNTING TEMPORARIES, INC.
1901 N. Moore Street
Suite 920
Arlington VA 22209
703/243-3600
Contact Kathleen A. Long, President. Temporary help agency. Appointment required. Founded 1985. Quality temporary Accounting personnel. Positions commonly filled include: Accountant; Bookkeeper; Data Entry Clerk; EDP Specialist; Financial Analyst. Company pays fee. Number of placements per year: 201-500.

MANPOWER TEMPORARY SERVICES OF VIENNA
8280 Greensboro Drive
Maclean VA 22102
703/821-0101
Contact Mindy Thomas, Office Manager. Temporary help service. Appointment requested. Founded 1948. Manpower Temporary Services has over 1000 offices worldwide. Specializes in the areas of: Clerical; Personnel and Human Resources; Word Processing. Positions commonly filled include: Administrative Assistant; Bookkeeper; Clerk; Customer Service Representative; Data Entry Clerk; Demonstrator; General Laborer; Legal Secretary; Office Worker; Secretary; Stenographer; Technical Writer/Editor; Typist; Word Processing Specialist. Company pays fee. Number of placements per year: 1001+.

MARKETA DAY & ASSOCIATES, INC.
5023-A Backlick Road
Annandale VA 22003
703/941-5242
Contact Marketa Day, President. Employment agency. Appointment required. Marketa day has been in the placement business for over 25 years. Specializes in the areas of: Accounting; Banking and Finance; Construction; Food Industry; Legal; Manufacturing; Nonprofit; Real Estate. Positions commonly filled include: Accountant; Administrative Assistant; Bookkeeper; Computer Programmer; Credit Manager; Customer Service Rep; Data Entry Clerk; EDP Specialist; Executive Secretary; Financial Analyst; Legal Secretary; Receptionist; Secretary; Stenographer; Systems Analyst; Typist; Word Processor. Company pays fee. Number of placements per year: 201-500.

MICRO/TEMPS AND EDP/TEMPS OF VIRGINIA
2095 Chain Bridge Road
Vienna VA 22182
703/893-2400
Temporary help service. No appointment required. Founded 1976. Branch offices located in: California; Connecticut; Illinois; Maryland; Massachusetts; Michigan; New York; Ohio; Pennsylvania. Specializes in the areas of: Accounting and Finance; Banking; Computer Hardware and Software; Engineering; Insurance; Manufacturing; MIS/EDP; Nonprofit; Personnel and Human Resources; Printing and Publishing; Technical and Scientific. Positions commonly filled include: Computer Operator; Computer Programmer; EDP Specialist; MIS Specialist; Systems Analyst; Technical Writer/Editor. Company pays fee. Number of placements per year: 1001+.

PAT DYER PERSONNEL
101 South Whiting Street
Suite 201
Alexandria VA 22304
703/751-7803
Contact Linda Dyer, General Manager. Employment agency. Appointment requested. Founded 1973. Member National Association of Personnel Consultants. Specializes in the area of: Clerical. Positions commonly filled include: Administrative Assistant; Bookkeeper; Clerk; Customer Service Representative; Data Entry Clerk; Legal Secretary; Medical Secretary; Office Worker; Receptionist; Secretary; Typist; Word Processing Specialist. Company pays fee. Number of placements per year: 201-500.

SALEM TECHNICAL SERVICES OF McLEAN
1483 Chain Bridge Road,
Suite 103
McLean VA 22101
703/827-0600
Contact Joanne Volak, Manager. Temporary help service. No appointment required. Founded 1967. Branch offices located in: Atlanta, GA; Austin, TX; Beloit, WI; Bloomington, MN; Burlington, MA; Charlotte, NC; Cincinnati, OH; Cleveland, OH; Dallas, TX; Grand Rapids, MI; Houston, TX; Milwaukee, WI; Phoenix, AZ; San Jose, CA; Golden, CO; San Jose, CA; Oak Brook, IL. Specializes in the areas of: Architecture; Computer Hardware and Software; Engineering; Manufacturing; MIS/EDP; Personnel and Human Resources; Technical and Scientific. Positions commonly filled include: Aerospace Engineer; Architect; Buyer; Chemical Engineer; Chemist; Civil Engineer; Commercial Artist; Computer Operator; Computer Programmer; Data Entry Clerk; Draftsperson; Driver; EDP Specialist; Electrical Engineer; Industrial Designer; Industrial Engineer; MIS Specialist; Manufacturing Engineer; Mechanical Engineer; Metallurgical Engineer; Operations and Production Specialist; Personnel and Labor Relations Specialist; Purchasing Agent; Quality Control Supervisor; Reporter and Editor; Software Engineer; Systems Analyst; Technical Illustrator; Technical Recruiter; Technical Writer/Editor; Technician; Word Processing Specialist. Number of placements per year: 201-500.

TAC/TEMPS INC. OF VIRGINIA
1700 North Moore Street
Arlington VA 22202
703/522-4988
Temporary help service. No appointment required. Branch offices located in: California; Connecticut; District of Columbia; Maryland; Massachusetts; New Hampshire; New York; Pennsylvania; Rhode Island. Specializes in the areas of: Accounting and Finance; Advertising; Banking; Clerical; Education; Health and Medical; Insurance; Legal; Manufacturing; Nonprofit; Personnel and Human Resources; Printing and Publishing; Sales and Marketing; Transportation. Positions commonly filled include: Bookkeeper; Clerk; Data Entry Clerk; Demonstrator; Driver; Factory Worker; General Laborer; Legal Secretary; Light Industrial Worker; Medical Secretary; Office Worker; Receptionist; Secretary; Typist; Word Processing Specialist. Company pays fee. Number of placements per year: 1001+.

TAC/TEMPS INC. OF VIRGINIA
2095 Chain Bridge Road
Vienna VA 22180
703/893-5260
Temporary help service. No appointment required. Branch offices located in: California; Connecticut; District of Columbia; Maryland; Massachusetts; New Hampshire; New York; Pennsylvania; Rhode Island. Specializes in the areas of: Accounting and Finance; Advertising; Banking; Clerical; Education; Health and Medical; Insurance; Legal; Manufacturing; Nonprofit; Personnel and Human Resources; Printing and Publishing; Sales and Marketing; Transportation. Positions commonly filled include: Bookkeeper; Clerk; Data Entry Clerk; Demonstrator; Driver; Factory Worker; General Laborer; Legal Secretary; Light Industrial Worker; Medical Secretary; Office Worker; Receptionist; Secretary; Typist; Word Processing Specialist. Company pays fee. Number of placements per year: 1001+.

TECH/AID OF VIRGINIA
2095 Chain Bridge Road,
Suite 300
Vienna VA 22182
703/893-6444
Temporary help service. No appointment required. Founded 1969. Tech/Aid is a division of Technical Aid Corporation and has branch offices located in: Arizona; California; Connecticut; Illinois; Maryland; Massachusetts; New Hampshire; Pennsylvania; Rhode Island; Texas. Specializes in the areas of: Architecture; Cable Television; Computer Hardware and Software; Construction; Engineering; Manufacturing; Technical and Scientific. Positions commonly filled include: Aerospace Engineer; Architect; Buyer; Ceramics Engineer; Chemical Engineer; Civil Engineer; Draftsperson; Electrical Engineer; Estimator; Factory Engineer; Industrial Designer; Industrial Engineer; Mechanical Engineer; Metallurgical Engineer; Mining Engineer; Operations and Production Specialist; Petroleum Engineer; Purchasing Agent; Quality Control Supervisor; Technical Writer and Editor; Technician. Company pays fee. Number of placements per year: 1001+.

TELESEC TEMPORARY PERSONNEL OF FALLS CHURCH
7309 Arlington Boulevard,
Suite 210
Falls Church VA 22042
703/641-0600
Temporary help service. No appointment required. Founded 1948. Branch offices located in: Washington, DC; Kensington, MD; Hyattsville, MD. Nonspecialized. Positions commonly filled include: Administrative Assistant; Bookkeeper; Claim Representative; Clerk; Customer Service Representative; Demonstrator; General Laborer; Legal Secretary; Librarian; Library Technician; Light Industrial Worker; Medical Secretary; Office Worker; Receptionist; Secretary; Stenographer; Typist; Word Processing Specialist.

VANTAGE PERSONNEL, INC.
2000 15th Street North
Suite 501
Arlington VA 22201
703/247-4100
Contact Mary Ann Wilkinson, President. Employment agency. Appointment required. Founded 1974. Offers professional recruitment, outplacement, training and organizational development services to private and public sector clients in the Washington, D.C. technical and international markets. We utilize a career counseling approach to develop meaningful career experiences to employees while meeting long-term staffing needs of our clients. Nonspecialized. Positions commonly filled include: Accountant; Administrative Assistant; Aerospace Engineer; Biochemist/Chemist; Bookkeeper; Computer Programmer; Draftsperson; EDP Specialist; Economist; Electrical Engineer; Executive Secretary; Financial Analyst; Legal Secretary; Logistics Analyst; Mechanical Engineer; Physicist; Receptionist; Secretary; Statistician; Systems Analyst; Technical Writer/Editor; Typist; Word Processor. Company pays fee. Number of placements per year: 0-50.

EXECUTIVE SEARCH FIRMS OF VIRGINIA

COMPUSEARCH OF FAIRFAX COUNTY SOUTH
8411 Arlington Boulevard
Suite 310
Fairfax VA 22031
703/573-2042
Contact Tony Ehrenzeller or Jennie Ehrenzeller, Co-Managers. Executive search firm. Appointment required; no phone calls; unsolicited resumes accepted. Founded 1965. World's largest contingency search firm. Five hundred offices nationwide, doing business under the names "Management Recruiters", "Sales Consultants", "CompuSearch" and "OfficeMates5". Specializes in mid-management/professional positions, $25,000-75,000. Specializes in the areas of: Accounting; Administration, MIS/EDP; Advertising; Affirmative Action; Architecture; Banking and Finance;

Communications; Computer Hardware and Software; Construction; Electrical; Engineering; Food Industry; General Management; Health and Medical; Human Resources; Industrial and Interior Design; Insurance; Legal; Manufacturing; Operations Management; Printing and Publishing; Procurement; Real Estate; Retailing; Sales and Marketing; Technical and Scientific; Textiles; Transportation. Contingency.

DUNHILL OF ALEXANDRIA
6491 Little River Turnpike
Post Office Box 11497
Alexandria VA 22312
703/354-7227
Contact Don J. Pitt, C.P.C., President. Executive search firm. Appointment requested. Founded 1976. Member of Dunhill Personnel System, which has 300 offices throughout the United States. Specializes in the areas of: Accounting and Finance; Banking; Computer Hardware and Software; Engineering; Food Industry; Health and Medical; Insurance; Manufacturing; MIS/EDP; Minorities; Nonprofit; Sales and Marketing; Technical and Scientific; Women. Number of searches conducted per year: 101-200.

EXECUTIVE RECRUITERS
6845 Elm Street
Suite 511
McLean VA 22101
703/556-9580
Contact Joseph Segal, President. Executive search firm. Appointment requested. Founded 1980. Specializes in the areas of: Food Industry; Hotel and Restaurant Industry. Number of searches conducted per year: 51-100.

KEY FINANCIAL PERSONNEL
1901 N. Moore Street
Suite 920
Rosslyn VA 22209
703/528-1010
Contact Michael A. Caggiano, President. Executive search firm. Appointment required. Founded 1985. Offers a professional, personalized Accounting recruitment service to the Washington/Baltimore region. Positions commonly filled include: Accountant. Company pays fee. Number of placements per year: 51-100.

MANAGEMENT RECRUITERS OF ALEXANDRIA
Seminary Plaza Building
Suite 514
4660 Kenmore Avenue
Alexandria VA 22304-1361
703/823-6600
Contact Mike Prentiss, Manager. Executive search firm. Appointment required; no phone calls; unsolicited resumes accepted. Founded 1965. World's largest contingency search firm. Five hundred offices nationwide, doing business under the names "Management Recruiters", "Sales Consultants", "CompuSearch" and "OfficeMates5". Specializes in mid-management/professional positions, $25,000-75,000. Specializes in the areas of: Accounting; Administration, MIS/EDP; Advertising; Affirmative Action; Architecture; Banking and Finance; Communications; Computer Hardware and Software; Construction; Electrical; Engineering; Food Industry; General Management; Health and Medical; Human Resources; Industrial and Interior Design; Insurance; Legal; Manufacturing; Operations Management; Printing and Publishing; Procurement; Real Estate; Retailing; Sales and Marketing; Technical and Scientific; Textiles; Transportation. Contingency.

MANAGEMENT RECRUITERS OF ARLINGTON
AFA Building
Suite 101
1501 Lee Highway
Rosslyn VA 22209-1109
703/522-1800

Contact Vic Viswanath, Manager. Executive search firm. Appointment required; no phone calls; unsolicited resumes accepted. Founded 1965. World's largest contingency search firm. Five hundred offices nationwide, doing business under the names "Management Recruiters", "Sales Consultants", "CompuSearch" and "OfficeMates5". Specializes in mid-management/professional positions, $25,000-75,000. Specializes in the areas of: Accounting; Administration, MIS/EDP; Advertising; Affirmative Action; Architecture; Banking and Finance; Communications; Computer Hardware and Software; Construction; Electrical; Engineering; Food Industry; General Management; Health and Medical; Human Resources; Industrial and Interior Design; Insurance; Legal; Manufacturing; Operations Management; Printing and Publishing; Procurement; Real Estate; Retailing; Sales and Marketing; Technical and Scientific; Textiles; Transportation. Contingency.

MANAGEMENT RECRUITERS OF BRISTOL
901 State Street
Suite 300
Bristol VA 24201-3815
703/466-5400
Contact Mike Williams or Marie Williams, Co-Managers. Executive search firm. Appointment required; no phone calls; unsolicited resumes accepted. Founded 1965. World's largest contingency search firm. Five hundred offices nationwide, doing business under the names "Management Recruiters", "Sales Consultants", "CompuSearch" and "OfficeMates5". Specializes in mid-management/professional positions, $25,000-75,000. Specializes in the areas of: Accounting; Administration, MIS/EDP; Advertising; Affirmative Action; Architecture; Banking and Finance; Communications; Computer Hardware and Software; Construction; Electrical; Engineering; Food Industry; General Management; Health and Medical; Human Resources; Industrial and Interior Design; Insurance; Legal; Manufacturing; Operations Management; Printing and Publishing; Procurement; Real Estate; Retailing; Sales and Marketing; Technical and Scientific; Textiles; Transportation. Contingency.

MANAGEMENT RECRUITERS OF FAIRFAX COUNTY SOUTH
8411 Arlington Boulevard
Suite 310
Fairfax VA 22031
703/573-2042.
Contact Tony Ehrenzeller, Office Manager. Executive search firm. Appointment required; no phone calls; unsolicited resumes accepted. Founded 1965. World's largest contingency search firm. Five hundred offices nationwide, doing business under the names "Management Recruiters", "Sales Consultants", "CompuSearch" and "OfficeMates5". Specializes in mid-management/professional positions, $25,000-75,000. Specializes in the areas of: Accounting; Administration, MIS/EDP; Advertising; Affirmative Action; Architecture; Banking and Finance; Communications; Computer Hardware and Software; Construction; Electrical; Engineering; Food Industry; General Management; Health and Medical; Human Resources; Industrial and Interior Design; Insurance; Legal; Manufacturing; Operations Management; Printing and Publishing; Procurement; Real Estate; Retailing; Sales and Marketing; Technical and Scientific; Textiles; Transportation. Contingency.

MANAGEMENT RECRUITERS OF LOUDOUN COUNTY
Suite 250
Six Pidgeon Hill Drive
Sterling VA 22170-5617
703/450-7770.
Contact Carol J. Poltorak, Manager. Executive search firm. Appointment required; no phone calls; unsolicited resumes accepted. Founded 1965. World's largest contingency search firm. Five hundred offices nationwide, doing business under the names "Management Recruiters", "Sales Consultants", "CompuSearch" and "OfficeMates5". Specializes in mid-management/professional positions, $25,000-75,000. Specializes in the areas of: Accounting; Administration, MIS/EDP; Advertising; Affirmative Action; Architecture; Banking and Finance; Communications; Computer Hardware and Software; Construction; Electrical; Engineering; Food Industry; General Management; Health and Medical; Human Resources; Industrial and Interior Design; Insurance; Legal; Manufacturing; Operations Management; Printing and Publishing; Procurement; Real Estate; Retailing; Sales and Marketing; Technical and Scientific; Textiles; Transportation. Contingency.

MANAGEMENT RECRUITERS OF McLEAN
Suite 301
1568 Spring Hill Road
McLean VA 22102
703/442-4842.

Contact Howard Reitkopp, Manager. Executive search firm. Appointment required; no phone calls; unsolicited resumes accepted. Founded 1965. World's largest contingency search firm. Five hundred offices nationwide, doing business under the names "Management Recruiters", "Sales Consultants", "CompuSearch" and "OfficeMates5". Specializes in mid-management/professional positions, $25,000-75,000. Specializes in the areas of: Accounting; Administration, MIS/EDP; Advertising; Affirmative Action; Architecture; Banking and Finance; Communications; Computer Hardware and Software; Construction; Electrical; Engineering; Food Industry; General Management; Health and Medical; Human Resources; Industrial and Interior Design; Insurance; Legal; Manufacturing; Operations Management; Printing and Publishing; Procurement; Real Estate; Retailing; Sales and Marketing; Technical and Scientific; Textiles; Transportation. Contingency.

MANAGEMENT RECRUITERS OF ROANOKE
Cave Spring Professional Center
Building E
Suite 2-A
3243 Electric Road SW
Roanoke VA 24018-6425
703/989-1676

Contact Daniel Dowdy, Manager. Executive search firm. Appointment required; no phone calls; unsolicited resumes accepted. Founded 1965. World's largest contingency search firm. Five hundred offices nationwide, doing business under the names "Management Recruiters", "Sales Consultants", "CompuSearch" and "OfficeMates5". Specializes in mid-management/professional positions, $25,000-75,000. Specializes in the areas of: Accounting; Administration, MIS/EDP; Advertising; Affirmative Action; Architecture; Banking and Finance; Communications; Computer Hardware and Software; Construction; Electrical; Engineering; Food Industry; General Management; Health and Medical; Human Resources; Industrial and Interior Design; Insurance; Legal; Manufacturing; Operations Management; Printing and Publishing; Procurement; Real Estate; Retailing; Sales and Marketing; Technical and Scientific; Textiles; Transportation. Contingency.

OERTH ASSOCIATES INC.
205 South Whiting Street
Suite 404
Alexandria VA 22304
703/823-3334

Contact Lorraine C. Oerth, President. Executive search firm. Appointment required. Founded 1985. Oerth Associates' client-base has grown to include the top names in Commercial Real Estate Development and Construction. We specialize in middle to executive level management placements. Most positions require technical degrees. All require minimum undergraduate degree from recognized school. Categories of personnel commonly filled by our firm: Construction Project Manager, Superintendent, Estimator and Property Manager. Also Asset, Acquisitions and Development Managers. Vice President and Regional Manager. Company pays fee. Number of placements per year: 51-100.

OFFICEMATES5 OF McLEAN
Suite 301
1568 Spring Hill Road
McLean VA 22102
703/442-4842

Contact Ellen Reitkopp, Manager. Executive search firm. Appointment required; no phone calls; unsolicited resumes accepted. Founded 1965. World's largest contingency search firm. Five hundred offices nationwide, doing business under the names "Management Recruiters", "Sales Consultants", "CompuSearch" and "OfficeMates5". Specializes in mid-management/professional positions, $25,000-75,000. Specializes in the areas of: Accounting; Administration, MIS/EDP; Advertising; Affirmative Action; Architecture; Banking and Finance; Communications; Computer Hardware and Software; Construction; Electrical; Engineering; Food Industry; General Management; Health and Medical; Human Resources; Industrial and Interior Design; Insurance; Legal; Manufacturing; Operations

Management; Printing and Publishing; Procurement; Real Estate; Retailing; Sales and Marketing; Technical and Scientific; Textiles; Transportation. Contingency.

PROFESSIONAL AND TRADE
ASSOCIATIONS

Anyone who has conducted a job search has heard the dictum, "It's not what you know, it's who you know." While the validity of this comment has just as often been exaggerated, it does contain more than a grain of truth. Connections can never replace good old hard work as the best method of finding employment, but they can't hurt.

If you don't have an uncle in high places who can set up some interviews for you with a few of his friends, don't worry. Most people don't. The important thing to remember is that in most instances, connections do not materialize out of thin air -- they are created. That means that anyone who works at it can make them.

One of the best ways to meet people in your area of interest is through professional trade associations. Trade associations exist so that professionals in an industry can meet, share information about trends in the field, and arrange new business. Many of them regularly publish newsletters and magazines that will help you stay abreast of the current state of your industry. In addition, many associations hold regular meetings, and these meetings may present you the opportunity not only to learn more about the field you hope to enter, but also to establish connections.

With this in mind, we have included this directory of professional associations. Many of the addresses listed are for headquarters offices only. Inquire about local chapters in your area.

ACCOUNTING

NATIONAL SOCIETY OF PUBLIC ACCOUNTANTS
1010 North Fairfax Street
Alexandria VA 22314
703/549-6400

For more information, contact:

**AMERICAN INSTITUTE OF
CERTIFIED PUBLIC ACCOUNTANTS**
1211 Avenue of the Americas
New York NY 10036
212/575-6200

THE EDP AUDITORS ASSOCIATION
P.O. Box 88180
Carol Stream IL
312/682-1200

INSTITUTE OF INTERNAL AUDITORS
P.O. Box 1119
249 Maitland Avenue
Altamonte Springs FL 32701
407/830-7600

NATIONAL ASSOCIATION OF ACCOUNTANTS
10 Paragon Drive
Box 433
Montvale NJ 07645
201/573-9000

ADVERTISING, MARKETING, PUBLIC RELATIONS

AMERICAN ADVERTISING FEDERATION
1400 K Street NW
Suite 1000
Washington DC 20005

For more information, contact:

AMERICAN ASSOCIATION OF ADVERTISING AGENCIES
666 Third Avenue
New York NY 10017
212/682-2500

AMERICAN MARKETING ASSOCIATION
250 South Wacker Drive
Suite 200
Chicago IL 60606
312/648-0536

BUSINESS-PROFESSIONAL ADVERTISING ASSOCIATION
Metroplex Corporate Center
100 Metroplex Drive
Edison NJ 08817
201/985-4441

PUBLIC RELATIONS SOCIETY OF AMERICA
33 Irving Place
New York NY 10003
212/995-2230

TELEVISION BUREAU OF ADVERTISING
477 Madison Avenue
New York NY 10022-5892
212/486-1111

APPAREL AND TEXTILES

AMERICAN APPAREL MANUFACTURERS ASSOCIATION
2500 Wilson Boulevard
Suite 301
Arlington VA 22201
703/524-1864

AMERICAN TEXTILE MANUFACTURERS INSTITUTE
1801 K Street NW
Suite 900
Washington DC 20006
202/862-0500

For more information, contact:

NATIONAL APPAREL DISTRIBUTORS
102 West 38th Street
New York NY 10018
212/768-2300

NORTHERN TEXTILE ASSOCIATION
230 Congress Street
Boston MA 02110
617/542-8220

TEXTILE RESEARCH INSTITUTE
Box 625
Princeton NJ 08540
609/924-3150

ARTS AND ENTERTAINMENT/LEISURE

NATIONAL ENDOWMENT FOR THE ARTS
1100 Pennsylvania Avenue NW
Washington DC 20506
202/682-5400

For more information, contact:

AMERICAN ASSOCIATION OF ZOOLOGICAL PARKS & AQUARIUMS
Oglebay Park
Wheeling WV 26003
304/242-2160

AMERICAN FEDERATION OF MUSICIANS
1500 Broadway
New York NY 10036
212/869-1330

AMERICAN FEDERATION OF TELEVISION AND RADIO ARTISTS
260 Madison Avenue
New York NY 10016
212/532-0800

THEATRE COMMUNICATIONS GROUP
355 Lexington Avenue
New York NY 10017
212/697-5230

BANKING/SAVINGS AND LOAN

AMERICAN BANKERS ASSOCIATION
1120 Connecticut Avenue NW
Washington DC 20036
202/663-5221

INDEPENDENT BANKERS ASSOCIATION OF AMERICA
One Thomas Circle NW
Suite 950
Washington DC 20005
202/659-8111

NATIONAL COUNCIL OF SAVINGS INSTITUTIONS
1101 15th Street NW
Suite 400
Washington DC 20005
202/857-3100

For more information:

BANK ADMINISTRATION INSTITUTE
60 Gould Center
Rolling Meadows IL 60008
609/424-3233

INSTITUTE OF FINANCIAL EDUCATION
111 East Wacker Drive
Chicago IL 60601
312/644-3100

BOOK AND MAGAZINE PUBLISHING

For more information:

AMERICAN BOOKSELLERS ASSOCIATION
137 West 25th Street
New York NY 10001
212/463-8450

ASSOCIATION OF AMERICAN PUBLISHERS
220 East 23rd Street
New York NY 10010
212/689-8920

MAGAZINE PUBLISHERS ASSOCIATION
575 Lexington Avenue
New York NY 10022
212/752-0055

WRITERS GUILD OF AMERICA EAST, INC.
555 West 57th Street
New York NY 10019
212/245-6180

WRITERS GUILD OF AMERICA WEST, INC.
8955 Beverly Boulevard
Los Angeles CA 90048
213/550-1000

BROADCASTING

BROADCAST EDUCATION ASSOCIATION
1771 N Street NW
Washington DC 20036
202/424-5355

CABLE TELEVISION ASSOCIATION
1724 Massachusetts Avenue NW
Washington DC 20036
202/775-3550

NATIONAL ASSOCIATION OF BROADCASTERS
1771 N Street
Washington DC 20036
202/429-5300

**NATIONAL ASSOCIATION OF BUSINESS
AND EDUCATIONAL RADIO**
1501 Duke Street
Suite 200
Alexandria VA 22314
703/739-0300

WOMEN IN RADIO AND TV, INC.
1101 Connecticut Avenue NW
Suite 700
Washington DC 20036
202/429-5102

For more information, contact:

INTERNATIONAL RADIO AND TV SOCIETY
420 Lexington Avenue
Suite 531
New York NY 10170
212/867-6650

TELEVISION BUREAU OF ADVERTISING
477 Madison Avenue
New York NY 10022-5892
212/486-1111

CHARITABLE, NON-PROFIT, HUMANITARIAN

NATIONAL ASSOCIATION OF SOCIAL WORKERS
7981 Eastern Avenue
Silver Spring MD 20910
301/565-0333

For more information, contact:

**NATIONAL ORGANIZATION FOR HUMAN
 SERVICE EDUCATION**
National College of Education
2840 Sheridan Road
Evanston IL 60201
312/256-5150

CHEMICALS & RELATED: PROCESSING, PRODUCTION, DISPOSAL

AMERICAN CHEMICAL SOCIETY
Career Services
1155 16th Street NW
Washington DC 20036
202/872-4600

AMERICAN INSTITUTE OF CHEMISTS
7315 Wisconsin Avenue
Bethesda MD 20814
301/652-2447

**ASSOCIATION OF STATE & INTERSTATE
 WATER POLLUTION CONTROL ADMINISTRATORS**
444 North Capital Street NW
Suite #330
Washington DC 20001
202/624-7782

WATER POLLUTION CONTROL FEDERATION
601 Wythe Street Avenue NW
Alexandria VA 22314
703/684-2400

For more information, contact:

AMERICAN INSTITUTE OF CHEMICAL ENGINEERING
345 East 47th Street
New York NY 10017
212/705-7338

DRUG, CHEMICAL, AND ALLIED TRADES ASSOCIATION
#2 Two Roosevelt Avenue
3rd Floor
Syosset NY 11791
516/496-3317

COLLEGES AND UNIVERSITIES/EDUCATION

AMERICAN ASSOCIATION OF SCHOOL ADMINISTRATORS
1801 North Moore Street
Arlington VA 22209
703/528-0700

ASSOCIATION OF AMERICAN UNIVERSITIES
One Dupont Circle NW
Suite 730
Washington DC 20036
202/466-5030

COMMUNICATIONS

COMMUNICATIONS WORKERS OF AMERICA
1925 K Street NW
Washington DC 20006
202/728-2300

UNITED STATES TELEPHONE ASSOCIATION
900 19th Street NW
Washington DC 20006
202/835-3100

COMPUTERS: HARDWARE, SOFTWARE AND SERVICES

ADAPSO/THE COMPUTER SOFTWARE AND SERVICES INDUSTRY ASSOCIATION
1300 North 17th Street
Arlington VA 22209
703/522-5055

IEEE COMPUTER SOCIETY
1730 Massachusetts Avenue NW
Washington DC 20036
609/722-4089

For more information, contact:

ASSOCIATION FOR COMPUTER SCIENCE
P.O. Box 19027
Sacramento CA 95819
916/421-9149

ASSOCIATION FOR COMPUTING MACHINERY
11 West 42nd Street
New York NY 10036
212/869-7440

PROFESSIONAL SOFTWARE PROGRAMMERS ASSOCIATION
1405 Civic Center Drive
Santa Clara CA 95050
408/985-2181

SEMICONDUCTOR INDUSTRY ASSOCIATION
4320 Stevens Clark Boulevard
San Jose CA 95129
408/246-1181

CONSTRUCTION

ASSOCIATED BUILDERS AND CONTRACTORS
729 15th Street NW
Washington DC 20005
202/832-1351

NATIONAL ASSOCIATION OF HOME BUILDERS
15th & M Streets NW
Washington DC 20005
202/822-0200

For more information, please contact:

**BUILDING OFFICIALS AND CODE
 ADMINISTRATORS INTERNATIONAL, INC**
4051 West Flossmoor Road
Country Club Hills IL 60477
312/799-2300

CONSTRUCTION INDUSTRY MANUFACTURERS ASSOCIATION
1111 East Wisconsin Avenue
Milwaukee WI 53202
414/272-0943

INTERNATIONAL CONFERENCE OF BUILDING OFFICIALS
5360 South Workman Road
Whittier CA 90601
213/699-0541

DEFENSE AND MILITARY RELATED

MILITARY OPERATIONS RESEARCH SOCIETY
101 South Whiting Street, Suite 202
Alexandria VA 22304
703/751-7290

ELECTRICAL AND ELECTRONICS

ELECTRONIC INDUSTRIES ASSOCIATION
1722 Eye Street NW
Suite 300
Washington DC 20006
202/457-4900

INTERNATIONAL BROTHERHOOD OF ELECTRICAL WORKERS
1125 15th Street NW
Washington DC 20005
202/833-7000

NATIONAL ELECTRICAL MANUFACTURERS ASSOCIATION
2101 L Street NW
Washington DC 20037
202/457-8400

For more information:

AMERICAN ELECTROPLATERS AND SURFACE FINISHERS SOCIETY
12644 Research Parkway
Orlando FL 32826
407/281-6441

ELECTROCHEMICAL SOCIETY
10 South Main Street
Pennington NJ 08534
609/737-1902

ELECTRONICS TECHNICIANS ASSOCIATION
825 East Franklin
Greencastle IN 46135
317/653-8262

INSTITUTE OF ELECTRICAL AND ELECTRONICS ENGINEERS
345 East 47th Street
New York NY 10017
212/705-7900

INTERNATIONAL SOCIETY OF CERTIFIED ELECTRONICS TECNICIANS
2708 West Berry
Ft. Worth TX 76109
817/921-9101

NATIONAL ELECTRONICS SALES AND SERVICES ASSOCIATION
2708 West Berry
Ft. Worth TX 76109
817/921-9061

ENGINEERING AND ARCHITECTURE

AMERICAN INTITUTE OF ARCHITECTS
1735 New York Ave NW
Washington DC 20006
202/626-7300

AMERICAN SOCIETY FOR ENGINEERING EDUCATION
11 Dupont Circle NW
Suite 200
Washington DC 20036
202/293-7080

AMERICAN SOCIETY OF LANDSCAPE ARCHITECTS
1733 Connecticut Avenue NW
Washington DC 20009
202/466-7730

NATIONAL ACADEMY OF ENGINEERING
2101 Constitution Avenue NW
Washington DC 20418
202/334-3200

NATIONAL SOCIETY OF PROFESSIONAL ENGINEERS
1420 King Street
Alexandria VA 22314
703/684-2800

For more information, contact:

AMERICAN SOCIETY OF CIVIL ENGINEERS
345 East 47th Street
New York NY 10017
212/705-7496

**AMERICAN SOCIETY OF HEATING, REFRIGERATING
AND AIR CONDITIONING ENGINEERS**
1791 Tullie Circle NE
Atlanta GA 30329
404/636-8400

AMERICAN SOCIETY OF NAVAL ENGINEERS
1452 Duke Street
Alexandria VA 22314
703/836-6727

AMERICAN SOCIETY OF PLUMBING ENGINEERS
3617 Thousand Oaks Boulevard
Suite #210
Westlake Village CA 91362-3625
805/495-7120

AMERICAN SOCIETY OF SAFETY ENGINEERS
1800 East Oakton Street
Des Plaines IL 60018
312/692-4121

ILLUMINATING ENGINEERING SOCIETY OF NORTH AMERICA
345 East 47th Street
New York NY 10017
212/705-7926

INSTITUTE OF INDUSTRIAL ENGINEERS
25 Technology Park
Atlanta GA 30092
404/449-0460

SOCIETY OF FIRE PROTECTION ENGINEERS
60 Batterymarch Street
Boston MA 02110
617/482-0686

UNITED ENGINEERING TRUSTEES
345 East 47th Street
New York NY 10017
212/705-7000

FABRICATED METAL PRODUCTS/PRIMARY METALS

AMERICAN CASTE METALS ASSOCIATION
455 State Street
Des Plaines IL 60016
312/299-9156

AMERICAN POWDER METALLURGY INSTITUTE
105 College Road East
Princeton NJ 08540
609/452-7700

ASSOCIATION OF IRON AND STEEL ENGINEERS
Three Gateway Center
Suite 2350
Pittsburgh PA 15222
412/281-6323

NATIONAL ASSOCIATION OF METAL FINISHERS
111 East Wacker Drive
Chicago IL 60601
312/644-6610

FINANCIAL SERVICES/MANAGEMENT CONSULTING

AMERICAN FINANCIAL SERVICES ASSOCIATION
Fourth Floor, 1101 14th Street NW
Washington DC 20005
202/289-0400

AMERICAN SOCIETY OF APPRAISERS
P.O. Box 17265
Washington DC 20041
202/478-2228

FEDERATION OF TAX ADMINISTRATORS
444 North Capital Street NW
Washington DC 20001
202/624-5890

NATIONAL ASSOCIATION OF CREDIT MANAGEMENT
8815 Centre Park Drive
Suite 200
Columbia MD 21045-2117
301/740-5560

NATIONAL ASSOCIATION OF REAL ESTATE INVESTMENT TRUSTS
1129 20th Street NW
Suite 705
Washington DC 20036
202/785-8717

For more information, contact:

AMERICAN MANAGEMENT ASSOCIATION
Management Information Service
135 West 50th Street
New York NY 10020
212/586-8100

ASSOCIATION OF MANAGEMENT CONSULTING FIRMS
230 Park Avenue
New York NY 10036
212/697-9693

FINANCIAL ANALYSTS FEDERATION
1633 Broadway
Room 1602
New York NY 10019
212/957-2860

FINANCIAL EXECUTIVES INSTITUTE
10 Madison Avenue
P.O. Box 1938
Morristown NJ 07960
201/898-4600

INSTITUTE OF FINANCIAL EDUCATION
111 East Wacker Drive
Chicago IL 60601
312/644-3100

INSTITUTE OF MANAGEMENT CONSULTANTS
19 West 44th Street
New York NY 10036
212/921-2885

NATIONAL ASSOCIATION OF BUSINESS ECONOMISTS
28349 Chagrin Boulevard
Suite 201
Cleveland OH 44122
216/464-7986

**NATIONAL CORPORATE CASH
 MANAGEMENT ASSOCIATION**
P.O. Box 7001
Newton CT 06740
203/426-3007

SECURITIES INDUSTRY ASSOCIATION
120 Broadway
New York NY 10271
212/608-1500

FOOD: PROCESSING, PRODUCTION AND DISTRIBUTION

DAIRY AND FOOD INDUSTRIES SUPPLY ASSOCIATION
Supply Association
6245 Executive Boulevard
Rockville MD 20852
301/984-1444

NATIONAL AGRICULTURAL CHEMICALS ASSOCIATION
1155 15th Street NW
Suite 900
Washington DC 20005
202/296-1585

**UNITED FOOD AND COMMERCIAL
WORKERS INTERNATIONAL UNION**
1775 K Street NW
Washington DC 20006
202/223-3111

For more information, contact:

AMERICAN ASSOCIATION OF CEREAL CHEMISTS
3340 Pilot Knob Road
St. Paul MN 55121
612/454-7250

AMERICAN SOCIETY OF AGRICULTURAL ENGINEERS
2950 Niles Road
St. Joseph MI 49085
616/429-0300

AMERICAN SOCIETY OF BREWING CHEMISTS
3340 Pilot Knob Road
St. Paul MN 55121
612/454-7250

NATIONAL DAIRY COUNCIL
6300 North River Road
Rosemont IL 60018
312/696-1020

GENERAL MERCHANDISE: RETAIL AND WHOLESALE

NATIONAL RETAIL MERCHANTS ASSOCIATION
100 West 31st Street
New York NY 10001
212/244-8780

HEALTH CARE AND PHARMACEUTICALS/HOSPITALS

AMERICAN ACADEMY OF PHYSICIAN ASSISTANTS
1117 North 19th Street
Suite 300
Arlington VA 22209
703/836-2272

AMERICAN ASSOCIATION FOR CLINICAL CHEMISTRY
2029 K Street NW, 7th Floor
Washington DC 20006
202/857-0717

AMERICAN HEALTH CARE ASSOCIATION
1200 15th Street NW
Washington DC 20005
202/842-4444

AMERICAN OCCUPATIONAL THERAPY ASSOCIATION
P.O. Box 1725
1383 Picard Drive
Rockville MD 20850
301/948-9626

AMERICAN PHARMACEUTICAL ASSOCIATION
2215 Constitution Avenue NW
Washington DC 20037
202/628-4410

AMERICAN PHYSICAL THERAPY ASSOCIATION
1111 North Fairfax Street
Alexandria VA 22314
703/684-2782

**AMERICAN SOCIETY FOR BIOCHEMISTRY
AND MOLECULAR BIOLOGY**
9650 Rockville Pike
Bethesda MD 20814
301/530-7145

AMERICAN SOCIETY OF HOSPITAL PHARMACISTS
4630 Montgomery Avenue
Bethesda MD 20814
301/657-3000

NATIONAL MEDICAL ASSOCIATION
1012 Tenth Street NW
Washington DC 20001
202/347-1895

For more information, contact:

AMERICAN ACADEMY OF FAMILY PHYSICIANS
8880 Ward Parkway
Kansas City MO 64114
816/333-9700

AMERICAN COLLEGE OF HEALTHCARE EXECUTIVES
840 North Lake Shore Drive
Chicago IL 60611
312/943-0544

AMERICAN DENTAL ASSOCIATION
211 East Chicago Avenue
Chicago IL 60611
312/440-2500

AMERICAN MEDICAL ASSOCIATION
535 North Dearborn Street
Chicago IL 60610
312/645-5000

AMERICAN VETERINARY MEDICAL ASSOCIATION
930 North Meacham Road
Schaumburg IL 60196
312/605-8070

CARDIOVASCULAR CREDENTIALING INTERNATIONAL
2801 Far Hills #309
Dayton OH 45419
513/293-0315

MEDICAL GROUP MANAGEMENT ASSOCIATION
1355 South Colorado Boulevard
Suite 900
Denver CO 80222
303/753-1111

NATIONAL HEALTH COUNCIL
622 Third Avenue 34th Floor
New York NY 10017
212/972-2700

HOTEL AND RESTAURANT RELATED

**COUNCIL ON HOTEL, RESTAURANT
AND INSTITUTIONAL EDUCATION**
1200 17th Street NW
Washington DC 20036
202/331-5990

For more information, contact

THE AMERICAN HOTEL AND MOTEL ASSOCIATION
888 7th Avenue
New York NY 10106
212/759-0570

**THE EDUCATION FOUNDATION OF
THE NATIONAL RESTAURANT ASSOCIATION**
20 North Wacker Drive
Suite 2620
Chicago IL 60606
312/853-2525

INSURANCE

AMERICAN COUNCIL OF LIFE INSURANCE
1001 Pennsylvania Avenue NW
Washington DC 20004
202/624-2000

AMERICAN INSURANCE ASSOCIATION
1130 Connecticut Avenue NW
Suite 1000
Washington DC 20036
202/828-7100

NATIONAL ASSOCIATION OF LIFE UNDERWRITERS
1922 F Street NW
Washington DC 20006
202/331-6000

For more information contact:

ALLIANCE OF AMERICAN INSURERS
1501 Woodfield Road
Suite 400 West
Schaumburg IL 60173
312/330-8500

INSURANCE INFORMATION INSTITUTE
110 William Street
New York NY 10038
212/669-9200

SOCIETY OF ACTUARIES
475 North Martingale Road
Suite 800
Schaumburg IL 60173
312/706-3500

LEGAL SERVICES

FEDERAL BAR ASSOCIATION
1815 H Street NW
Washington DC 20006
202/638-0252

NATIONAL ASSOCIATION FOR LAW PLACEMENT
440 First Street NW, Suite 302
Washington DC 20001
202/667-1666

For more information, contact:

AMERICAN BAR ASSOCIATION
750 North Lake Shore Drive
Chicago IL 60611
312/988-5000

ASSOCIATION OF LEGAL ADMINISTRATORS
104 Wilmot
Suite 205
Deerfield IL 60015-5195
312/940-9240

NATIONAL ASSOCIATION OF LEGAL ASSISTANTS
1420 South Utica
Tulsa OK 74104
918/587-6828

NATIONAL ASSOCIATION OF LEGAL ADMINISTRATORS
2250 East 73rd Street
Suite 550
Tulsa OK 74136
312/940-9240

NATIONAL FEDERATION OF PARALEGAL ASSOCIATIONS
Suite 201, 104 Wilmot Road
Deerfield IL 60015-5195
312/940-8800

NATIONAL PARALEGAL ASSOCIATION
P.O. Box 629
Doylestown PA 18901
215/297-8333

MISCELLANEOUS ASSOCIATIONS

NATIONAL COOPERATIVE BUSINESS ASSOCIATION
1401 New York Ave. NW
Suite #1100
Washington DC 20005
202/638-6222

NATIONAL SMALL BUSINESS UNITED
1155 15th Street NW
Suite 710
Washington DC 20005
202/293-8830

For more information, contact:

AMERICAN FEDERATION OF SMALL BUSINESS
407 South Dearborn Street
Chicago IL 60605
312/427-0206

MISCELLANEOUS MANUFACTURING

NATIONAL ASSOCIATION OF MANUFACTURERS
1331 Pennsylvania Avenue, NW
Suite 1500
Washington DC 20004-1703
202/637-3000

NATIONAL MACHINE TOOL BUILDERS
7901 Westpark Drive
McLean VA 22102
703/893-2900

NATIONAL TOOLING AND MACHINING ASSOCIATION
9300 Livingston Road
Fort Washington MD 20744
301/248-1250

For more information, contact:

NATIONAL SCREW MACHINE PRODUCTS ASSOCIATION
6700 West Snowville Road
Breckville OH 44141
216/526-0300

THE TOOLING AND MANUFACTURING ASSOCIATION
1177 South Dee Road
Park Ridge IL 60068
312/693-2347

NEWSPAPER PUBLISHING

AMERICAN NEWSPAPER PUBLISHERS ASSOCIATION
11600 Sunrise Valley Drive
Reston VA 22091
703/648-1000

AMERICAN SOCIETY OF NEWSPAPER EDITORS
P.O. Box 17004
Washington DC 20041
202/620-6087

INTERNATIONAL CIRULATION MANAGERS ASSOCIATION
11600 Sunrise Valley Drive
Reston VA 22091
703/620-9555

NATIONAL NEWSPAPER ASSOCIATION
1627 K Street NW
Suite 400
Washington DC 20006
202/466-7200

NATIONAL PRESS CLUB
529 14th St. NW
Washington DC 20045
202/662-7500

THE NEWSPAPER GUILD
Research and Information Department
1125 15th Street NW
Washington DC 20005
301/585-2990

For more information, contact:

THE DOW JONES NEWSPAPER FUND
P.O. Box 300
Princeton NJ 08543-0300
609/520-4000

PAPER PRODUCTS AND PACKAGING/CONTAINERS

AMERICAN PAPER INSTITUTE
260 Madison Avenue
New York NY 10016
212/340-0600

TECHNICAL ASSOCIATION OF THE PULP AND PAPER INDUSTRY
P.O. Box 105113
Atlanta GA 30348
404/446-1400

PETROLEUM AND ENERGY RELATED/MINING AND DRILLING

AMERICAN GAS ASSOCIATION
1515 Wilson Boulevard
Arlington VA 22209
703/841-8400

AMERICAN GEOLOGICAL INSTITUTE
4220 King Street
Alexandria VA 22302
703/379-2480

AMERICAN PETROLEUM INSTITUTE
1220 L Street NW
Washington DC 20005
202/682-8000

For more information, contact:

AMERICAN ASSOCIATION OF PETROLEUM GEOLOGISTS
1444 South Boulder
Tulsa OK 74119
918/584-2555

AMERICAN INSTITUTE OF MINING,
 METALLURGICAL AND PETROLEUM
345 East 47th Street
New York NY 10017
212/705-7695

AMERICAN NUCLEAR SOCIETY
555 North Kensington Avenue
La Grange Park IL 60525
312/352-6611

AMERICAN SOCIETY OF TRIBOLOGISTS
AND LUBRICATION ENGINEERS
838 Busse Highway
Park Ridge IL 60068
312/825-5536

CLEAN ENERGY RESEARCH INSTITUTE
P.O. Box 248294
Coral Gables FL 33124
305/284-4666

GEOLOGICAL SOCIETY OF AMERICA
3300 Penrose Place
P.O. Box 9140
Boulder CO 80301
303/447-2020

PETROLEUM EQUIPMENT INSTITUTE
3739 East 31st Street
P.O. Box 2380/74101
Tulsa OK 74135
918/743-9941

SOCIETY OF EXPLORATION GEOPHYSICISTS
P.O. Box 702740
8801 South Yale
Tulsa OK 74170-2740
918/493-3516

PRINTING

PRINTING INDUSTRIES OF AMERICA
1730 North Lynn Street
Arlington VA 22209
703/841-8100

For more information, contact:

BINDING INDUSTRIES OF AMERICA
70 East Lake Street
Chicago IL 60601
312/372-7606

REAL ESTATE

BUILDING OWNERS AND MANAGERS ASSOCIATION
1521 Ritchie Highway
Arnold MD 21012
301/261-2882

NATIONAL ASSOCIATION OF REAL ESTATE INVESTMENT TRUSTS
1129 20th Street NW
Suite 705
Washington DC 20036
202/785-8717

For more information, contact:

APARTMENT OWNERS AND MANAGERS ASSOCIATION
65 Cherry Plaza
Watertown CT 06795
203/274-2589

INSTITUTE OF REAL ESTATE MANAGEMENT
430 North Michigan Avenue
Chicago IL 60611
312/661-1930

**INTERNATIONAL ASSOCIATION OF CORPORATE
 REAL ESTATE EXECUTIVES**
Suite 8, 471 Spencer Drive South
West Palm Beach FL 33409
407/683-8111

INTERNATIONAL REAL ESTATE INSTITUTE
8383 East Evans Road
Scottsdale AZ 85260
602/998-8267

NATIONAL ASSOCIATION OF REALTORS
430 North Michigan Avenue
Chicago IL 60611
312/329-8200

RUBBER AND PLASTICS

SOCIETY OF PLASTICS INDUSTRY
355 Lexington Avenue
New York NY 10017
212/370-7340

SOCIETY OF PLASTIC ENGINEERS
14 Fairfield Drive
Brookfield Centre CT 06804
203/775-0471

TRANSPORTATION/SHIPPING/AUTOMOTIVE

AIR TRANSPORT ASSOCIATION OF AMERICA
1709 New York Ave NW
Washington DC 20006
202/626-4000

AMERICAN SOCIETY OF TRAVEL AGENTS
1101 King Street
Alexandria VA 22314
703/739-2782

AMERICAN TRUCKING ASSOCIATION
2200 Mill Road
Alexandria VA 22314
703/838-1700

ASSOCIATION OF AMERICAN RAILROADS
50 F Street NW
Washington DC 20001
202/639-2100

INSTITUTE OF TRANSPORTATION ENGINEERS
Suite 410
525 School Street NW,
Washington DC 20024
202/554-8050

MARINE TECHNOLOGY SOCIETY
1825 K Street NW
Suite 203
Washington DC 20009
202/775-5966

NATIONAL AERONAUTIC ASSOCIATION OF USA
1763 R Street NW
Washington DC 20005
202/265-8720

NATIONAL AUTOMOTIVE DEALERS ASSOCIATION
8400 Westpark Drive
McLean VA 22102
703/821-7000

NATIONAL INSTITUTE FOR AUTOMOTIVE SERVICE EXCELLENCE
1920 Association Drive
Suite 400
Reston VA 22091
703/742-3800

SHIPBUILDERS COUNCIL OF AMERICA
1110 Vermont Ave. NW
Washington DC 20005
202/775-9060

For more information, contact:

AIR LINE EMPLOYEES ASSOCIATION
5600 South Central Ave
Chicago IL 60638
312/767-3333

AMERICAN INSTITUTE OF AERONAUTICS AND ASTRONAUTICS
555 West 57th Street
New York NY 10019
212/247-6500

AUTOMOTIVE SERVICE ASSOCIATION
P.O. Box 929
Bedford TX 76021-0929
817/283-6205

AUTOMOTIVE SERVICE INDUSTRY ASSOCIATION
444 North Michigan Avenue
Chicago IL 60611
312/836-1300

AVIATION MAINTENANCE FOUNDATION
P.O. Box 2826
Redmond WA 98073
206/828-3917

FUTURE AVIATION PROFESSIONAL OF AMERICA
4291 J. Memorial Drive
Atlanta GA 30032
1-800/GET-JOBS

MOTOR VEHICLE MANUFACTURERS ASSOCIATION
7430 2nd Avenue
Suite 300
Detroit MI 48202
313/872-4311

NATIONAL MARINE MANUFACTURERS ASSOCIATION
401 North Michigan Avenue
Suite 1150
Chicago IL 60611
312/836-4747

PROFESSIONAL AVIATION MAINTENANCE ASSOCIATION
P.O. Box 248
St. Ann MO 63074
314/739-2580

UTILITIES

AMERICAN WATER WORKS ASSOCIATION
6666 West Quincy Avenue
Denver CO 80235
303/794-7711

ALPHABETICAL EMPLOYER INDEX

COMPANY **PAGE**

District of Columbia Employers

Major Maryland Employers

Major Northern Virginia Employers